THE BOOK OF RUTH
INTERLINEAR EDITION

ARTSCROLL SERIES
34 YEARS OF LITERARY ACCOMPLISHMENT
1976-2010

In honor of Shavuos

Mesorah Heritage Foundation

presents this first edition of the

Interlinear Book of Ruth

The Foundation was created
to break down the barriers
of language and time —
to bring the classics of Jewish wisdom
to today's English-speaking Jews.

Read on.
See what WE do —
and how YOU can help…

Mesorah Heritage Foundation

FIRST EDITION
First impression … April 2010

THE ARTSCROLL SERIES® / SCHOTTENSTEIN EDITION
MEGILLAS RUTH / THE INTERLINEAR BOOK OF RUTH

© *Copyright 2010, by MESORAH PUBLICATIONS, Ltd.*
4401 Second Avenue / Brooklyn, N.Y. 11232 / (718) 921-9000 / www.artscroll.com

ISBN 10: 1-4226-0974-x   ISBN 13: 978-1-4226-0974-3

Mesorah Heritage Foundation

What have we accomplished so far?

*I*magine that you are standing in front of a vault filled with gold, silver, and precious stones. They are yours for the taking.

But the vault is locked and you don't know the combination!

If you have no access to all that wealth, it might as well be on another planet. How much would you give to unlock it?

There is a treasure far more valuable than the contents of any safe, but it has been locked away from millions of Jews. **That treasure is our Jewish literary heritage:** the Torah, the Talmud, the Mishnah, the Midrash, the Siddur and Machzor, our history, the stories and values that connect us to our past and lay the foundations of our future.

But most of this wealth is in ancient Hebrew and Aramaic, and presented in a manner that is incomprehensible to most modern readers. **Our authentic Jewish heritage has been locked away from English-speaking Jews for too long.**

The **Mesorah Heritage Foundation** was created to "unlock the vault." *Our goal is to remove the language barrier and make the riches of Jewish eternity available to English-speaking Jews.* Here is what we do:

❖ **Sponsor literature** that celebrates the rich Jewish heritage

❖ **Create works** of intensive scholarship and unexcelled beauty

❖ **Produce books** that will be read, studied, and cherished for generations

How does the Foundation do it?

The **Mesorah Heritage Foundation** recruits accomplished translators, scholars, writers, and editors who bring our classic texts to English-speaking Jews in books that are beautifully produced and literarily graceful.

At this writing, *more than a hundred scholars in America, Israel, and Europe are producing an English-language Torah literature that will endure for generations.*

Catalog of Accomplishment

❖ The English-language edition of the **Schottenstein Edition of the Babylonian Talmud** — a monumental 73-volume work, fifteen years in the making — is universally acknowledged as, in the words of Lord Immanuel Jakobovits ע״ה, the late Chief Rabbi of the British Commonwealth, "one of the most momentous publishing efforts gracing the entire length of Jewish history." A **Hebrew Schottenstein Edition of the Babylonian Talmud** is nearing completion.

These two editions have "enrolled" many tens of thousands of people in Talmud study every day. In offices, homes, synagogues, commuter trains, on airliners — everywhere, throughout the world — volumes of the Schottenstein Talmud are proving that Jews thirst for Torah, and these editions are quenching that thirst.

Compiled about 1650 years ago, the **Jerusalem Talmud** has long been the most neglected of our great classics. Never elucidated in the vernacular, very complex and difficult, it has been closed to all but exceptional scholars. The new **Schottenstein Editions of the Jerusalem Talmud**, in **English and Hebrew**, are opening eyes and minds to this treasure.

All this has been made possible thanks to the vision and generosity of **Jay and Jeanie Schottenstein and family** of Columbus, Ohio, and more than 200 patrons who have dedicated volumes in these historic projects.

❖ Now, **the Talmud is being published in French, The Edmond J. Safra Edition,** in a new and truly historic venture, and

is bringing our Torah heritage to thousands of French-speaking Jews worldwide.

❖ The **Schottenstein Interlinear Series** — This innovative series presents the Torah and liturgy with the translation directly under the Hebrew words, in addition to a commentary. An ingenious, *patented format* helps readers view the Hebrew and English texts simultaneously. **The Book of Ruth** is the newest addition to this trailblazing series.

More than ever before, this series enables the reader to understand every word as he prays and studies.

The series began with the **Siddur** and **Machzor**. So enormously popular were they that many more works were provided in this new format, including the recently completed **5-volume Interlinear Chumash**.

❖ The **Stone Edition of the Chumash** is the *Chumash* of choice throughout the English-speaking world. This new translation of the Five Books of Moses and its flowing, inspiring commentary speak to today's Jews. It is sparking renewed interest in the Torah as it has been studied for thousands of years.

Now in progress is a contemporary Hebrew edition to benefit Israelis who appreciate its readability and extensive elucidation.

❖ The **Edmond J. Safra Edition of the Chumash**, with translation and commentary in French, is now well under way.

❖ The **Sapirstein Edition of Rashi** shines new light on the premier commentary on the Torah. Acclaimed by scholars and students, this edition is the most acclaimed phrase-by-phrase translation and elucidation of its kind.

❖ **Ramban on Chumash**

This seminal, extraordinary commentary belongs on the study list of anyone who is serious about understanding the Torah. ArtScroll's new 7-volume treatment, which has quickly been acknowledged as a classic, makes this work accessible to all.

❖ The ***Davis Edition Baal Haturim on Chumash*** is a much-admired but insufficiently understood early classic on the Chumash. In the ArtScroll Edition — thoroughly researched and annotated — this great work comes to life.

❖ The ***Stone Edition of Tanach*** is a one-volume translation, with an annotated, concise commentary, of all twenty-four Books of the Bible.

❖ The ***Rubin Edition of the Early Prophets*** is doing for the Books of the Prophets what the Stone Edition is doing for the *Chumash*. The commentary sheds light on the framework of our history. The Books of Joshua, Judges, Samuel and Kings are in print.

❖ Most books of the ***Later Prophets and the Writings*** are available with clear translations and illuminating commentaries.

❖ The ***ArtScroll Mishnah Series*** with the ***Yad Avraham*** commentary translates and explains the Mishnah with unparalleled clarity. This series is scheduled for completion in the fall, and a **pocket-sized slipcased edition** is available as well.

❖ The ***ArtScroll Siddur and Machzor Series*** has become standard in home and synagogue thanks to its clear translations, inspirational and informative commentaries, and user-friendly instructions. These *Siddurim* and *Machzorim* have become indispensable to experienced users and beginners alike. That is why a **Russian Edition** and the ***Fischmann Edition Spanish Siddur*** were published.

❖ The *Seif Edition Transliterated Series* rolls out a welcome mat to people with difficulty reading Hebrew. The *Siddurim*, *Machzorim*, *Tehillim/Psalms*, and *Haggadah* in this series have enabled those who are not yet familiar with Hebrew to pray using the original text.

❖ The Foundation sponsors a host of other projects, including works of **practical Halachah, Torah commentary**, and even **High School literature textbooks** that teach literature, analytical reading and writing skills on the highest level, while incorporating the values and morals that are increasingly absent from many modern textbooks.

❖ *The Kleinman Edition of Limud Yomi —*
  A Daily Dose of Torah

   This revolutionary new English-language learning program, dedicated by **Elly and Brochie Kleinman**, provides a systematic daily regimen presenting core areas of Torah study. Each volume provides four weeks of stimulating study. In only 18 minutes a day, the reader gets an insight on the weekly Torah reading, a Mishnah, an adaptation from the Talmud, a *mussar* thought, a halachah, and a section of the *Siddur*. *Limud Yomi* provides an inspirational boost to anyone's day.

❖ *The Kleinman Mishkan Interactive DVD*

   More than four *parashiyos* in the Torah are devoted to the construction of the Tabernacle/*Mishkan*. Thanks to modern technology, this new Interactive DVD enables us to "build" a virtual *Mishkan*. This DVD visually depicts and explains the Torah, verse by verse, item by item, vessel by vessel, and includes an audio explanation of the verses by a master teacher. We see all the components, move them around, put them together, and thoroughly understand the *Chumash* and *Rashi*. Produced by our scholars in conjunction with artists who create virtual models for NASA and the Air Force, this is an unprecedentedly effective and fascinating teaching and learning tool. *A full-color, deluxe, coffee-table volume on the Mishkan is in progress.*

What's next? Major new projects are in progress:

❖ The *Schottenstein Edition of the Jerusalem Talmud in English and Hebrew*

For centuries, this basic text has been a closed book. Now, in a projected 49-volume set, the world-class scholars who produced the renowned Schottenstein Edition of the Babylonian Talmud are bringing the Talmud of the Land of Israel to world Jewry in English and Hebrew. Dedicated by **Jay and Jeanie Schottenstein** and with the support of generous patrons, our staff is opening the door to one of Judaism's great treasures.

❖ The Kleinman Edition of Kitzur Shulchan Aruch

Familiarly known as *the Kitzur*, this authoritative digest of the Code of Laws, was first published in 1864, and has been reprinted scores of times. The new translation and elucidation explains the *Kitzur*, and cites the *Mishnah Berurah* and Rabbi Moshe Feinstein (in *Igros Moshe*) where they differ with or expand upon the *Kitzur*. This trailblazing 5-volume work, dedicated by **Elly and Brochie Kleinman**, is bringing a classic halachic work to new generations of readers and scholars.

❖ The Kleinman Edition of Midrash Rabbah

Midrash Rabbah is the sourcebook of Torah commentary, stories, ethical illumination, and insightful interpretation of the great figures and events of the Chumash. Work is now in full swing on a 15-volume treatment of the Midrash. The elucidation follows the pattern of the Schottenstein editions of the Talmud, and it will be augmented by interpretations from classic works of Chassidus and Mussar.

❖ The Wasserman Edition of the ArtScroll Siddur

Since it was published in 1984, the ArtScroll Siddur has become the standard prayer book in countless communities. Now it will be published in a new revised edition, dedicated by **Stanley and Ellen Wasserman**, with larger type, a new Overview, a newly edited translation, and many new features, including the laws and customs relating to the Land of Israel.

The original classic ArtScroll Siddur, dedicated by **Joseph and Lea Berliner**, will continue to enlighten and inspire new generations. The names Berliner and Wasserman will always be joined in the annals of those who raised prayer to a new plateau.

Why the need for a Foundation to do this?

The amount of research and intensive review necessary to produce such a voluminous literature cannot be supported by the commercial market. Look at the most important secular cultural undertakings: great universities, libraries, orchestras, even

medical research — all must have substantial public and private support. The production of a great Torah literature is no different. Without generous public participation, it cannot be created.

What can you do to help this work go on?

Everyone can be a part of this monumental undertaking. People of vision and means can do more. Everyone can contribute something. There are many alternatives:

❖ **Dedicate a volume** in honor or memory of a loved one. **All dedications are in perpetuity.** Talmud dedications are mentioned **in every single volume,** so your dedication will appear **in millions of volumes** over the years. The same applies to the Mishnah and all other volumes.

❖ If you can't undertake a dedication on your own, you may wish to **join family and friends** in doing so.

❖ **Be acknowledged** in an individual volume, for a relatively modest contribution.

❖ Be a contributor so that Jews from Jerusalem to Johannesburg, from Moscow to Melbourne, from London to Los Angeles, will benefit from your generosity for generations.

Look at it this way:

Whatever your means, you can be a partner in projects that have been acclaimed by great scholars and leaders throughout the world as "the greatest English-language Torah dissemination undertaking in history." Your help will bring Torah literacy to countless Jews.

Your contribution is tax-deductible

The **Mesorah Heritage Foundation** is an IRS-recognized, not-for-profit 501(c)(3) trust. Every contribution is tax-deductible to the full extent permitted by law. And every dollar goes to support the work of bringing Torah to all of the People of the Book.

Join the Mesorah Heritage Foundation
in making Jewish history.

Help us bring pride to our people and inspiration
to future generations by supporting the scholars
who are returning the legacy of our past
to the builders of our future.

To send your generous contribution,
for further information
about dedication opportunities
and about the Foundation and its activities,
or to request a catalogue including
the ArtScroll volumes sponsored by the Foundation,
please write or call:

Mesorah Heritage Foundation

4401 SECOND AVENUE ❖ BROOKLYN, N.Y. 11232
Phone: 718 / 921-9000 ❖ Fax: 718 / 680-1875
email: heritage@mesorah.com
web: www.MesorahHeritage.org

FOR YOUR CONVENIENCE:
You can now charge
your tax-deductible donation
to your credit card online at:
www.MesorahHeritage.org

Mesorah Heritage Foundation is a 501(c)(3) not-for-profit organization.

THE SCHOTTENSTEIN EDITION

מגילת רות

THE BOOK OF RUTH

The ArtScroll Series®

WITH AN INTERLINEAR TRANSLATION

Rabbi Meir Zlotowitz / Rabbi Nosson Scherman
General Editors

מגילת רות

OF RUTH

ARTSCROLL SERIES
34
YEARS OF LITERARY
ACCOMPLISHMENT
1976-2010

FIRST INTERLINEAR EDITION

Published by

Mesorah Publications, ltd

THE SCHOTTENSTEIN EDITION

THE BOOK

A NEW INTERLINEAR TRANSLATION
BASED ON THE CLASSIC
ARTSCROLL EDITION OF THE BOOK OF RUTH
WITH A COMMENTARY ANTHOLOGIZED FROM
THE TALMUD, MIDRASH, AND RABBINIC WRITINGS

Original translation and commentary by
Rabbi Meir Zlotowitz

Overviews by
Rabbi Nosson Scherman

New interlinear translation edited by
Rabbi Menachem Davis

Designed by
Rabbi Sheah Brander

⋐ Publisher's Preface to the Interlinear Edition

Thirty-four years have gone by since *Megillas Esther* inaugurated the ArtScroll Series, in 1976. It is no secret that no one expected the overwhelming response to that volume. Since then, the English-speaking Jewish community has demonstrated an increasing thirst for an authentic Torah literature in the vernacular. All areas of Torah have been made available to those to whom our eternal tradition is precious. And countless thousands more have been introduced to it for the first time — and been astonished and gratified by what they see and learn.

The spark within the Jewish soul can never be extinguished, even after it has lain dormant for generations. The works of the ArtScroll Series are succeeding in feeding that spark and turning it into a flame that illuminates hearts and minds.

In recent years, the SCHOTTENSTEIN INTERLINEAR SERIES, dedicated by JAY AND JEANIE SCHOTTENSTEIN, has brought a new level of comprehension to Torah and *tefillah,* enabling people to understand their learning and prayers word for word and phrase by phrase. Now, on the 34th anniversary of the original ArtScroll Edition of *the Book of Ruth*, this new *Schottenstein Interlinear Edition* brings an enhanced level of comprehension to the Book.

This volume incorporates the anthologized commentary approach that has been enormously useful and popular for more than a generation. It includes a new Overview, in addition to the one that helped make the original volume so useful to so many people. We are confident that, with Hashem's help, this innovative interlinear approach to translation will be a boon to multitudes and we look forward to further volumes of this sort.

Many, many people have contributed to enable the production of over 1,200 titles now in the ArtScroll Series. We cannot enumerate them all, but we must thank RABBI MENACHEM DAVIS, who provided the interlinear translation and adapted the commentary for this volume. And we must thank REB SHEAH BRANDER, whose graphics genius has shaped the distinctive ArtScroll "look" since its first day.

We pray that Hashem will continue to make our colleagues and us the quills that record His word and bring it to His people.

Rabbis Meir Zlotowitz and Nosson Scherman

Rosh Chodesh Iyar 5770 / April 2010
Brooklyn, NY

✂️ Author's Preface

The predecessor of this enhanced Interlinear Edition was published in 1976.
We present the Author's Preface to that volume.

הַמַּתְחִיל בְּמִצְוָה אוֹמְרִים לוֹ גְמֹר

This volume marks the second in a planned series to be presented to the Jewish public.

The overwhelming response, with which the previous offering — *Megillas Esther*, published two months ago — has been received, has clearly indicated that the Torah audience is anxious for unadulterated traditional commentaries, lucidly, dignifiedly, and literately presented, and aesthetically and attractively packaged.

With this in mind, I approached my good friend REB NOSSON SCHERMAN and asked him again to take part in such a noble project: to make accessible to the Torah public a Chazal's-eye view of another of the twenty-four sacred Books of the Bible, a book that is deceiving in its seeming simplicity, but which holds the inscrutable secrets of Mashiach and the Kingship of the Davidic Dynasty.

I approached Reb Nosson with some trepidation, knowing how deeply involved he is in chinuch and service to the klal and how precious little personal time he has.

But his erudition and flowing style, as well as his insights and philosophical presentation of the sublime thoughts of our Sages, were indispensable to the success of this venture. He consented to put the public's needs before his own and gave freely of himself.

The resulting work is prima facie evidence of his erudition: his association has raised its level beyond description.

✂️ Scope of the Commentary

The commentary was meant to appeal to the needs of a large cross section of people: from the early-teenage day school student to the Hebrew teacher; from the college student with a limited Hebrew background to the young Kollel scholar who has neither access to all the sources in their original nor the time to investigate them individually. Therefore, a serious attempt has been made to bridge the very wide gap and fill the unique individual needs of each reader.

The *Book of Ruth* was more difficult than *Esther* in this area. The commentary on every nuance of every word is more copious and

abundant; the *Book of Ruth* is more laden with halachic implications; the Book is more "compact" in its narrative — the first few verses alone condensing ten years of events into a few words — the commentators are, on the whole, more esoteric and require more elaboration and interpretation. There were many concepts such as the sin of Elimelech and his sons, the conversion of Ruth, Moabite marriage, the period of the Judges, Davidic monarchy, etc., which needed a fuller treatment in order for the reader to comprehend the *Book of Ruth* — not as a "love story," God forbid — but as a Book of the Holy Scripture aglow with inner meaning and understandable only in the light of our Sages who expounded every word בִּקְדֻשָׁה וּבְטָהֳרָה — with sanctity and purity.

To this end a new, free-flowing translation of the main text — not literal, but true to the interpretation of our Sages — was prepared. This new translation, designed to be as readable as possible, eliminated many of the "surface difficulties" dealt with by the *Midrash*, *Rashi*, and *Ibn Ezra* because their interpretations were incorporated directly into the translation.

Continuing with the method used in *Esther*, the Talmud, *Midrashim*, and *Zohar Chadash* were then consulted and virtually every Chazal directly concerned with פְּשָׁט — the literal and intended meaning of the text, which could be meaningfully incorporated into the framework of an English-language commentary — was included.

The classic commentaries — *Rashi, Ibn Ezra, Alshich,* and *Vilna Gaon* — were then painstakingly culled for essential comments not suggested in the translation or quoted in the Talmudic source.

Next, the major commentaries were consulted: primarily the monumental *Iggeres Shmuel* by Rav Shmuel de Uzeda; *Meishiv Nefesh* by the Bach; *Akeidas Yitzchak* by Rav Yitzchak Arama; *Simchas HaRegel* and *Nachal Eshkol* by the Chida; *Kol Yaakov* by the Dubno Maggid; and the Malbim.

What was sorely missed is the encyclopedic and erudite commentary of *Me'am Loez* on *Ruth* which is not at this time available.

[In response to many readers of *Esther*, an extensive bibliography — with enlarged biographical description of the authorities quoted — has been added to the back of this volume as well.]

The major problem here was limiting and condensing the vast amount of commentary on every word into a book of meaningful and intelligible proportions that would satisfy both the scholar and the casual reader. Often, concepts briefly noted in the commentary are treated fully in the Introduction/Overview. I hope the resulting volume does justice both to these readers and to the Geonim whose sublime writings are quoted.

◄§ Hᴀsʜᴇᴍ's **Name**

It was decided that wherever the Hebrew Four-Letter Name of God appears, it would be translated in large and small caps: "Hᴀsʜᴇᴍ," i.e., "The" Name — the Holy Name of God. Where the Hebrew has *Elokim*, the more general and less "personal" Name of the Diety, it was translated "God." Although the Name of the Creator is generally written "G-d" and not spelled out in its entirety, since this Book is a portion of the Holy Scripture and the full Four-Letter Name of Hᴀsʜᴇᴍ appears in the Hebrew, it would have been ludicrous to abbreviate the spelling of the English word God. אֶרֶץ יִשְׂרָאֵל was translated *Eretz Yisrael* (Land of Israel). Where the word Israel is found, it refers to the Jewish people.

A cross between the Sephardi and Ashkenazi transliteration of Hebrew words was used: Ashkenezi consonants, so to speak, with Sephardi vowels. Thus: Yisrael, not Yisroel; *Iggeres Shmuel*, not *Iggeret Shmuel*, etc. Proper names that have become generally accepted have been retained; thus: Ruth, Bethlehem, Jesse were retained and not changed to conform to our method of transliteration. Although there are several inconsistencies, the style has generally been held throughout the work.

◄§ **Author's Acknowledgments to the Original Edition**

This work is not entirely my own. That it is in any way worthy of the reader's attention is because I have the honor of benefiting from the friendship and counsel of some of the most scholarly and intellectually gifted personalities on the contemporary Torah scene. They have graciously given of their free time and genius to read the manuscript in its evolutionary stages, saving me, in many cases, from my own ignorance. I am indebted to:

My father HARAV HAGAON ARON ZLOTOWITZ (שליט"א (זצ"ל who has reviewed the work and allowed me to benefit from his *hashkafah* and erudition. May he and my dear mother, תחי', be rewarded בְּכָל מִילֵי דְמֵיטַב.

A very great note of thanks is due רַבִּי אֱלוּפִי וּמְיוּדָעִי, RAV DAVID FEINSTEIN, who, seeing the importance of such a series, again made an exception to his general policy, to assist in the preparation of this work. He graciously allowed me to remain in constant communication with him, and he patiently clarified many difficult Chazals, reading the entire manuscript and offering most sensitive suggestions. He allowed me the freedom to decide what to include and what to omit — and hence

is absolved from any responsibility for the final redaction — but his scholarship and בְּקִיאוּת are something I could not have done without.

RAV JOSEPH ELIAS kindly consented to read through the whole manuscript and spent hours offering many concepts from the storehouse of his vast scholarship and in many ways raising the level of the work.

My very good friend, RAV DAVID COHEN, graciously took time from his hectic schedule to read and comment upon the entire manuscript, guiding me to thoughts and interpretations, elucidating upon many of the underlying concepts and tenderly removing many stumbling blocks. He performed "constant righteousness" — עוֹשֶׂה צְדָקָה בְּכָל עֵת, by lending me many of the volumes I needed for researching this anthology. He freely gave of his time, allowing me to "air out" important insights before committing them to writing. I am grateful for his loving concern and friendship through the years.

RABBI RONALD GREENWALD, a dear and devoted friend, has been kind enough to make invaluable and encouraging suggestions, many of which were incorporated into the final work. His wife, MIRIAM תחי', was kind enough to read the manuscript, and offered several suggestions.

My dear friend and colleague, REB AVI SHULMAN, along with his wife, תחי', made many very important stylistic and conceptual observations on portions of the commentary. Avi shouldered the burden at ArtScroll during my involvement with this work and, seeing the need for such a commentary, almost single-handedly ensured its dissemination on a broad scale.

The efforts of my friend REB ZUNDEL BERMAN, *sefarim* dealer and publisher, are deeply acknowledged. He envisioned the *harbatzas-Torah* value of this series and he undertook to distribute it to the broad spectrum of *bnei yeshivah* with whom he enjoys a fine reputation, and with whom he is so intimately involved. He has gone out of his way to cooperate in every way possible.

A note of thanks is due to my friends at ARTSCROLL STUDIOS, LTD., whose high degree of professionalism and self-sacrificing devotion and loyalty ensured a beautiful production.

To be adequately appreciated, spirituality must be esthetically clothed, and my חָבֵר נֶאֱמָן REB SHEAH BRANDER is the "master-tailor." The finished volume could not possibly have attained this degree of graphic excellence were it not for his efforts. He labored strenuously to assure a perfect product בִּפְנִים וּבַחוּץ, inside and out. He has my eternal gratitude for his every kindness, patience, and courtesy — both in the

compilation of the anthology — which he (and his wife, HENNY תחי׳) were kind enough to read with a most critical eye — and the final layout and design. He let nothing stand in the way of ensuring a beautiful production. Words do not adequately express my appreciation.

My devoted wife, RACHEL, is the recipient of my most profound blessings. Her patience continues to mystify me. She creates a home for me and our children which is conducive to Torah study, and which, to her delight, has become a בֵּית וַעֵד לַחֲכָמִים, a gathering place for scholars. She inspires my efforts for *harbatzas Torah*; in that merit may she be abundantly rewarded. תְּהִי מַשְׂכָּרְתָּהּ שְׁלֵמָה מֵעִם ה׳.

I again end with a prayer that work be received by the Torah world as a tool toward understanding and appreciating yet another one of the Sacred Books of the Bible as our Sages wanted us to understand and appreciate it; without recourse to so-called "scientific" or other untraditional sources, so that the hidden depths of the Torah will become the possession also of non-Hebrew-reading Jews — too many of whom have been condemned to varying degrees of spiritual pauperdom — so that "their souls will be drawn to HASHEM and His Torah."

Meir Zlotowitz

Rosh Chodesh Nissan, 5736
Brooklyn, N.Y.

✍ Overviews

Ruth and Shavuos

Ruth and the Seeds of Mashiach

◌§ An Overview /
Ruth and Shavuos*

אִלּוּ יָדַע רְאוּבֵן שֶׁהַקָּדוֹשׁ בָּרוּךְ הוּא מַכְתִּיב עָלָיו "וַיִּשְׁמַע רְאוּבֵן
וַיַּצִּלֵהוּ מִיָּדָם", בִּכְתֵפוֹ הָיָה מוֹלִיכוֹ אֵצֶל אָבִיו. וְאִלּוּ יָדַע אַהֲרֹן
שֶׁהַקָּדוֹשׁ בָּרוּךְ הוּא מַכְתִּיב עָלָיו "הִנֵּה הוּא יֹצֵא לִקְרָאתֶךָ",
בְּתוּפִּים וּבִמְחוֹלוֹת הָיָה יוֹצֵא לִקְרָאתוֹ. וְאִלּוּ הָיָה יוֹדֵעַ בּוֹעַז
שֶׁהַקָּדוֹשׁ בָּרוּךְ הוּא מַכְתִּיב עָלָיו "וַיִּצְבָּט לָהּ קָלִי וַתֹּאכַל וַתִּשְׂבַּע
וַתֹּתַר", עֲגָלוֹת מְפוּטָמוֹת הָיָה מַאֲכִילָהּ.

*Had Reuben known that the Holy One Blessed
is He would write about him, "Reuben heard and
rescued [Joseph] from their hand"(Genesis 37:21),
he would have carried him on his shoulders and
brought him back to [Jacob]. Had Aaron known
that the Holy One blessed is He would write about
him, "Behold [Aaron] is going out to meet you
[Moses]" (Exodus 4:14), [Aaron] would have gone
to meet him with drums and dances. And if Boaz
had known that the Holy One Blessed is He would
write about him, "He handed [Ruth] parched grain
and she ate and was satisfied, and had some left
over" (Ruth 2:13), he would have fed her fatted
calves (Midrash Rabbah, Ruth 5:6).*

לְשֶׁעָבַר הָיָה אָדָם עוֹשֶׂה מִצְוָה וְהַנָּבִיא כּוֹתְבָהּ. וְעַכְשָׁיו כְּשֶׁאָדָם
עוֹשֶׂה מִצְוָה מִי כּוֹתְבָהּ? אֵלִיָּהוּ כּוֹתְבָהּ וְהַמֶּלֶךְ הַמָּשִׁיחַ וְהַקָּדוֹשׁ
בָּרוּךְ הוּא חוֹתֵם עַל יְדֵיהֶם.

*In the past, a person would perform a command-
ment and a prophet would record it. And now, when
a person performs a commandment, who records
it? Elijah will record it and the King Messiah and
the Holy One Blessed is He will seal it (ibid. 5:7).*

*It is an almost
universal Jewish
custom to read
the Book of Ruth
on Shavuos.*

IT IS AN ALMOST UNIVERSAL JEWISH CUSTOM TO READ
the Book of *Ruth* on Shavuos. Various reasons are
given. *Vilna Gaon* (*Orach Chaim* 490:), citing *Avudra-
ham*, explains that just as the newly liberated nation

* Except where otherwise noted, the overview is based on *Sfas Emes*.

came to Mount Sinai to accept the Torah, the people "converted" to Judaism, as it were. So, too, Ruth converted to Judaism.

Magen Avraham (ibid. 490:8) cites *Yalkut Shemini* (996) that just as one can acquire the Torah only through struggle and hardship, so, too, Ruth elevated herself to Jewishness through struggle and hardship.

Ruth elevated herself to Jewishness through struggle and hardship.

Others explain that King David died on Shavuos, and since Ruth was his great-grandmother, it is fitting for Shavuos to be the day when we read how she joined the nation of Israel.

Magen Avraham (494:1) wonders why we celebrate Shavuos on the *sixth* day of Sivan when, according to the accepted version in the Talmud, the Ten Commandments were given on the *seventh* of Sivan. He answers that we observe the sixth day since, as the Torah prescribes, it is the fiftieth day of the Counting of the Omer. However, the Torah was originally given on 7 Sivan, the fifty-first day of the Omer count, to allude to the future second day of Yom Tov, which would be observed outside of *Eretz Yisrael* when the Temples were destroyed and the nation was cast into exile.

Woven together, the above four threads will give us an understanding of the relationship between Shavuos and Ruth.

I. The Oral Law

Implanted Within Us

TWO BLESSINGS ARE RECITED WHEN ONE IS CALLED TO the Torah. The first one blesses God for choosing Israel to receive His Written Torah. The second one blesses God for חַיֵּי עוֹלָם נָטַע בְּתוֹכֵנוּ, *implanting eternal life within us.* Just as plants grow, the Torah can "grow." This alludes to the Oral Torah, by means of which a Jew has the capacity to delve into the Oral Law that Moses received from God, and apply its principles to obtain deeper understandings and deal with new phenomena (*Tur Orach Chaim* 139). There is no greater intellectual exercise than the study of the Talmud with the classic commentators. The analytical brilliance of Rabbi Chaim Soloveitchik's work on the Talmud is breathtaking. The

Just as plants grow, the Torah can "grow."

There is no greater intellectual exercise than the study of the Talmud with the classic commentators.

halachic responsa of Rabbi Moshe Feinstein demonstrate how the Talmudic principle of millennia ago can be applied to modern inventions that were undreamt of even a generation ago.

Their works are all luxuriant outgrowths of the eternal life that God implanted within us.

Their works and the thousands upon thousands of rabbinic volumes that line the shelves of great libraries — not to mention the infinite number of volumes and manuscripts that were destroyed in the Holocaust, Inquisition, and Crusades — are all luxuriant outgrowths of the eternal life that God implanted within us. That "eternal life" is the Oral Torah, the inseparable companion of the Written Torah.

To Accept Ruth

THE STORY OF RUTH BEARS WITNESS TO THIS. AS WILL BE noted in more detail in the next Overview, Ruth's passion to become a Jew and to produce Jewish generations was clouded by a Scriptural restriction. The Torah commands לֹא יָבֹא מוֹאָבִי בִּקְהַל ה', *a Moabite may not enter the congregation of Hashem* (*Deuteronomy* 23:4), meaning that although a Moabite may convert and become a member of the Jewish people, he may not intermarry into the nation. Ruth was a Moabite princess. Noble though her conversion was, how could she be permitted to marry a Jew, in violation of the Torah's prohibition? The answer was in the Oral Law. When God taught the prohibition to Moses, He added the explanation: only a *male* Moabite was forbidden, but not a Moabitess. Thus, the prohibition did not apply to Ruth, and she was permitted to marry Boaz.

When God taught the prohibition to Moses, He added the explanation.

The law was not well known, presumably because such a case had rarely if ever come up.

The law was not well known, presumably because such a case had rarely if ever come up in the centuries since the Torah had been given. This was why Ploni Almoni, the closest relative of Ruth's late husband, refused to marry her. He declared פֶּן אַשְׁחִית (*Ruth* 4:6), how can I enter into a "forbidden" marriage, a marriage that will produce halachically blemished children? As for the Rabbinically taught interpretation that the verse did not apply to Ruth, Ploni Almoni could not overcome his doubts about its validity. Did not the Scriptural verse forbid the seed of Moab? Could he have confidence in a Rabbinic teaching that the "obvious" meaning was not the true meaning?

Boaz and Power

BOAZ WAS DIFFERENT. HE HAD A POWERFUL FAITH IN THE teaching of the Sages. If the Oral Law taught that Ruth was permitted to him, there was no room for doubt, any more than there was room to doubt that the rising of the sun signaled the beginning of a new day. The Holy Zohar teaches that his faith was signified by his name. Boaz is a combination of the two words בּוֹ עֹז, *in him there is power*. Others might question the veracity of the Sages, but Boaz had no questions. If the Sages taught that he was permitted to marry Ruth, then he would stand at the gate of his city, in the presence of the court, and declare his desire to do so. He had a powerful faith. It may well be that this is the very reason why the Book of *Ruth* refers to him as Boaz, although his real name was Ivtzan (*Bava Basra* 91a). The great-grandfather of King David, who, with Ruth, would be the ancestor of the Messianic dynasty, was renamed Boaz in tribute to his exemplary faith in the sages and his courage to act on it publicly. His new name was intended to recognize his newly elevated mission; just as Abram became Abraham and Jacob became Israel, Ivtzan became Boaz.

The great-grandfather of King David was renamed Boaz in tribute to his exemplary faith in the sages and his courage to act on it publicly.

II. Deeds Have Meaning

Ripples and Righteous Deeds

JUST AS A JEW CAN USE HIS GOD-GIVEN WISDOM AND sanctity to draw new knowledge from the Oral Torah, so he can even add to the Written Torah by means of his dedication and good deeds. In tribute to the heroic dedication of Esther and Mordechai, a new Book of the Torah was created. In tribute to the faith and courage of Ruth and Boaz, a new book of the Torah was created. God wants Jews to know that the deeds of the righteous have an enormous impact. The world was created for the sake of the Torah (see *Rashi* to *Genesis* 1:1) and it remains in existence thanks to the Torah. Thus, righteous deeds are not limited to the ledger of those who perform them. Those who imbue the material world with a spiritual dimension become partners in creation. The soul gives life

God wants Jews to know that the deeds of the righteous have an enormous impact.

The soul gives life to the body; allegiance to the Torah gives life to the world. to the body; allegiance to the Torah gives life to the world.

Only during the era of prophecy could such deeds be immortalized in the Torah. But we do not act in a vacuum. As expressed eloquently in the Midrashic passage quoted to introduce this essay, the spiritual strides of Jews in exile are recorded by Elijah in the presence of God and King Messiah. Deeds have consequences that stretch to the Heavenly spheres — for good or evil — especially the deeds of God's Chosen People. As *Nefesh HaChaim* sets forth in very stark terms, the evil fantasies of a Jew cause greater harm in Heaven than did the monstrous lechery of Titus, who had the audacity to commit immoral acts in the Holy of Holies, before *At present, we do not understand the import of our actions, but in the Messianic era we will.* he destroyed the Second Temple. At present, we do not understand the import of our actions, but in the Messianic era we will. As the Sages put it, וְכָל מַעֲשֶׂיךָ בַּסֵּפֶר נִכְתָּבִים, *all your deeds are inscribed in a book* (*Avos* 2:1), and that book will be read and understood when the Messianic Era dawns.

The Midrash cited above states that Reuven, Aaron, and Boaz would have done much more had they known that their deeds would be inscribed in the Torah. This does not mean that they would have acted differently for the sake of popularity; historically great tzaddikim do not fashion their behavior to win public acclaim. Rather the Midrash means that they did not realize that their good deeds could have such repercussions that they were worthy of inclusion in God's eternal Torah. If *If they could have known the significance of something that to them was no more than "the right thing to do," they would have done much more.* they could have known the significance of something that to them was no more than "the right thing to do," they would have done much more.

The same applies to all of us. Our deeds have meaning. Their ripples go far beyond our awareness. They are recorded in the Heavenly ledger and attract the attention of even God, Elijah, and the Messiah.

Magnetic Power AN ILLUSTRATION OF THIS CONCEPT IS FOUND IN *OR HA-Chaim* (*Exodus* 19:5) and elaborated upon in *Or Gedalyahu* (*Likkutim LiShavuos* 7). The Sages teach that Israel was exiled among the nations to "gather up the sparks of holiness" that God spread throughout the world. What would have happened if Jews

had never sinned and never been exiled? Who would have wandered from country to country gathering the holy sparks? The answer is that the power of Torah is so great that if Israel in its own land had lived up to its infinite potential, the nation would have been like a magnet drawing to itself all those spread-out sparks. As a very mundane example, לְהַבְדִּיל, we see that outstanding personages — "stars" — can fill halls and stadiums with people traveling from afar and buying expensive tickets to hear or watch them. The power of absolute holiness is far greater. The Torah of the Jewish people would have drawn seekers of truth to *Eretz Yisrael* from everywhere.

The Torah of the Jewish people would have drawn seekers of truth to Eretz Yisrael from everywhere.

Ruth, the future mother of Jewish majesty, came to the Holy Land, where she would fulfill her mission to become the mother of the Messianic dynasty. Had her father-in-law Elimelech, who had been one of the great figures of the land, been as great as he should have been, she would somehow have felt an urge to come to Bethlehem. But Elimelech fell short. So he and his family left the Land for a self-imposed exile in Moab, where Ruth was attracted to his son and forged a close tie to her mother-in-law Naomi and the Jewish people. So great was her love for Naomi and the Divine ideal that she embodied, that Ruth left her land and family to adopt the destiny of Israel — and then she was drawn to Boaz, as if by a magnet.

Ruth left her land and family to adopt the destiny of Israel — and then she was drawn to Boaz, as if by a magnet.

Had Elimelech and his sons been worthy and remained in *Eretz Yisrael*, Ruth's quest for holiness would have drawn her to them. But they were not worthy. Boaz was. So, without knowing why, she was attracted to him, and they earned a place in the Almighty's Scriptures.

Effort Rewarded ROTE BEHAVIOR HAS LITTLE VALUE. AS THE SAGES SAY, לְפוּם צַעֲרָא אַגְרָא, *the greater the difficulty, the greater the reward* (*Avos* 5:26). No one becomes great in Torah without effort. The paramount sages of every generation — including our own — may well have become fine scholars based on their natural ability, but they become great only because they exerted maximum effort, constantly. So, too, Ruth. Her struggles with identity, odyssey, hunger, poverty, and loneliness were enough

Ruth earned a place alongside that of august Torah sages. to break the spirit of even a strong woman. But Ruth persevered, and thereby earned a place alongside that of august Torah sages.

III. Shavuos and the Oral Law

What the Torah Means

HISTORICALLY, STUDY OF THE ORAL TORAH HAS BEEN emphasized in Jewish life, because without it the commandments of Written Torah are incomprehensible. There was a deviant Jewish sect that sat in the dark and did not leave their homes throughout Shabbos because the Torah says that one may not kindle a fire and should remain in his place on the seventh day. Had the Oral Law not explained what the verses mean, that sect would have seemed to be justified. Similarly, what are tefillin and how should animals be slaughtered?

Without the Oral Law, we would be at a loss to understand the Torah properly. The list of such questions is endless. Without the Oral Law, we would be at a loss to understand the Torah properly.

The decision to postpone the acceptance of the Torah from the sixth of Sivan to the seventh was made by Moses, with God's approval. That was a classic instance of a sage's use of the Oral Law, and Israel's acceptance of his authority. This is what *Magen Avraham* means when he says that the second day of Shavuos in the diaspora alludes to the power of the Oral Law.

Exemplified by Ruth

THE STORY OF RUTH AND BOAZ EXEMPLIFIES THIS PRINCIPLE. It is true, as some commentators have noted, that there was no second day of the festivals until many centuries after the Torah was given and after the story of Ruth. *R' Tzaddok Hacohen* (*Pri Tzaddik*) explains

The greatest flowering of the Oral Law took place in Babylonia, during the period of the Mishnah and the Talmud. that, as noted above, the Oral Law is an essential component of the Torah. The greatest flowering of the Oral Law took place in Babylonia, during the period of the Mishnah and the Talmud. Since the oral fortress of the Torah was developed primarily in the Diaspora, it is fitting that this phenomenon be conspicuously marked on Shavuos, when the Torah was given.

The story of Ruth and the festival of Shavuos are inseparable.

The story of Ruth and the festival of Shavuos are inseparable, not only because of the personal experience of the great woman who became the Mother of Royalty, but because her achievement still resonates and will become most pronounced when the Davidic dynasty reaches it zenith with the coming of Messiah and the universally acknowledged sovereignty of the Torah and its Giver.

Rabbi Nosson Scherman

Iyar 5770 / April 2010

✑ An Overview / Ruth and the Seeds of Mashiach

בִּשְׁבִיל שְׁתֵּי פְרֵידוֹת טוֹבוֹת [רוּת הַמּוֹאֲבִיָּה וְנַעֲמָה הָעַמּוֹנִית] חָס הַקָּדוֹשׁ בָּרוּךְ הוּא עַל שְׁתֵּי אוּמוֹת גְּדוֹלוֹת וְלֹא הֶחֱרִיבָן (בבא קמא לח:)

Because of two good "doves" [pure and righteous Ruth the Moabite and Na'amah the Ammonite], the Holy One, Blessed is He, had mercy on two great nations [Ammon and Moab] and did not destroy them (Talmud).

שְׁתֵּי נָשִׁים הָיוּ שֶׁמֵּהֶם נִבְנָה זֶרַע יְהוּדָה וְיָצָא מֵהֶם דָּוִד הַמֶּלֶךְ שְׁלֹמֹה הַמֶּלֶךְ וּמֶלֶךְ הַמָּשִׁיחַ ... תָּמָר וְרוּת ... וּשְׁתֵּיהֶם עָשׂוּ בְכַשְׁרוּת כְּדֵי לַעֲשׂוֹת טוֹבָה עִם הַמֵּתִים (זהר)

There were two women from whom were built the seed of Judah and from whom descended King David, King Solomon, and the King Mashiach. . . Tamar and Ruth . . . . Both acted properly in order to do good with the dead (Zohar).

שְׁבָטִים הָיוּ עוֹסְקִים בִּמְכִירָתוֹ שֶׁל יוֹסֵף, יוֹסֵף הָיָה עָסוּק בְּשַׂקּוֹ וְתַעֲנִיתוֹ, רְאוּבֵן הָיָה עָסוּק בְּשַׂקּוֹ וְתַעֲנִיתוֹ, יַעֲקֹב הָיָה עָסוּק בְּשַׂקּוֹ וְתַעֲנִיתוֹ, וִיהוּדָה הָיָה עָסוּק לִיקַּח לוֹ אִשָּׁה, וְהַקָּדוֹשׁ בָּרוּךְ הוּא הָיָה עוֹסֵק בּוֹרֵא אוֹרוֹ שֶׁל מֶלֶךְ הַמָּשִׁיחַ (בראשית רבה)

The tribes were occupied with the sale of Joseph, Joseph was occupied with his sackcloth and fast, Reuben was occupied with his sackcloth and fast, Jacob was occupied with his sackcloth and fast, and Judah was occupied with taking a wife. And the Holy One, Blessed is He, was occupied in creating the light of the King Mashiach (Bereishis Rabbah).

I. The Period — A Moral Perspective

THE BOOK OF *RUTH* BEGINS WITH A PHRASE THAT, AT first glance, appears designed to place the story in a historical time frame: בִּימֵי שְׁפֹט הַשֹּׁפְטִים — *And it happened in the days when the Judges judged.* Upon

closer examination, however, we see that Samuel, author of *Megillas Ruth,* has, in fact, told us very little. The
period of Judges began with the death of Joshua and
extended until King Saul introduced monarchy to *Eretz*

By telling us that *Yisrael* — a period of roughly 350 years. By telling us
the story of Ruth that the story of Ruth occurred during the period of the
occurred during Judges, the prophet is hardly telling us when the events
the period of took place.
the Judges, the
prophet is hardly True, the Talmud says אִבְצָן זֶה בֹּעַז — the Judge Ivtzan
telling us when was Boaz (*Bava Basra* 91a), in which case the marriage
the events took of Ruth and Boaz took place in the year 2792 (968 BCE),
place. 304 years after Joshua led *Bnei Yisrael* into the Land and
259 years after the period of Judges began (*Toldos Am
Olam*). Nevertheless, *Scripture* does not declare explicitly that Boaz and Ivtzan were one and the same, a statement that would be of utmost necessity if the opening
phrase of *Megillas Ruth* were indeed intended to establish the chronology of the succeeding events.

Thus it is that our Sages interpret the phrase "when
the Judges judged" not as a historical, but as a moral
statement (see *Commentary* 1:1). Ruth emerged during
a chaotic period in Jewish history. It was a time when
When there are people did not respond to their leaders and too many
no leaders and of the leaders did not earn the allegiance of the people.
no followers, the During such a period, famine struck the land — not
soul of Judaism only physical but spiritual; when there are no leaders
hungers with and no followers, the soul of Judaism hungers with
pangs no less pangs no less severe or lethal than those of an emaci-
severe or lethal ated body (*Or Yohel*).
than those of an
emaciated body.

When There ALTHOUGH *MEGILLAS RUTH* IS A SEPARATE BOOK OF THE
Was No Twenty-Four, it is strikingly similar in many ways to two
King of the sorriest tales in Scripture, both at the conclusion
of the Book of *Judges:* (a) פִּלֶגֶשׁ בְּגִבְעָה, The Concubine
in Giv'ah [*Judges* Ch. 19], the story of an atrocity that
led to a civil war resulting in over 80,000 dead and the
virtual decimation of the tribe of Benjamin; and, (b)
פֶּסֶל מִיכָה, The Idol of Michah, that led astray a sizable
portion of the tribe of Dan [*Judges* Ch. 18]. Those episodes, too, are placed in an indefinite time frame and
the commentators disagree concerning when they occurred. But the author of the Book of *Judges* describes
the respective periods very pithily:

בַּיָּמִים הָהֵם אֵין מֶלֶךְ בְּיִשְׂרָאֵל אִישׁ הַיָּשָׁר בְּעֵינָיו יַעֲשֶׂה

In those days there was no king in Israel, every man did what was right in his own eyes (Judges 17:6, 18:1, 19:1, 21:25).

How striking! The precise year of the event is unimportant. Even the name of the contemporary Judge matters not at all .... The Scripture is not a history book.

How striking! The precise year of the event is unimportant. Even the name of the contemporary Judge matters not at all. Were we to know these historical curiosities, they would not add to our understanding of the episodes or instruct us for the future. And, in the final analysis, Scripture is not a history book. The narratives are often incomplete and the chronology indefinite. Any number of inspirational and miraculous tales are told only in the *Talmud* and *Midrash*. Why aren't they in Scripture? They aren't because they needn't be; the Torah is neither a history book nor a story book. God in His infinite wisdom gave us the סֵפֶר תּוֹלְדוֹת אָדָם, *the "Book of the Generations of Man" (Genesis 5:1)*, and included in it what was necessary for us to know. The Jewish people produced over a million prophets until the period of prophecy came to an end with the Babylonian Exile, but only fifty-five are mentioned in the Twenty-Four Books of the Torah. Only those stories and prophecies needed by posterity were recorded. The others, too, were manifestations of the mind, hand, and word of God, but, needed only in the period when they were revealed, they were not immortalized in the eternity of Torah *(Maharal)*.

The Jewish people produced over a million prophets ... but only fifty-five are mentioned in the Twenty-four Books of the Torah ... Only those stories and prophecies needed by posterity were recorded.

But the closing tragedies of the Book of *Judges* — the concubine in Giv'ah and the idol of Michah — were. They were indelibly inscribed in Jewish thought because they are more than tales. They are expressions of what can occur when *"there is no king in Israel, every man did what is right in his own eyes."* As such, they are timeless and eternal. The Jew in every age must know what his fate can become if he refuses to accept authority and leadership. *Ruth* is of a piece with those other illustrations of what can happen when there is no vested authority in Israel. *Megillas Ruth*, too, begins with a cryptic phrase, *"in the days when the Judges judged."* The prophet, in three Hebrew words, captures the attitude of an era. As the Talmud interprets, it indicates that the people judged, criticized, flouted their judges. Under such conditions authority breaks down. When that happens, there is famine: physical

The Jew in every age must know what his fate can become if he refuses to accept authority and leadership.

and spiritual. When that happens, even so great a man as Elimelech — learned, honored, wealthy — can cast off his responsibility to his people and flee to the fields of Moab (see *Commentary*).

The Story of Ruth

Ruth, princess of Moab, might never even have seen a Jew, much less married one, had it not been for the lapse of Elimelech and the Jewish people.

... She became the matriarch of the family that produced David, bearer of God's glory on earth.

The seeds of salvation can often be planted in a greenhouse of tragedy.

SEEN IN THIS LIGHT, THE STORY OF RUTH AS THE BACK-ground of מַלְכוּת בֵּית דָּוִד, the kingship of the House of David, takes on a new perspective. Ruth, princess of Moab, might never even have seen a Jew, much less married one, had it not been for the lapse of Elimelech and the Jewish people. Because there was relative an-archy, a family from Bethlehem went to Moab and set in motion a chain of events that resulted in a princess from Moab becoming אִמָּהּ שֶׁל מַלְכוּת, the mother of Jew-ish royalty, matriarch of the family that produced David, bearer of God's glory on earth, and will ultimately pro-duce *Mashiach* who will lead Israel and all mankind to the spiritual splendor intended by God when He said, יְהִי אוֹר, "*Let there be light!*"

It is axiomatic in Jewish belief that God's hand is ev-erywhere and that the seeds of salvation can often be planted in a greenhouse of tragedy. Joseph was sold into slavery and his righteous father grieved for twenty-two years, but meanwhile God was preparing for Joseph to become the gracious and merciful viceroy who would ease the way into an Egyptian exile that had to be. A Jewish baby was placed in a basket to die in the sea, but he became Moses, the ward of Pharaoh's daughter and the faithful shepherd of the Jewish people. Elimelech fled his destiny and we can only imagine how mortified the tribe of Judah must have been that its most illustri-ous son deserted it in its time of desperate need, but God was preparing the genesis of the Davidic house which would bring to Judah at long last the glory that Jacob pledged it in his final blessing.

II. The Sins of the Ancients

A Frame of Reference

BEFORE PROCEEDING FURTHER, IT IS IMPORTANT TO UN-derstand that the sins of the ancients cannot even be mentioned in the same breath as ours. The Torah

creates no cult of hero worship; it freely and frankly discloses the transgressions and shortcomings of the Jewish people as a whole and of the most exalted figures in its history. When such greats as Moses and David fall short of the exacting standards expected of them, they are criticized in a way that can make modern-day readers smug and complacent in their own fantasies of self-righteousness. Superficial readings of Torah have resulted in the images of violence, cruelty, and lust profitably merchandised by writers and producers who dare to cheapen history's greatest souls to turn an easy profit. Yet one of our great scholars and righteous men of recent generations expressed the Torah view succinctly and well when he said, "If only our *mitzvos* could be as holy as their *aveiros* (transgressions)." It is ingrained in our system of belief that earlier generations — because they were closer to the wellsprings of revelation and to Sinai — were infinitely more holy than ours. So much so that, even in halachah, the outstanding decisors of any era can only interpret and compare, but never dispute, the findings of their predecessors of a previous period. The demarcations of periods were decreed by the leading scholars of a generation when they, themselves, realized that they did not approach the stature of the preceding greats. Thus it was that the Sages of the Talmud decided that the illustrious period of the Mishnaic *Tannaim* had come to an end. In the same way, the personal conduct of the ancients — and especially of the greatest among them — was measured by a standard infinitely higher and more exacting than ours.

When such greats as Moses and David fall short of the exacting standards expected of them, they are criticized in a way that can make modern-day readers smug and complacent in their own fantasies of self-righteousness.

It is ingrained in our system of belief that earlier generations — because they were closer to the wellsprings of revelation and to Sinai — were infinitely more holy than ours.

The personal conduct of the ancients — and especially of the greatest among them — was measured by a standard infinitely higher and more exacting than ours.

Such a concept should not be entirely foreign to us. We expect higher standards of conduct from people holding positions of responsibility. One might feel extreme annoyance at the sight of a drunken bicyclist; after all, he could collide with someone or something, endangering himself and others. But we would be appalled at the thought of a drunken airline pilot with hundreds of passengers, and of untold innocents below, at the mercy of his inebriated mind and uncontrollable hands. Similarly, succeeding generations have learned to shrug at the corruption of leaders and magnates, but *Baruch Hashem*, we could not even

conceive of such behavior on the part of our Torah giants.

One does not expect big things of small people, nor should one be indulgent of "human" weakness in mighty figures.

Conversely, because more is expected of greater people, their lapses must be judged by a higher standard as well. The standard the Torah imposes on the holy figures of ancient times is harsh and unforgiving, and it is proof of their greatness: one does not expect big things of small people, nor should one be indulgent of "human" weakness in mighty figures.

Condemnation — But No Sin

וַיֵּלֶךְ רְאוּבֵן וַיִּשְׁכַּב אֶת־בִּלְהָה פִּילֶגֶשׁ אָבִיו
And Reuben went and slept with Bilhah, his father's concubine (Bereishis 35:22).

The Talmud explains that Reuben did not commit the sin of adultery: "Whoever says Reuben sinned is mistaken."

A HORRIBLE SIN! THE CHILDREN OF JACOB HAD ONLY RE-cently exterminated the city of Shechem for a lesser abomination, and yet Reuben remained a son in good standing, a respected father of the Jewish nation. The Talmud explains that Reuben did *not* commit the sin of adultery; מִי שֶׁאָמַר רְאוּבֵן חָטָא אֵינוֹ אֶלָּא טוֹעֶה, "Whoever says Reuben sinned is mistaken" *(Shabbos 55b)*. After the death of Rachel, who had had the status of Jacob's principal wife, Leah and her children felt that the honor of family primacy was due her. When, instead, Jacob's personal belongings were moved to the tent of Bilhah, Reuben felt that his mother had been slighted. To right the wrong, he removed Jacob's things to the tent of Leah. An understandable, even commendable, deed by most standards. But for a person of Reuben's stature to tamper with his father's privacy, to interfere in the personal life of the patriarch Jacob, was a gross, coarse act. By the standard of behavior expected of a Reuben, such an indiscretion is tantamount to adultery and the Torah so labels it.

But for a person of Reuben's stature to tamper with his father's privacy, to interfere in the personal life of the patriarch Jacob, was a gross, coarse act.

וַיְהִי לְעֵת זִקְנַת שְׁלֹמֹה נָשָׁיו הִטּוּ אֶת־לְבָבוֹ אַחֲרֵי אֱלֹהִים
אֲחֵרִים . . . וְלֹא שָׁמַר אֵת אֲשֶׁר צִוָּה ה'
And it happened when Solomon was old that his wives turned his heart away to other gods . . . and he kept not that which HASHEM commanded (I Kings 11:4-10).

Scripture apparently makes it clear that the aging Solomon became an idol worshiper. Again, the Talmud says no *(Shabbos 56b)*. His wives attempted to draw

Solomon's wives attempted to draw him after the idols, but he did not heed them. Just the same, Solomon is condemned as an idolater.

him after the idols, but he did not heed them. Just the same, Solomon is condemned as an idolater, the harshest approbrium the Torah can confer, because, by his indulgent attitude toward the sins of his foreign wives, he allowed them to think that they could sway his heart from the service of God. This might be excusable in lesser men, but never in Solomon.

An Exalted Nation

Higher standards are expected of the Jewish people, especially during the period of Scripture when they were witness to miracles, audience to prophecy.

SIMILARLY, HIGHER STANDARDS ARE EXPECTED OF THE JEWish people, especially during the period of Scripture when they were witness to miracles, audience to prophecy. The classic, indisputable case in point is the incident in *Joshua* Ch. 7, which tells of the shocking, demoralizing defeat suffered by Israel in their attack upon the small town of Ai. After the miracle of Jericho and the Divine promises that they would conquer the land without a casualty, this setback cast a pall upon the entire people. Joshua and the elders tore their clothes, put ashes on their heads, and fell before the Holy Ark pleading with God to tell them why the tragedy happened.

God responded with a shocking and frightening litany of the transgressions of His once holy and righteous people:

חָטָא יִשְׂרָאֵל וְגַם עָבְרוּ אֶת־בְּרִיתִי ... וְגַם לָקְחוּ מִן
הַחֵרֶם וְגַם גָּנְבוּ וְגַם כִּחֲשׁוּ וְגַם שָׂמוּ בִּכְלֵיהֶם

Israel has sinned and they have also violated My covenant ... and they have also taken from the consecrated property, and have also stolen, and denied, and they have also placed [it] in their vessels.

How bold and all-encompassing a condemnation! Israel had become a nation of traitors and thieves!

Joshua investigated and it was discovered that Achan — only one man from an entire nation — had violated Joshua's prohibition against looting the spoils of Jericho. Because of one man's lapse, the nation was castigated in the sharpest terms and doomed to defeat in the wars commanded by God. Because of only one man's frailty, the Divine pledge to the patriarchs and their children was jeopardized.

Because of only one man's frailty, the Divine pledge to the patriarchs and their children was jeopardized.

Did Scripture not tell the story explicitly, we could not imagine that Achan's deed could even be considered

How great was the nation that could be so stringently judged for the failure of one of its insignificant members, because of its malfeasance in winking at his act.

a serious sin, much less imperil a nation. That it was considered so grievous an act points up to an inspiring and unimaginable degree how great was the nation that, because of its malfeasance in winking at his act, could be so stringently judged for the failure of one of its insignificant members. (For a fuller treatment of the above concept and further examples of it, see *Michtav Me'Eliyahu I* p. 162.)

Ruth in Perspective

It is a valid indication of the depth of ignorance and the shallowness of scholarship with which most of Tanach is studied, or, better said, read.

Even during its period of deepest decline, Israel was far, far above the moral, ethical, scholarly, and religious standards of the twentieth century.

MEGILLAS RUTH HAS BEEN REFERRED TO IGNORANTLY AND sacrilegiously by people far from Torah as history's first love story. That such a statement makes any Torah Jew shudder with disgust and bristle with anger goes without saying. Just the same, it is a valid indication of the depth of ignorance and the shallowness of scholarship with which most of *Tanach* is studied, or, better said, read. True, a literal reading of much of *Tanach* presents a blood-and-guts, lust-and-transgression picture of the Jewish people in what should have been the most spiritual and fulfilling period of its history. To be sure, Israel fell short of the goals set for it, but let us never forget that it fell short of *its* goals, not of ours. Even during its period of deepest decline, Israel was far, far above the moral, ethical, scholarly, and religious standards of the twentieth century which so enjoys basking in the self-anointed status of occupant of civilization's highest rung.

Our Sages make it clear that Ruth's visit to Boaz in the dark of night was, in truth, the dawn of the blazing sun of the Davidic dynasty. Far from lusting after a Moabite woman, Boaz dedicated the last day of his life and the last strength of his aging body to the holy task of preparing the source of *Mashiach* with the righteous and pure "dove" for whose sake God spared incestuous, selfish, iniquitous Moab for over seven hundred years. Even the sins of a generation judging its judges, the shortcomings of judges unequal to their responsibilities (see *Commentary* 1:1), and the lapse of the great Elimelech and his family (*Commentary* 1:1-5) cannot be understood in terms of the corruption, cowardice, and rebellion to which we have become inured in recent years.

The Book of *Judges* is called סֵפֶר הַיָּשָׁר, *The Book of the Just,* because during the three-and-a-half centuries

of the Judges, the Jewish people, as a rule, did what was
Their sins, "upright in the eyes of God" (*Avodah Zarah* 25a). This in
however real, no way contradicts the many tales of sinfulness found
were defined in the pages of *Judges*. The years of sin were relatively
by a standard as few, they did not enmesh the entire nation, and the
elevated from sins, however real, were defined by a standard as el-
ours as is heaven
from earth. evated from ours as is heaven from earth.

III. Monarchy in Israel

A A S IS MADE CLEAR IN THE OPENING OF *MEGILLAS RUTH*
Command- and the references to the lack of a king in the chap-
ment ters of the concubine in Giv'ah and the idol of Michah,
Deferred the rule of Judges was not the ideal condition of Israel,
and the absence of a king was, from time to time, sorely
There is a basic felt. Clearly there is a basic difference between a king
difference and a judge and, in order to understand the period, we
between a king must understand the difference. Further, if monarchy
and a judge is the ideal condition of Jewish government, why was
and, in order to it not established as soon as Israel entered *Eretz Yis-*
understand the *rael?* And why, when the Jews finally asked Samuel to
period, we must give them a king, did he criticize them so bitterly for
understand the doing so? The Torah ordains as one of the Six Hundred
difference. Thirteen Commandments that Israel request a king
(*Deuteronomy* 17:14-15) according to the halachically
accepted view of Rabbi Yehudah (*Sanhedrin* 20b, *Ram-*
bam Hilchos Melachim) that:

> שָׁלֹשׁ מִצְוֹת נִצְטַווּ יִשְׂרָאֵל בִּכְנִיסָתָם לָאָרֶץ: לְהַעֲמִיד
> לָהֶם מֶלֶךְ, וּלְהַכְרִית זַרְעוֹ שֶׁל עֲמָלֵק, וְלִבְנוֹת לָהֶם בֵּית
> הַבְּחִירָה
>
> *The Jews were charged with three com-*
> *mandments upon entering the Land: to ap-*
> *point a king, to cut off the seed of Amalek,*
> *and to build the Beis Hamikdash . . . .*

If so, why did God scathingly describe the request
for a king as:

> לֹא אֹתְךָ מָאָסוּ כִּי אֹתִי מָאֲסוּ מִמְּלֹךְ עֲלֵיהֶם
> *Not you [Samuel] have they rejected, but*
> *Me have they rejected that I should not*
> *reign over them (I Samuel 8:7)?*

Government in Israel THE JEWISH CONCEPT OF GOVERNMENT IS UNIQUE AND always has been. Josephus Flavius put it this way:

> Some nations place the sovereignty of their land in the hands of a single ruler (monarchy), some in the hands of a small number of rulers (oligarchy), and some in the hands of the people (democracy). Moses our Teacher taught us to place our faith in none of these forms of government. He taught us to obey the rule of God, for to God alone did he accord kingship and power. He commanded the people always to raise their eyes to God, for He is the source of all good for mankind in general and for each person in particular and in Him will people find help when they pray to Him in their time of suffering, for no act is hidden from His understanding and no hidden thought of man's heart is hidden from Him (Contra Appion).

Josephus's description of Jewish government is often mistakenly described as theocracy, but it is not that at all. Jewish government was never the province of priests, an exchange of ermine for cassock. The Chashmonaim established a royal dynasty after their overthrow of the Syrian-Greeks, it is true, but the attempted perpetuation of that priestly monarchy was in violation of Jewish law in that it usurped the prerogative of the House of David and perverted the purpose of the priesthood. For their persistence in occupying the seat of power, the Chashmonaim were punished with extermination in a slave rebellion (*Ramban, Genesis* 49:10).

Jewish government was never the province of priests, an exchange of ermine for cassock.

The government described by Josephus is not one of priests, but of God. It mattered not whether the throne was occupied by a king or, as in earlier days, the accepted authority was a Judge: the true King of Israel is God; whatever human hands hold the reins of government are but His tools.

The true King of Israel is God; whatever human hands hold the reins of government are but His tools.

King Too Soon WHY, THEN, THE COMMANDMENT TO INSTALL A KING?

כִּי תָבֹא אֶל הָאָרֶץ אֲשֶׁר ה' אֱלֹקֶיךָ נֹתֵן לְךָ וִירִשְׁתָּהּ וְיָשַׁבְתָּה בָּהּ וְאָמַרְתָּ אָשִׂימָה עָלַי מֶלֶךְ כְּכָל הַגּוֹיִם אֲשֶׁר סְבִיבֹתָי

> When you come to the land that HASHEM, your God, gives you, and possess it, and

settle in it, and you will say "I set a king over myself like all the nations that around me (Deuteronomy 17:14).

The commandment makes it clear that it is *not* the purpose of a king to serve as a charismatic conqueror uniting the nation behind him, meting out judgment to the enemy, and conquering and securing the land for his people *(Kiddushin 37b)*. For it was only *after* having conquered and inhabited the land that a king was to be sought. Israel needed no mighty warlord to win its land, for had not God Himself promised them speedy conquest and total victory? הֹ' אִישׁ מִלְחָמָה ה' שְׁמוֹ, *God is a Man of war, with His Name* HASHEM — what need had they of a mortal conqueror? Security, prosperity, fruitfulness, happiness, and health were to be theirs as a natural consequence of observing the commandments, not for allegiance to a becrowned head or awe of a bemedaled breast *(Deuteronomy 28:1-14).*

Israel needed no mighty warlord to win its land, for had not God Himself promised them speedy conquest and total victory?

Security, prosperity, fruitfulness, happiness, and health were to be theirs as a natural consequence of observing the commandments, not for allegiance to a becrowned head or awe of a bemedaled breast.

For Israel upon its entry into *Eretz Yisrael* to have a king with all his royal trappings would have cheapened itself and its king. Had Israel been a conquering army with a king at its head, the presence and assistance of God would have been obscured by the glitter of a crown and the plush of royal robes. The fiction would indeed have been created that Israel had won its land by force of arms rather than *by grace of God; that the foe had been slain by a* flesh-and-blood king rather than by the King of kings, blessed is He.

Had Israel been a conquering army with a king at its head, the presence and assistance of God would have been obscured by the glitter of a crown and the plush of royal robes.

During the days of Samuel, significant stretches of *Eretz Yisrael* had not yet been conquered. Indeed, it was to the enduring shame and centuries-long discredit of Israel that it allowed such a condition to persist. Rather than take advantage of Divine assistance and heed the Divine command that it purge the Holy Land of its profane inhabitants and turn it in its entirety into the land of Abraham, Isaac, and Jacob, Israel was content to settle what had been won, retire to its vineyards and fig trees, and allow the less-fortunate tribes — those whose inheritance was still in alien hands — to bemoan their fate in isolation. For not uniting as a nation and carrying out its destiny, it was condemned to endure the presence and invasions of its enemies in a centuries-long cycle of fall, punishment, repentance, and deliverance *(Judges* Ch. 2).

Rather than take advantage of Divine assistance ... Israel was content to settle what had been won, and allow the less-fortunate tribes to bemoan their fate in isolation.

It was a weary people fearing invasion by Ammon and seeking a defender and military leader that confronted aging Samuel and demanded a king. But it was not for defense and conquest that God ordained royalty upon Israel; for those purposes, Israel had to worry less about the weaknesses of its fortresses than about the stubbornness of its spirit; less about crumbling the defenses of its enemies than about shattering its own nature-conditioned heart.

It was not for defense and conquest that God ordained royalty upon Israel

So it was an angry and disappointed Samuel who recited the catalog of miraculous Divine interventions in behalf of Israel, interventions that should have been more than sufficient to clarify the road of deliverance from their enemies. Samuel said:

וַתֹּאמְרוּ לִי, לֹא כִּי מֶלֶךְ יִמְלֹךְ עָלֵינוּ וַה' אֱלֹקֵיכֶם מַלְכְּכֶם

And you said to me, "No; but a king shall reign over us!" But HASHEM, your God, is your King! (I Samuel 12:12).

Yes, the Torah indeed commands Israel to request a king, but, in Samuel's day, the request was premature.

Yes, the Torah indeed commands Israel to request a king, but, in Samuel's day, the request was premature. They got their king, Saul — a great and righteous man, head and shoulders above the rest of the nation — but his monarchy ended in tragedy because the people were wrong in demanding it then.

The Role of a King

The king is the living embodiment of Torah and how its statutes and holiness ennoble man.

The king does not rest until his people know the rigors of Torah study and a discipline of honesty and morality ... that would earn sainthood in any other nation.

THE IDEAL JEWISH KING ASCENDS HIS THRONE IN A TIME OF tranquility. The nation is secure and prosperous because its ultimate King, God, has made it so, and its way of life is charted by the Torah. The king plays a unique role. He, as first citizen of the nation, is the living embodiment of Torah and how its statutes and holiness ennoble man. Holder of immense and almost unbridled power, he submits to the laws in the *Sefer Torah* which he carries with him at all times; required by his duty to the nation to hold wealth and exhibit pomp, he acquires what he must, but shuns excess; enabled by his station to indulge his passions, he sets an example of sobriety and self-control; inhibited by no mortal restraint, he turns his energies to the self-less service of his people; able to establish the absolute dominion of his own will, he does not rest until his people know the rigors of Torah study and a discipline of honesty and morality in their personal and

business lives that would earn sainthood in any other nation.

When the nation sought its king, it had not yet attained the stature it needed to be worthy of that type of monarch. Nevertheless, it did possess a man suited to the role: David, an unknown shepherd who was unappreciated even by his own family. Had Israel been worthy, David would have become the final *Mashiach* and the eternal *Beis HaMikdash* would have been built by him. As it was, he became the father of the dynasty whose ultimate heir will one day proclaim the kingdom of heaven upon earth. (Although there are many sources for the above treatment of Jewish monarchy, it is based primarily upon *Rav S.R. Hirsch, Deuteronomy* 17:14).

Had Israel been worthy, David would have become the final Mashiach *and the eternal* Beis HaMikdash *would have been built by him.*

Powers of the King

IT IS THE FUNCTION OF THE KING TO SAFEGUARD THE TORAH and see to it that the people study it and obey its commandments. Nor is he to be considered above the halachah; on the contrary, it is his duty to be a model of scrupulous adherence to the laws of the Torah. His office, however, carries with it a unique legal status which may be divided into two categories:

a) As the sovereign embodiment of the nation, the king is entitled to respect and reverence exceeding anyone else's. All must step aside to make way for him and even property may be destroyed for his convenience. Nor may the king voluntarily forfeit any of his prerogatives; to do so is to demean the nation he leads. He is as obligated to exercise his claim upon the awe of the nation as is each of its members to grant it.

b) The king has extralegal powers to confiscate, punish, and condemn to execution. A Jewish court of law may not execute a murderer save under a set of extraordinarily strict rules of evidence and testimony; a king may have the murderer killed, so long as he is satisfied that sufficient proof of guilt exists, even if the evidence is circumstantial. Whoever is disrespectful or defiant of the king is liable to the death penalty upon his command and at his pleasure.

All this is to insure that he has the power to inspire the fear of, and destroy the capacity of evildoers (*Rambam, Hilchos Melachim* 3).

In the exercise of his extralegal powers, the king is guided by one consideration: *"to correct any situation, as required by the times"* (ibid).

Thus it becomes clear why Samuel, author of *Judges*, explains the worst aberrations of the people with the unadorned statement, *In those days there was no king in Israel, every man did what was right in his own eyes.* A king would not have permitted the barbaric city of Giv'ah to go unpunished after its *act of wantonness against a helpless concubine* innocently seeking nothing more than a place to rest her head before going on with her craven Levite husband. Nor would a king have allowed the Levite, in his grief and anger, to incite the other tribes against Benjamin. Nor would he have allowed a jurisdictional dispute between the Sanhedrin of Benjamin and the rest of the nation to result in such tragic bloodshed. The existing legal system at the time could not cope with the travail engendered by the atrocity of Giv'ah, but a king transcends and overrides the legal system.

Nor would a king have allowed the marauders of Dan to make off with Michah's idol and carve out a little kingdom of their own up north. His duty to maintain the spiritual standard of the nation would have forced him to act; no lack of power or jurisdiction could have stood in his way.

The defection of Elimelech, too, at the beginning of *Megillas Ruth* was a result of the "judging of the Judges" — a lack of constituted, accepted, powerful leadership. Elimelech, great and wealthy, felt a *responsibility but feared its burden.* He would be expected to establish some sort of order to cope with the ravages of famine and his treasury would have to be thrown open to the poor and hungry. Elimelech felt unequal to the task — and fled. Trying to conserve his fortune and peace of mind, he lost both — and his Jewish identity. Save for the sacrifice and idealism of Ruth, he would have lost his posterity, as well. Had there been a king — who knows? The responsibility upon Elimelech might not have been so overwhelming and the majesty of the throne might have been employed to prevent the flight of the erstwhile patron of Bethlehem.

Extralegal powers are not the province of a king alone. The Sanhedrin, too, has the power to ordain

A king would not have permitted the barbaric city of Giv'ah to go unpunished.

A king transcends and overrides the legal system.

Elimelech, great and wealthy, felt a responsibility but feared its burden ... he felt unequal to the task — and fled.

Had there been a king — who knows?

coercive measures in defense of the nation and its mission. There were such courts in the days before the monarchy. The Torah commands that judges and officers of the court be established in all cities (*Deuteronomy* 16:18). They were, and they performed valiantly throughout the period. even under foreign occupation and terror; these were the judges whom Deborah praised several times in her song (*Judges* Ch. 5). But the courts were loath to exercise their extralegal powers, as is shown from the formula, *In those days there was no king*, to explain how such tragedies could have happened.

But the courts were loath to exercise their extralegal powers.

For there is a basic difference between the residual power of the monarchy and the Sanhedrin:

כָּל אֵלּוּ הָרַצְחָנִים שֶׁאֵינָם חַיָּיבִים מִיתַת בֵּית דִּין אִם יִרְצֶה מֶלֶךְ יִשְׂרָאֵל לְהוֹרְגָם בְּדִין מַלְכוּת וְתַקָּנַת עוֹלָם הָרְשׁוּת בְּיָדוֹ. וְכֵן אִם רָצוּ בֵּית דִּין לְהוֹרְגָם בְּהוֹרָאַת שָׁעָה, אִם הָיְתָה הַשָּׁעָה צְרִיכָה לְכָךְ יֵשׁ רְשׁוּת לָהֶם כְּפִי מַה שֶּׁיִּרְאוּ

All these murderers who are not liable to execution — if a Jewish king wishes to kill them using his regal powers and for the benefit of society, he may do so. So, too, if a court wishes to execute them by an extraordinary decree, if the times require it, the court has the right as it sees fit (Rambam, Hilchos Rotzei'ach 2:4).

Rav Tzvi Hirsch Chayes (in *Toras Nevi'im* 7) deduces from the subtle differences in Rambam's descriptions of the respective authority of king and court, that the king's powers, while identical to those of the court in the case under discussion, may be more freely exercised. Rambam (*Hilchos Sanhedrin* 18:6) differentiates between הוֹרָאַת שָׁעָה, *extraordinary decree*, and דִּין מַלְכוּת, *the law of the king*. This further indicates a presumption of authority that is automatically attributed to the king purely by virtue of his office; an authority that the court cannot exercise unless it is absolutely convinced by the particular circumstances that the national interest and severity of the situation require it to act extralegally.

The king's powers, while identical to those of the court in the case under discussion, may be more freely exercised.

Plainly, any Sanhedrin, local or national, would be most cautious in annexing such powers to itself. Only in the most serious of cases would it tamper

It is no small matter for a court of Torah law to go beyond the strictures of Torah law.

with the laws of the Torah; it is no small matter for a court of Torah law to go beyond the strictures of Torah law.

The king is bound by no such restrictions. His very position and resultant responsibility to the nation demand and require that he exercise the powers of his position. A weak king does the nation no good; he becomes an invitation to religious lassitude and the paralysis of leadership that results in spiritual famine, atrocity, and idolatry. Indeed, the constant obligation to respect the king's personal majesty — the neglect of which can result in the death penalty — is in order to strengthen his position as national leader so that he can better serve the nation.

The judges of old were national leaders, but their leadership was based on law and public acceptance. They did not have the power inherent in the office of the king.

The judges of old were national leaders, but their leadership was based on law and public acceptance. They did not have the power inherent in the office of the king. They could lead if the people followed and they could exercise the extralegal powers of a Sanhedrin under such conditions as allowed a court to exercise those powers. But the ability to lead varies with many factors, and Jewish judges did not exercise extralegal powers with impunity.

There was another circumstance conferring power on a judge. The people could accept him upon themselves with all the rights and powers of a monarch — including the right to execute the disrespectful and disobedient. Joshua was given such acceptance (*Joshua* 1:16-18) and the people were anxious to establish a Gideonic dynasty (*Judges* 8:22).

The period of the judges was one of striving imperfectly toward goals that were never achieved.

The result was the turbulence of the period of judges and flawed monarchy aiming at a spiritual summit that has, for millennia, awaited the coming of Mashiach.

Generally, however, the period of the judges was one of striving imperfectly toward goals that were never achieved: the goal of national unity under God, sovereignty over all of *Eretz Yisrael*, the attainment of the Divine blessings of peace, prosperity, and security. Had that goal been achieved, the people could have gone on to the fulfillment of the Torah's commandment that they ask God to select a king to lead them to even greater spiritual heights. It was not achieved. The result was the turbulence of the period of judges and flawed monarchy aiming at a spiritual summit that has, for millennia, awaited the coming of *Mashiach.*

IV. The Murky Roots of Monarchy

The Kingship of Judah

JEWISH MONARCHY IS NO MERE POLITICAL SYSTEM; WHEN it is ordered according to the Divine Will, it is an end unto itself. It is this end which is particularly represented by the kingdom of Judah. The final one of the Ten *Sefiros*, the stages through which God's will is carried out in creation, is מַלְכוּת, *malchus* (kingship). *Malchus* represents the final revelation, the coming to fruition of His will. To the extent to which His will is obscured by the human fiction of *"my strength and the power of my hand has created for me all this accomplishment,"* His rule on earth fails to find expression in our lives.

Jewish monarchy is no mere political system; when it is ordered according to the Divine Will, it is an end unto itself.

When Leah's fourth child was born, she named him Judah, saying הַפַּעַם אוֹדֶה אֶת ה', *now I will praise HASHEM*. Rashi explains that she gave special praise then, rather than previously with the birth of her first three sons, שֶׁנָּטַלְתִּי יוֹתֵר עַל חֶלְקִי, *for I have taken more than my share*. The matriarchs knew that Jacob would have twelve sons; that should have meant three sons for each of Jacob's four wives. When Leah gave birth to her fourth son, she gave special thanks because God had given her more than her share. That is why Jews are called *Yehudim* (implying that they are descended from Judah) no matter what tribe they belong to. Even Mordechai, a Benjamite, is referred to in *Megillas Esther* as *Mordechai HaYehudi*. We are *Yehudim* because we always thank God for giving us more than our share, more than we deserve. The Jew is ever conscious of the graciousness and mercy of God. To him, health, prosperity — life itself — are never his by right; he thanks God for everything, for it is all an undeserved gift (*Chiddushei HaRim* in *Sefer HaZechus*).

The matriarchs knew that Jacob would have twelve sons; that should have meant three sons for each of Jacob's four wives. When Leah gave birth to her fourth son, she gave special thanks because God had given her more than her share.

To the Jew, health, prosperity — life itself — are never his by right.

The strength of Judah lay in his readiness to be a willing receptacle of God's talent, blessing, and responsibility while ascribing nothing to himself. His very name indicates this quality. The Hebrew spelling of Judah's name, יְהוּדָה, contains the sacred Four-Letter Name of God plus one more letter, a ד, *dalet*. The word דַּל, *dal*, in Hebrew means a pauper. Judah has within himself the majesty of his Creator; his kingship is no less than the kingship, in a mortal guise, of God Himself; in his

own eyes, Judah remains דָּל, a pauper. No matter how exalted his position, whatever he has is an undeserved gift of God.

David, first of the Judean kings and model for all his successors, embodies the same concept in his name. It begins with *dalet* and ends with *dalet*. For all his grandeur and achievement, for all the love his Maker bore for him and the holiness that made even the blood of his war victims seem like holy offerings before the altar of God, David, from beginning to end, considered himself a pauper, an impoverished mortal who carried only the gifts of God, but nothing of his own. The future *Mashiach* is described by Zechariah as עָנִי וְרוֹכֵב עַל חֲמוֹר, *a poor man riding a donkey*. He will finally fulfill the purpose of creation by bringing the kingdom of heaven to earth and by crowning God as King of all mankind, but he is a pauper riding the humblest of domestic beasts of burden.

For all the holiness that made even the blood of his war victims seem like holy offerings before the altar of God, David considered himself a pauper who carried only the gifts of God.

Such kings represent the final stage of revelation. They are themselves but an embodiment of God's will on earth (*Sfas Emes, Vayigash*).

Tainted Origins

IT IS NO LESS THAN ASTOUNDING THAT THE CONCEPTION OF the Davidic dynasty was shrouded in mists of impropriety.

Lot and his daughters were miraculously saved from the destruction of Sodom. His daughters, thinking they were the only people left on earth, intoxicated him, lived with him, and gave birth to Ammon and Moab. Centuries later, Ruth the Moabite became the great-grandmother of David. Even later, Naamah the Ammonite became the wife of King Solomon and mother of his successor, Rehoboam. True, the righteousness of Ruth and Naamah was of such magnitude that their nations were spared by God for all the centuries spanning traditions of selfishness and cruelty, but why was it necessary for God to defile His servant David by planting his origin in a guise of incest? And what luster could it add to the Holy Name for His מַלְכוּת, *kingship*, to trace its source to so ignoble a beginning?

Lot's daughters, thinking they were the only people left on earth, intoxicated him, lived with him, and gave birth to Ammon and Moab.

Why was it necessary for God to defile His servant David by planting his origin in a guise of incest?

After the sale of Joseph into slavery, Judah left his brothers to found his own family. First his oldest and then his second son married Tamar. Each of the young men died because of his own sin (see

Genesis Ch. 38). Judah, fearing that Tamar had some blame in the unusual pair of tragedies, delayed the יִבּוּם, *levirate marriage,* of Tamar to his youngest son, Shelah. She realized that Judah would not allow her to marry Shelah but she wanted to share in building God's Kingdom, so, posing as a harlot, she lured Judah into spending a single night with her. She conceived and gave birth to twins, Perez and Zerah. Her ambition was fulfilled: Perez was the ancestor of David.

Tamar's ambition was fulfilled: Perez was the ancestor of David.

> *Rabbi Yochanan said, Judah sought to pass by Tamar. The Holy One, Blessed is He, dispatched the angel of lust to waylay him. The angel said to Judah, "Where are you going? From where will kings arise, from where will great men arise?" "Then he [Judah] turned to her by the way" — he was coerced, against his good sense (Bereishis Rabbah 85:8).*

Not only did Judah father the twins in an apparently illicit manner, the shame of his action became public knowledge by his own admission in an act of moral courage that remains a shining example of honesty even under the most distasteful circumstances. But Judah's tryst with Tamar left him no less righteous and chaste than before. It was more than Divinely inspired; it was forced by the Hand of God. But why? Why did God's design require so convoluted an execution; why did His plan require such unbecoming conduct?

Judah's tryst with Tamar left him no less righteous and chaste than before. It was more than Divinely inspired; it was forced by the Hand of God.

The next episode in the strange Divine scheme was the marriage of Ruth and Boaz. (See *Commentary* 3.) Why a Moabite? Why a blot in the family — לֹא יָבֹא 'מוֹאָבִי בִּקְהַל ה . . ., *"a Moabite may not come into the Assembly of HASHEM"* — that took years to erase? Why a stealthy nighttime visit by the Moabite woman to the field where the righteous, aged judge slept guarding his harvest? Why so profane a method to carry out so sacred a mission?

A Bribe for the Satan THE ETERNAL STRUGGLE BETWEEN GOOD AND EVIL REvolves essentially around man. It is not God who struggles with evil; the Satan exists only as long as he

That evil exists and that it has the ability to becloud the senses of even the wisest of men is in order to create the battleground for man's free-will struggle to choose correctly.

suits God's purpose. That evil exists and that it has the ability to becloud the senses of even the wisest of men is in order to create the battleground for man's free-will struggle to choose correctly. People are rewarded only for having prevailed in the struggle to choose right over wrong; if the emptiness of evil and the virtues of good are so obvious that the choice becomes automatic, then there is no justification for rewarding the righteous. One does not reward a child for not reaching into a blazing fire; the consequences of doing so are so plain that no sane person would try it. On the other hand, the child who is all alone with a tempting cookie jar and conquers his greed is amply deserving of recognition. Had there been no prophets of Ba'al with their "miracles" and appearance of rectitude, no one would have been fool enough to reject Elijah. The forces of evil must have the power to confuse, confound, convince; otherwise, man's mission would be an exercise in the obvious *(Derech Hashem)*.

The forces of evil must have the power to confuse, confound, convince; otherwise, man's mission would be an exercise in the obvious.

A direct frontal attack on the יצר הרע, the *evil inclination*, is too often doomed to failure. The powers of the Satan are usually too great for mortal man. Indeed, his own flesh-and-blood drives and desires are too strong to be vanquished and sublimated without a long, complex, and devious struggle.

But there are ways. The evil inclination is far from invincible; in fact, it is eminently deceivable. The Sages have an interesting expression: שוחד לשטן, *a bribe for the Satan*. All of us know the popular methods for developing self-control. "I won't allow myself a piece of cake until I finish forty-five minutes of study." "I will take a vacation if I am successful." To a serious thinker these ploys are ridiculous, except that they work! People have an awesome capacity for self-deception: the sincere and intelligent person uses this capacity for the good; the self-indulgent and shallow person uses this same capacity to cause his own downfall. The old witticism, "It's the easiest thing in the world to stop smoking — I've done it thousands of times," is all too true!

The strategems in the battle against evil are like one step backward and two steps forward.

The strategems in the battle against evil are like one step backward and two steps forward. They are a means of utilizing the frailities of human nature to combat,

weaken, and eventually conquer the evil inclination that is part of the very humanness of man.

Man is fully capable of knowing and understanding himself well enough to cope with his urges, and to utilize rather than be defeated by them. Even base desires — like greed and vanity — can be sublimated by using money for charity or accepting honor only for worthwhile accomplishments (see *Ramban, Leviticus* 16:8 and *Michtav Me'Eliyahu I* p. 262):

But it remains true that our world is a balance of good and evil with every person facing the challenge of choosing one over the other.

But it remains true that our world is a balance of good and evil with every person facing the challenge of choosing one over the other. And man seldom succeeds by directly attacking the forces of evil; in order to maintain the balance, they were given too much power to be easily defeated. They will bounce back with a counterattack that will leave the presumed victor bloodied and disarrayed.

No greater good exists than the Kingdom of God on earth and its champions, the tribe of Judah with its most distinguished son, David. Its development began with Judah's apparently inexplicable weakness in straying from the path — literally and figuratively — after Tamar in harlot's disguise. The episode illustrates that the Satan will not — cannot — permit spiritual heights to be scaled without a fierce struggle. To take the direct path would be to court failure by inviting the Satan ferociously to thwart the attainment of good. The Satan must be appeased. Judah's act had the appearance of a lamentable fall as the great leader of Jacob's sons was powerless to control his lust for a stranger. Satan laughed, the Canaanites snickered, Judah was ashamed, but God was doing His work by striking the spark that would ultimately become the brilliant light of *Mashiach* (*Chafetz Chaim on Torah*).

The Satan will not — cannot — permit spiritual heights to be scaled without a fierce struggle.

Satan laughed, the Canaanites snickered, Judah was ashamed — but God was doing His work by striking the spark that would ultimately become the brilliant light of Mashiach.

Drawing Out the Sparks

מִי יִתֵּן טָהוֹר מִטָּמֵא?

"Who can withdraw purity from impurity?" (*Job* 14:3).

Abraham came from Terach, Hezekiah from Achaz, Yoshiah from Omon, Mordechai from Shim'i, Israel from the nations, the world to come from this world. Who could do this? Who could command this? Who could decree this? No one but [God] the only One on earth! (Bamidbar Rabbah 19:1).

IN A DEEPER SENSE, THERE IS MORE TO THE STRANGE AND distasteful circumstances surrounding Lot, Judah, and Ruth than a bribe to the Satan. There is a constant refrain in Kabbalist and esoteric literature that this world is a mixture of good and evil symbolized by עֵץ הַדַּעַת טוֹב וָרָע, *the Tree of Knowledge of Good and Evil.* In all evil there is some good; otherwise it could not exist. Man's highest purpose is to extract the sparks of good from the evil. Obviously this is no simple task. It demands a high degree of self-perfection before it can even be attempted, but the mission of mankind on earth is to withdraw the spiritual good from its captivity.

Man's highest purpose is to extract the sparks of good from the evil. Obviously this is no simple task.

> *It is known to all who have been given understanding that the soul of David was clothed in the shell of Moab and that it was freed from Moab through Ruth. Concerning this, too, Scripture says: Who could withdraw purity from impurity* [see Midrash above]. *These were the intentions of the inscrutable wisdom of the Creator in guiding His world to bring every act to its proper path. Every act of God travels through byways, often in complex, crooked ones . . . . For such has occurred to all great souls as they go among the "shells" of impurity to capture and extract the good* (Rabbi Moshe Chaim Luzatto in Megillas Sesarim).

The sparks of goodness are scattered throughout creation. One was in Lot and remained glimmering even in the moral filth of Sodom. To salvage that spark, God sent the angel Rafael, who, after healing Abraham, went to Sodom to save Lot, bearer of the spark that would become the soul of David. It went down the generations until the time came for it to leave the impurity of Moab and enter the Jewish nation through Ruth.

There was a spark in Canaan and it was lodged in Tamar. Judah had to unite with her, but of his own free will he would never have done it.

There was a spark in Canaan and it was lodged in Tamar. Judah had to unite with her, but of his own free will he would never have done it. An angel forced Judah into the path of a harlot when God was ready to begin the creation of the Davidic dynasty.

Lot's spark traveled through his Moabite descendants for seven centuries until it reached its ultimate destination. When the proper time came, Ruth went from the

field of Moab to the field of Boaz. While popular wisdom held that no Moabite could ever enter the community of God, the scion of Judah, leader of his people, unearthed the long-neglected law that a Moabitess was not forbidden to marry a Jew. One fateful night, the last one of Boaz's life, the spark of Lot and the brilliance of Judah were united as Ruth and Boaz were married. That night, Obed, the grandfather of David, was conceived.

V. The Marriage — Levirate and Moabite

THE TORAH'S FIRST MENTION OF THE OBLIGATION OF יִבּוּם, *levirate marriage,* appears when Er, firstborn son of Judah, died and Judah instructed his second son, Onan, to marry the widow וְהָקֵם זֶרַע לְאָחִיךָ, *and raise up seed for your brother (Genesis 38:8).*

The *Holy Zohar (Vayeishev* 177) explains that the death of a person does not remove him from his eternal roots on earth because his children carry on his role in life. When someone dies without children, his mission on earth would go uncontinued and unfulfilled. To prevent this tragedy and maintain the departed's link in the chain of life, the Divine Wisdom ordained that his widow and his brother marry and produce children . . . . The newborn child becomes the receptacle for the soul of the departed so that his mission in life can be completed through the children of his widow and closest relative.

Shaar Bas Rabim (Vayeishev) explains further that man and wife are considered like one body, one unit. It is her duty to perpetuate his life through levirate marriage because, with the death of her husband, it is as if part of her own body had died. The closest relative is a brother, because he and the deceased are products of the same parents. Therefore, the commandment of levirate marriage applies to the brother.

In early generations, לִפְנֵי מַתַּן תּוֹרָה, *before the Torah was given,* the secret of levirate marriage was known to wise men of the caliber of Judah. They knew that in the absence of a brother to marry the widow, the closest blood relatives, too, could function to make "whole" the disrupted family unit. Therefore, Judah's unwitting marriage

Man and wife are considered like one body, one unit.

In early generations, לִפְנֵי מַתַּן תּוֹרָה, before the Torah was given, the wise men knew that in the absence of a brother to marry the widow, the closest blood relatives, too, could function to make "whole" the disrupted family unit.

to Tamar was legal, even commendable. Only its mode — the apparent wanton act with a "harlot" and the resulting humiliation of Judah — was degrading. When the Torah was given with the statutes that most forms of family marriages were incestuous, a relationship such as that of Judah and Tamar became forbidden. Still, levirate marriage was so holy that God continued to permit, even command, it in its highest form: that of a brother marrying his widowed, childless sister-in-law *(Ramban)*.

Boaz was a "redeemer" and a potential participant in a levirate marriage with Ruth by virtue of the fact that *It is apparent from* he was a close relative, but not so close that a marriage *Megillas Ruth, that* would be forbidden as incestuous. He was second in *in those days, Jews* line; the closest relative was Tov, a brother of Elimelech *acknowledged a* and an uncle of Mahlon. The next relative was Boaz, a *moral obligation* cousin of Mahlon. True, the Torah does not ordain levi- *to provide a* rate marriage except for a brother of the deceased, but, *resting place* as is apparent from *Megillas Ruth,* in those days, Jews *for the soul of* acknowledged a moral obligation to provide a resting *the departed* place for the soul of the departed by providing an off- *by providing an* spring from his wife (see *Commentary* 3:1; 3:10). *offspring from his*
wife

Moabite IN PROHIBITING CONVERTS FROM AMMON AND MOAB
But Not from ever marrying into the "congregation of God," the
Moabitess Torah explains the reason why:

עַל דְּבַר אֲשֶׁר לֹא קִדְּמוּ אֶתְכֶם בַּלֶּחֶם וּבַמַּיִם בַּדֶּרֶךְ
בְּצֵאתְכֶם מִמִּצְרָיִם

*Because of the fact that they did not greet
you with bread and water on the road when
you were leaving Egypt (Deuteronomy 23:5).*

The Sages interpret the verse to indicate that עַמּוֹנִי
וְלֹא עַמּוֹנִית, מוֹאָבִי וְלֹא מוֹאָבִית, only male Ammonite and
Moabite converts may marry into the nation *(Ye-
vamos* 76b). This interpretation is implicit in the verse *The Torah gives* itself. The Torah gives us a reason for the prohibi- *us a reason for* tion: the accused nations failed to show simple hu- *the prohibition:* man decency in not greeting the travel-weary Jews *the accused* with food and drink. It is customary for men to travel *nations failed* into the desert to meet travelers, point out our Sages, *to show simple* but it is not proper for women to do so. Therefore, *human decency* women were absolved from the national guilt and *in not greeting* hence welcome to convert and marry into the Jewish *the travel-weary* nation. *Jews with food*
and drink.

Like all interpretations that modify Scriptural prohibitions, this one was transmitted to Moses by God.
The Sages did not legislate; they merely pointed out the
Scriptural basis for an apparently incongruous law; no-
where do we find a law of this type that applies to one
sex, but not to the other. Egyptian converts, male and
female alike, are forbidden to enter the congregation
of God until their third generation as Jews. *Mamzeirim* (people born of incestuous or adulterous unions
which can never be legitimized by marriage) are forbidden to marry other Jews no matter what their sex. Why,
then, should the Ammonite and Moabite nations be
different? The answer — our Sages *explain,* but do not
originate — is found in Scripture itself as cited above.

The Sages did not legislate; they merely pointed out the Scriptural basis for an apparently incongruous law.

This law was known to Moses and his disciples. During the three centuries between Israel's entry into the
Land and the time of Ruth and Boaz, the law gradually
became forgotten, probably because it fell into disuse.
Those were the times when the Oral Law was still oral
— the interpretations of Scripture were not committed
to writing; they passed from teacher to student down
through the generations. If no Ammonites or Moabites
sought to convert — a natural consequence of the
long-standing hostility between them and Israel — the
legal question of their marital status would never have
required decision by a court. And the average Jew, even
most scholars, would have assumed that the prohibition upon them was as sexless as those upon Egyptians
and *mamzeirim.* Of course, had the question come
before the Great Sanhedrin or any of the other distinguished courts of the Land, it is virtually certain that
a decision would have been rendered in favor of Ammonite and Moabite women. Indeed, it *did* arise in the
court of Boaz at that pivotal time in Jewish history and
it *was* so decided. Many legal concepts become hazy
with disuse, however, and this was one of them. So it
was that it was almost universally thought, even by a
minority of the greatest sages, that Ruth's marriage to a
Jew was prohibited.

Those were the times when the Oral Law was still oral — the interpretations of Scripture were not committed to writing; they passed from teacher to student down through the generations.

Many legal concepts become hazy with disuse, however, and this was one of them.

An analogy can be found in the prohibition against
eating certain species of birds. The Torah specifies that
only twenty kinds of fowl may not be eaten. All others — the overwhelming majority of all birds on earth

— are permitted. With the passing of time, successive exiles, and the increasing disuse of the Scriptural Hebrew names of the forbidden birds, the exact identities of the forbidden fowl were forgotten. Not knowing with any degree of certainty which birds are forbidden, the Jewish people have refrained from eating any fowl save for those which were in constant use down through the centuries. Those are permitted only because uninterrupted traditions guarantee that they are not among the forbidden twenty. Turkey, for example, was once of doubtful status until it was learned that in some areas such a tradition existed; that being established, the permitted status of turkey was accepted by the overwhelming majority of Jews.

Not knowing with any degree of certainty which birds are forbidden, the Jewish people have refrained from eating any fowl save for those which were in constant use down through the centuries.

Boaz's proclamation that any Jew might marry Ruth must be understood in this way. Boaz permitted nothing new; he merely popularized a law that had been forgotten by the majority of the population. That many found it difficult to accept this repudiation of the popular misconception is obvious from the reaction of Tov, the *Ploni Almoni* of *Megillas Ruth* who refused to marry Ruth on the grounds that he would be tainting his posterity by marrying a forbidden Moabitess (*Ruth* 4:6).

Boaz permitted nothing new; he merely popularized a law that had been forgotten by the majority of the population.

An ensuing tragedy lent credence to those who disputed Boaz and his court. Righteous Boaz married Ruth and lived with her for only one night; the next day he was dead. The wags of the generation were convinced they knew why: Boaz had publicly defied the Torah's prohibition by marrying a forbidden daughter of Moab; for that he was struck dead. The truth, of course, was just the opposite. God kept an aging Boaz alive and in good health so that the centuries-old design could come to fruition. The holiness lodged in the seed of Lot, the holiness lodged in the seed of Tamar, and the holiness lodged in the seed of Judah joined that night to produce the grandfather of David. But the truth is not always visible. When Ruth's baby was born, the birth was celebrated by few because, for many, it was not a blessed event at all, this product of a "forbidden" marriage (*Ruth* 4:14-17; see *Commentary*).

The holiness lodged in the seed of Lot, the holiness lodged in the seed of Tamar, and the holiness lodged in the seed of Judah joined that night to produce the grandfather of David.

This popular misconception died hard; it hung like a black cloud over the family until the time of David, and very nearly changed and embittered the course of Jewish history.

Marriage in Moab

THE FLIGHT OF ELIMELECH AND HIS FAMILY TO MOAB IN ITself is enough to strain the credulity of even the casual reader. The simple text makes abundantly clear that Elimelech's was a most distinguished family. The Sages go even further in extolling Elimelech and in pointing out the enormity of his sin in deserting his people. Imagine the blow to them when the great man to whom they looked for encouragement, guidance, and material support during the famine defected to an antagonistic neighbor. But the marriage of Mahlon and Chilion to Ruth and Orpah hurt even more. How could they intermarry with Moabites? Whatever their lack of loyalty to their people, surely there was no justification for the marriages that kept them anchored in Moab until their deaths!

Whatever their lack of loyalty to their people, surely there was no justification for the marriages that kept them anchored in Moab until their deaths!

The commonly known view is that of Rabbi Meir as expounded in the *Midrash*:

לֹא גִּיְּירוּם וְלֹא הִטְבִּילוּ אוֹתָם

"They neither converted nor ritually immersed them" (Ruth Rabbah 1:4).

In that view, the marriage is but one more unpleasant indication of how far lapsed people can sink once they cut loose from their moorings. Support is lent to this view by the Talmud (*Yevamos* 47b) which derives the laws of proselytes from the exchange between Naomi and Ruth (see *Commentary* 1:16). It would also explain why Naomi tried so hard to encourage Ruth and Orpah to return home rather than go to *Eretz Yisrael* with her. If her daughters-in-law had converted prior to their marriages, Naomi would have had no right to send them back to idolatry.

It would also explain why Naomi tried so hard to encourage Ruth and Orpah to return home rather than go to Eretz Yisrael with her.

On the other hand, if, indeed, the Moabite brides were unconverted during their marriage, several other difficulties arise. Scripture repeatedly refers to Naomi as the mother-in-law of Ruth. Had Ruth been a Moabite during her marriage to Mahlon, the marriage would not have been legally binding under Jewish law, thus rendering incongruous the references to "mother-in-law." But the problems are more than semantic. If Ruth was never legally married to Mahlon, then much of the succeeding story of Ruth is incomprehensible. Boaz was a redeemer of Ruth's property; what property? Under Jewish law she had no right to

If Ruth was never legally married to Mahlon, then much of the succeeding story of Ruth is incomprehensible.

any property of Mahlon. Boaz accepted a moral responsibility to enter into a levirate marriage with Ruth, but only the widow of a Jewish marriage falls within the purview of the levirate relationship. A non-Jewish Ruth would no more obligate Boaz than any other widowed Moabite.

Indeed, there is a second view, that of *Zohar Chadash* that Ruth and Orpah *did*, in fact, convert to Judaism prior to their marriages:

> *Rabbi P'dos asked the son of Rav Yosi, a man from Socho: Since Ruth was a proselyte, why did they not call her by another [Jewish] name? He answered him: So have I heard — she did have another name and when she married Mahlon, they renamed her Ruth and from then on she used that name. For her conversion came when she married Mahlon, and not afterward.*
>
> *He said to him: But it is written later, "where you lodge, I will lodge, and your God is my God," etc. (Ruth 1:16). Naomi gave her many warnings [against the rigorous life of a Jew] as we have learned, and Ruth accepted them all. If she had already converted previously, why was all this necessary at that time?*
>
> *He replied to him: God forbid that Mahlon married her while she was still a gentile. Rather, when she married she converted and she remained under the presumption of אֵימַת בַּעֲלָה, fear of her husband, she and Orpah, in this matter. When their husbands died, Orpah returned to her abominable ways, and Ruth remained in her goodness, as it is written, "'Look, your sister-in-law has returned to her people and to her god,' but Ruth clung to her" (Ruth 1:15,14) as she had earlier. When her husband died, [Ruth] cleaved to her of her own free will (Zohar Chadash Ruth 180-182).*

When Ruth married, she converted and remained under the presumption of אֵימַת בַּעֲלָה, fear of her husband.

According to this view, how could Naomi have allowed, much less urged, the widows to return to Moabite idolatry?

It may be that the key words in solving this serious difficulty are אֵימַת בַּעֲלֵיהֶן, "the fear of their husbands." Mahlon and Chilion came to Moab as very wealthy, highly eligible young אֶפְרָתִים, "Ephrathites," distinguished citizens of Judah's leading city [see *Commentary* 1:2]. So esteemed was the family of Elimelech that the royal family of Moab wanted two of its daughters to marry the newly arrived Jewish brothers. In those days, the prospective bride had little say in such an arrangement, especially when it was a marriage of state made for considerations transcending personal preferences. If Mahlon and Chilion had insisted that their brides convert to Judaism as a condition of marriage, the young women would surely have felt compelled to accede.

This could well have constituted a coerced conversion. In the case of such a conversion, the mere fact that the marriage took place and that the converted woman lived as a Jewess would not in and of itself prove that the conversion was valid. Should she have become widowed and then — newly freed — declared her refusal to continue her fiction of Jewishness, her conversion would have been proven invalid from the start.

When Mahlon and Chilion died, Naomi put Ruth and Orpah to the test. Was their original conversion sincere? Had they become committed Jews in the course of their marriages? Or were they accompanying her back to *Eretz Yisrael* merely out of pity? Orpah turned her back with a parting kiss, thereby proving that her conversion had never been sincere. Ruth withstood the test; she demonstrated her commitment, thus proving that her membership in the Jewish nation was entirely unfeigned.

The problem of conversion was not limited to Mahlon and Chilion. A similar, though not identical, question was raised concerning far-greater *tzaddikim* than they, Solomon and Samson, who also married non-Jewish wives. Rambam raises the question in *Hilchos Issurei Biah* 13:14-16. He states categorically that it is inconceivable that those two great men married unconverted women. Their wives were converted. Rambam explains that a convert must demonstrate that

In those days, the prospective bride had little say in such an arrangement, especially when it was a marriage of state.

If Mahlon and Chilion had insisted that their brides convert to Judaism as a condition of marriage, the young women would surely have felt compelled to accede.

This could well have constituted a coerced conversion.

Ruth withstood the test — she demonstrated her commitment, thus proving that her membership in the Jewish nation was entirely unfeigned.

Rambam explains that a convert must demonstrate that his conversion is sincerely motivated ....

his conversion is sincerely motivated: that it is not done for money, prestige, or fear, and that it is not done for love of man or woman. If there are no ulterior motives, the rabbinical court teaches the would-be convert the responsibilities of Torah and its commandments. When the court is convinced of his sincerity, he is accepted.

As an example of the sincere convert, Rambam cites Ruth.

As an example of the sincere convert, *Rambam* cites Ruth.

During the reigns of David and Solomon, *Rambam* continues, converts were not accepted because the lures of conversion were too great to insure that sincerity was present. Despite this ban, many non-Jews did join Israel thanks to conversions performed by uninformed, unsophisticated, makeshift courts. Those converts were ignored by the legitimate courts — not ostracized, and not embraced — until time and experience showed whether or not they were truly sincere.

Those converts were ignored by the legitimate courts — not ostracized, and not embraced — until time and experience showed whether or not they were truly sincere.

The wives of Samson and Solomon, *Rambam* concludes, converted for the sake of marriage, without any true motivation for Jewishness. For this reason Scripture refers to them as non-Jews; in terms of the standards expected of sincere converts, they were. Their outcomes told the story; they remained idolaters, proving that their conversions were but a sham.

The wives of Samson and Solomon, Rambam concludes, converted for the sake of marriage, without any true motivation for Jewishness.

It may be that it was this knowledge that motivated Naomi's attempts to dissuade her daughters-in-law. Were they truly her daughters-in-law or were they merely the Moabite common-law widows of her sons? She performed her task well. Orpah was never truly a Jew; Ruth was one of the finest daughters — and mothers — Israel ever had.

(It should be unmistakably clear that the above discussion is not meant and must not be taken as the basis for any halachic decision. The laws of conversion, like most areas of halachah, are based on a two-thousand-year accumulation of Mishnaic, Talmudic, and post-Talmudic literature. Especially in so sensitive an area as conversion, only highly qualified rabbis are competent to render decisions.)

VI. The Emergence of David*

O BED, SON OF RUTH AND BOAZ, AND JESSE, SON OF Obed, were outstandingly righteous men, among the greatest of their age. Inevitably, people began to feel that such people could not have been the progeny of a sinful marriage; surely God would not invest holiness so promiscuously. So Jesse's family was the most respected in Bethlehem.

Surely God would not invest holiness so promiscuously.

God revealed to Samuel that the successor to King Saul would be a son of Jesse the Bethlehemite. The prophet was commanded to go to Bethlehem where God would show him the future king (*I Samuel* Ch. 16). Samuel asked Jesse to come with his sons to a feast. As we can well imagine, the great prophet's invitation was a rare privilege. Jesse came with seven of his sons; David was left behind. David — red of complexion, short of stature, tender of sheep, desert hermit — could not possibly become God's anointed. There wasn't a soul in Bethlehem, not even his father or brothers, who thought that. No one knew that he was not alone in the fields, that he was attuning his soul to his Maker; that his very being was a harp in the hands of holiness, reverberating with the sweet songs that would become part of one of Israel's most precious legacies: *The Book of Tehillim.* No one knew that the love he would later lavish on his people was being nurtured in his care of helpless sheep. No one knew that the fearless warrior of the future was single-handedly slaying lions and bears, learning that only God is to be feared. The moment of anointment came and Samuel asked that Jesse's sons come before him one by one. They were outstanding products of an outstanding family. The great prophet was impressed with Eliab, Jesse's firstborn; he was sure that he was in the presence of God's chosen anointed, only to be told by God:

No one knew that the love he would later lavish on his people was being nurtured in his care of helpless sheep.

> *Look not on his countenance nor on the height of his stature, because I have refused him: for it is not as a man sees, for a man looks on the outward appearance, but God looks on the heart (ibid. 16:7).*

* A superlative treatment of this topic can be found in *Sefer haTodaah* by Eliyahu Ki Tov. Much of his essay is beyond the scope of this paper, but is highly recommended reading.

So it was. One by one, each was rejected. Finally, Samuel asked Jesse if he had any more sons and Jesse answered strangely, "*The youngest one is still left; and he is tending the sheep now.*" Samuel ordered that he be brought. He was — and he was anointed David, King of Israel.

"The youngest one is still left; and he is tending the sheep now."

As soon as he arrived, Samuel knew that they were in the presence of God's chosen. Samuel knew that this was to be no temporary, transitory king like Saul. When Samuel picked up the horn of the holy oil, it began to bubble as though it could not wait to drop on the forehead of David. When Samuel anointed him, the oil hardened and glistened like pearls and precious stones, and the horn remained full (*Yalkut HaMakiri Tehillim* 118).

As soon as he arrived, Samuel knew that they were in the presence of God's chosen.

But the taint on David's origin was a stubborn one:

וְכִרְאוֹת שָׁאוּל אֶת דָּוִד יֹצֵא לִקְרַאת הַפְּלִשְׁתִּי אָמַר אֶל
אַבְנֵר שַׂר הַצָּבָא בֶּן מִי זֶה הַנַּעַר אַבְנֵר

When Saul had seen David going forth toward the Philistine [Goliath], he said to Abner, the minister of the army, "Abner, whose son is this lad?"(I Samuel 17:55).

Didn't Saul know who David was? The Talmud asks (*Yevamos* 76b): Scripture says (*I Samuel* 16:21) that Saul loved David very much and appointed him his personal armor-bearer. Obviously Saul knew him well!

Saul became apprehensive and began to fear that David was more than a talented singer and devoted shepherd.

Saul became apprehensive and began to fear that David was more than a talented singer and devoted shepherd. When David volunteered to defend the honor of Israel by facing Goliath in combat, Saul offered the young man his own armor. David put it on and it fit, but Saul was head and shoulders above even the tallest of Israel and David was shorter than average! That the royal armor fit could well be a Divine indication that David was to be Saul's successor as king. He asked Abner which branch of Judah David was from. If he was from Zerah, then he would be illustrious, but no threat to Saul. But if he was from Perez, then he was royalty, for it was from Perez that the kings of Judah would descend.

Then, Doeg the Edomi stepped forward. Doeg was one of the greatest scholars of the age, head of the Sanhedrin, and a close friend and adviser to the king. Doeg said,

"Instead of asking whether or not he is worthy of kingship, ask whether or not he is fit to enter the congregation of God! He is descended from Ruth the Moabitess."

Abner defended David's legitimacy with the dictum expounded by the court of Boaz and reaffirmed by the court of Samuel.

Abner defended David's legitimacy with the dictum expounded by the court of Boaz and reaffirmed by the court of Samuel: A Moabite, but not a Moabitess, is forbidden to enter the congregation of God. Doeg fought back and, halachic great that he was, no one was able to refute his arguments against the fitness of David. Then Amasa, son of Yisra, arose and declared,

"Whoever refuses to acknowledge this law will be stabbed with my sword. This I have learned from the court of Samuel of Ramah: a Moabite, but not a Moabitess!"

Finally it was only through a violent insistence upon the unshakable Jewish belief in its tradition as transmitted by the Torah greats that the royal house of David — embodiment of God's kingdom on earth — could come into being.

These were the passions awakened by David. The greatest men of his generation questioned and agonized over his status. Finally it was only through a violent insistence upon the unshakable Jewish belief in its tradition as transmitted by the Torah greats that the royal house of David — embodiment of God's kingdom on earth — could come into being.

Doeg did not rest. Throughout the reign of Saul he was David's nemesis; inflaming Saul against the young Judean shepherd whose love for, and loyalty to the king were unmatched. He urged Saul to kill David as a rebel (see above, "Powers of the King") and he succeeded in having eighty-five priests of the city of Nob executed for having harbored David (*I Samuel* Ch. 22)

David endured patiently all the barbs slung at him throughout his lifetime. Yet even this patient, long-suffering model of righteousness lashed out at Doeg in a passionate, poignant appeal to conscience and decency:

The true hero is the one who sees his fellow at the brink and pulls him back to safety!

"You, a powerful and wealthy man, head of the Sanhedrin, stoop to such a low level of evil and slander! Is it a show of strength to see someone teetering at the edge of an abyss and push him over? Or to see someone at the edge of a roof and throw him down? The true hero is the one who sees his fellow at the brink and pulls him back to safety! You saw how Saul became angry

with me and you attacked me further. Is this how one serves his God? Do you think that if Ahimelech [High Priest of Nob] had not yet welcomed me and given me a crust of bread that no one in all Israel would have given me food? A man who is occupied with God's goodness, the study of Torah, has no right to act this way. Why did you do this?" (Midrash Shocher Tov).

The Talmudic Sages [*Sanhedrin* 106b] hold Doeg up to rebuke as a person who made a mockery of his learning. "His learning was from the lips outward"; it had no inner meaning. God asked him, "Wicked one, why do you study My statutes? What will you say when you come to the sections of the Torah that forbid murder and slander?"

Brilliant man though he was, Doeg was condemned to prove by his own downfall that his tirades against David were baseless. He forgot his learning before his death and lost the respect of even his own students. Scintillating Doeg, who held sway over the great minds in Israel, died in disgrace as a ridiculed caricature of a Torah scholar. Of him the Talmud says: אַנְשֵׁי דָמִים וּמִרְמָה לֹא יֶחֱצוּ יְמֵיהֶם, *men of bloodshed and deceit shall not live out half their days* (Psalms 55:24). Doeg died when he was only thirty-three.

Not until then could David hold up his head without fear that the canard "Moabite" would be slung at him.

Not until then could David hold up his head without fear that the canard "Moabite" would be slung at him.

But his days of adversity were not numbered; they lasted throughout his life. War, betrayal, personal tragedy, rebellion, abuse — all of these were his constant lot, but he responded with a life that became אֲנִי תְפִלָּה, *I am prayer;* David became the very embodiment of prayer, his entire being became a song of praise. In the end, David's greatness was acknowledged. He was worthy of his people, but his people were unworthy of him.

In the end, David's greatness was acknowledged. He was worthy of his people, but his people were unworthy of him.

> David asked God: "Why can I not build the Holy Temple?"
> God answered: "Because if you build it, it will endure and never be destroyed" (*Yalkut Shimoni, II Samuel* 145).

The Jewish people were not yet worthy of a Temple built by David. It would be too great, too permanent.

David was so great, so consistent, that any act of his had to endure forever. The Jewish people were not yet worthy of a Temple built by David. It would be too great, too permanent, because it would be his, and his people would not rise to such a level until the coming of *Mashiach* (see *Michtav Me'Eliyahu II,* p. 275).

When he died, he left us with two treasures:

His *Tehillim,* the songs of praise and prayer that have sustained countless Jewish sparks amid constant storms and holocausts;

And his sacred seed, nurtured through millennia — just as the seed of Moab, Judah, Tamar, Boaz, and Ruth were nurtured — waiting for the time when it would explode into the flame of the seven days of creation;

Waiting for the day when a poor man will come riding on a donkey; possessing all talents and blessing, but ascribing nothing to himself and everything to God.

waiting for the day when a poor man will come riding on a donkey; possessing all talents and blessing, but ascribing nothing to himself and everything to God; leading all the world under the protective wings of Divine Presence when HASHEM will be King over the entire universe, on that day when HASHEM will be One and His Name will be One.

Rabbi Nosson Scherman

מְגִילַּת רוּת

THE BOOK OF RUTH

פרק א

א וַיְהִי בִּימֵי שְׁפֹט הַשֹּׁפְטִים וַיְהִי

⟨ that ⟪ of the Judges, ⟨ of the ⟨ in the ⟨ And it **1**
there was   judging   days   happened

I.

1. וַיְהִי — *And it happened.* Wherever in the Bible we find the term וַיְהִי בִּימֵי, *And it happened in the days*, it indicates the approach of trouble. Thus, *And it came to pass in the days of Ahasuerus*, that there was Haman. *And it came to pass in the days of the judging of the Judges*, that there was a famine (*Megillah* 10b).

שְׁפֹט הַשֹּׁפְטִים — *Of the judging of the Judges.*

The story of Ruth occurred before the reign of King Saul, when the Jews were governed by Judges. The Judge at the time was Ivtzan [*Judges* 12:8] — whom the Sages identify as Boaz of *Megillas Ruth* [*Bava Basra* 91a] (*Rashi*).

According to *Seder HaDoros* and *Tzemach David*, the episode happened approximately in the year 2787 (973 B.C.E.).

Iggeres Shmuel quotes *Rav Yosef ibn Yichiah* that Ivtzan was not *specifically* named in our verse in deference to his righteousness, for Scripture did not wish to implicate him in Elimelech's sin.

According to the *Malbim*, these events transpired between the days of the Judges, a period of which it was written [*Judges* 21:25]: בַּיָּמִים הָהֵם אֵין מֶלֶךְ בְּיִשְׂרָאֵל אִישׁ הַיָּשָׁר בְּעֵינָיו יַעֲשֶׂה, *In those days there was no king in Israel; every man did that which was right in his own eyes.*

No *specific* Judge ruled at the time; it was during an interval *between* Judges, when no one individual exercised control over the Jews, that Elimelech came to leave the country — a time when power was seized by lesser men, unable to earn position through their personal merit, and everyone acted independently.

Some understand שְׁפֹט הַשֹּׁפְטִים as the period when "God judged the Judges," for they were the cause of the famine (*Ibn Ezra; Vilna Gaon*).

It was a generation which judged its Judges. If the judge said to a man, "Take the splinter from between your teeth," he would retort, "Take the beam from between your eyes" (*Bava Basra* 15b).

"Woe unto the generation whose Judges are judged," bewails the *Midrash*, "and woe to the generation whose Judges deserve to be judged."

All the above interpretations are suggested by the use of the phrase בִּימֵי שְׁפֹט הַשֹּׁפְטִים [*in the days of the judging of the Judges*], instead of the more direct בִּימֵי הַשֹּׁפְטִים, *in the days of the Judges* (*Torah Temimah*).

A different approach is taken by *Iggeres Shmuel*: The *Midrash* states that a famine comes only upon a strong and righteous people that can withstand the test. Therefore, we can say that the generation was not lawless. On the contrary, it was a time

I
1

רָעָב בָּאָרֶץ וַיֵּלֶךְ אִישׁ מִבֵּית לֶחֶם

⟨ from Bethlehem ⟨ a man ⟨ and there ⟨⟨ in the ⟨ a famine
went land,

when שָׁפֹט הַשֹּׁפְטִים — *the Judges judged* — and the people listened. It was to *this* generation that God, knowing they would withstand the test and not flee or be rebellious against the Desirable Land [Eretz Yisrael], brought a famine upon them. And it was so. No one left Eretz Yisrael, except for the single family mentioned by Scripture.

וַיְהִי רָעָב בָּאָרֶץ — *That there was a famine in the land.* ["The" land, *par excellence*, Eretz Yisrael.]

[The judges in those days, say the commentaries, were devoid of Torah knowledge, and it was due to their laxity in rebuking the multitude who strayed from the Torah path that God punished the Jews with a famine.]

The word וַיְהִי is repeated twice in this verse to imply that there were two famines in the days of the Judges: a famine for bread and a famine for Torah. This teaches us that in any generation where there is a lack of Torah, famine must ensue (*Yalkut Shimoni; Midrash Zuta*).

"At that moment the Holy One, blessed is He, said: 'My children are rebellious; yet to destroy them is impossible, to take them back to Egypt is impossible, exchange them for another people I cannot; what then shall I do to them? I will punish them and purify them with famine'" (*Midrash*).

וַיֵּלֶךְ אִישׁ — *And there went a man.* [The appellation אִישׁ, *man*, throughout the Bible signifies prominence.]

The *Targum* here translates "גַּבְרָא רַבָּא," *a great man.*

Elimelech was very wealthy and the פַּרְנָס הַדּוֹר, provider of that generation, who left Eretz Yisrael because he was selfish and was afraid that all the impoverished people would come and knock at his door for help. For this he was punished (*Rashi*).

He was punished because he struck despair into the hearts of Israel. When the famine came, he arose and fled (*Midrash*).

Elimelech may have rationalized his departure by claiming that he could not bear to witness the corruption of the judges while powerless to correct the situation, or that he was not required to dispense more than a fifth of his resources to charity, hardly enough to feed all of the hungry (*Kol Yehudah*).

Ima Shel Malchus notes that in those days, the Jews had settled in Eretz Yisrael according to their tribal divisions, their families' and fathers' houses. An added insight into Elimelech's misdeed can be gained if we remember that all the inhabitants of Bethlehem were related to one another in some manner, and that now, in the days of trouble, Elimelech's family had deserted its relatives and fled.

[The *Midrash* notes that nothing is said about the wealth he took with him; surely he did not go empty-handed!]

And there went a man — like a "dead stump" [to which nothing is

פרק א
ב   יְהוּדָה לָגוּר בִּשְׂדֵי מוֹאָב הוּא וְאִשְׁתּוֹ

⟨ in Judah ⟨ to sojourn ⟨ in the fields ⟨⟨ of Moab, ⟨ he, ⟨ and his wife,

attached]! See how the Holy One, blessed is He, favors the entry *into Eretz Yisrael* over the departure *from it*! When the Jews returned from Babylon it is written: *Their horses ... their mules ... their camels*, etc. [*Ezra* 2:66]. But here the verse simply tells us: *and there went a man* — like a mere stump. He left the country, and Scripture makes no mention of his property, as though he left empty-handed (*Midrash*).

The word וַיֵּלֶךְ, *went* [lit., *walked*], not וַיִּסַּע, *traveled*, is used. This indicates that he originally planned only a temporary stay (*Kol Yehudah*).

The phrase וַיֵּלֶךְ אִישׁ, *and there went a man*, appears twice in Scripture: here, and in *Exodus* 2:1 [referring to Moses' father]. Esoterically speaking, just as there — וַיֵּלֶךְ אִישׁ מִבֵּית לֵוִי, *and there went a man of the house of Levi*, resulted in the first Redeemer, Moses — so here, too, did וַיֵּלֶךְ אִישׁ מִבֵּית לֶחֶם יְהוּדָה, *and there went a man from Bethlehem in Judah*, resulted in the final Redeemer: the House of David (*Alshich; Baal HaTurim*).

מִבֵּית לֶחֶם יְהוּדָה — *From Bethlehem in Judah*. [The verse could also be translated *A man from Bethlehem in Judah went ...*, that a man, who was a resident of Bethlehem, went (the phrase being adjectival).]

[Bethlehem was one of the finest and most fruitful areas of Eretz Yisrael.]

[Perhaps יְהוּדָה, *in Judah*, is men-

tioned to distinguish it from the other Bethlehem in Zevulun (*Joshua* 19:15).]

Why is the phrase *from Bethlehem in Judah to sojourn in the fields of Moab* inserted here [between *a man* and *he, his wife, and his two sons*]? Grammatically, the verse should read: *And there went a man, along with his wife and his two sons, from Bethlehem in Judah to sojourn in the fields of Moab ....*

This verse, structured as it is, seems to imply that leaving Eretz Yisrael at that time was his decision alone. וַיֵּלֶךְ אִישׁ, *And there went a man* — the decision to *leave* בֵּית לֶחֶם יְהוּדָה was his alone — and he compelled his wife and two sons to follow. Having unilaterally made the decision to leave, Elimelech asked his family where they wished to go. The ultimate choice — לָגוּר בִּשְׂדֵי מוֹאָב, *to sojourn in the fields of Moab* — was made with the unanimous consent of אִשְׁתּוֹ וּשְׁנֵי בָנָיו, *his wife and his two sons* (*Iggeres Shmuel*).

לָגוּר בִּשְׂדֵי מוֹאָב — *To sojourn in the fields of Moab*. "Fields" are in plural because it was Elimelech's original intention to sojourn and wander about the many fields and cities; not to establish himself permanently in any one place in Moab (*Alshich*).

Elimelech's sin was compounded by his choice of a new homeland. Had he gone elsewhere, his sin would not have been as severe. Our verse spe-

I
2

וּשְׁנֵי בָנָיו: בּ וְשֵׁם הָאִישׁ אֱלִימֶ֫לֶךְ

« and his two sons. **2** The < of the man < was
name Elimelech,

cifically elaborates on his shameful act by telling us his destination: the detestable Moab of whom God cautioned us: לֹא־יָבֹא עַמּוֹנִי וּמוֹאָבִי בִּקְהַל ה' ... עַד־עוֹלָם, *There shall not enter an Ammonite or a Moabite into the congregation of* Hashem *... to eternity* [*Deut.* 23:4], and also: לֹא־תִדְרֹשׁ שְׁלוֹמָם וְטוֹבָתָם כָּל־יָמֶיךָ לְעוֹלָם, *Do not seek their peace or their well-being all your days, forever* (ibid. v. 7). And yet, Elimelech went to live among them, where he would greet them every morning with "Shalom" or would at the very least respond to them, "Shalom"! (*Iggeres Shmuel*).

Elimelech perhaps rationalized that it was better for him to dwell in open fields among Moabites than to remain in Eretz Yisrael under the circumstances of lawlessness prevalent during the famine (*Pri Chaim*).

הוּא וְאִשְׁתּוֹ וּשְׁנֵי בָנָיו — *He, and his wife, and his two sons.* He was the prime mover, his wife secondary to him, and his two sons secondary to both of them (*Midrash*).

Elimelech's additional sin was that he took only his nearest kin — his wife and two sons — along with him not being concerned about anyone else (*Iggeres Shmuel*).

2. וְשֵׁם הָאִישׁ אֱלִימֶלֶךְ — *The name of the man was Elimelech.* The *Midrash* explains that his name signified his arrogant attitude; he would boast: אֵלַי תָּבוֹא מַלְכוּת, "To me shall kingship come ...."

Being a member of the tribe of Judah and a descendant of Nahshon ben Amminadab, its prince, he reasoned that royalty would descend from him (*Torah Temimah*).

Elimelech considered himself to be a prominent individual, always boasting, "To me shall kingship come." Therefore, he should have considered the consequences of his desertion of the Land, and so, he deserved to be punished (*Kol Yehudah*).

[The holiness of Eretz Yisrael is such that a sin on its holy earth is more serious and more significant than a sin elsewhere. For this reason the punishment for sins committed in Eretz Yisrael is quicker in coming and more stringent. (See *Lev.* 18:25-28, and *Ramban* there.) In attempting to flee from Divine judgment, Elimelech wanted to leave the Holy Land in the belief that if he were in a foreign, non-sacred land, his sins would be of lesser magnitude and less deserving of punishment.]

Elimelech wanted to flee from the Divine Decree, but was unsuccessful in escaping from it. This is implied in the words וַיֵּלֶךְ אִישׁ, *there went a man*, anonymously, *incognito.* But מִדַּת הַדִּין — God's Attribute of Judgment — recognized and identified him, as the verse continues: וְשֵׁם הָאִישׁ אֱלִימֶלֶךְ, *the name of the man was Elimelech*, the prominent and famous Elimelech, leader of that generation; one who could have protested the injustices of the time but

פרק א
ג

וְשֵׁם אִשְׁתּוֹ נָעֳמִי וְשֵׁם שְׁנֵי־בָנָיו |

⟨ of his two sons ⟨ and the ⟪ was ⟨ of his ⟨ and the
names Naomi, wife name

מַחְלוֹן וְכִלְיוֹן אֶפְרָתִים מִבֵּית לֶחֶם

⟨ of Bethlehem ⟨ Ephrathites ⟪ and ⟨ were
Chilion, Mahlon

did not. Judgment was then visited upon him and his sons, and they died (*Zohar Chadash*).

וְשֵׁם אִשְׁתּוֹ נָעֳמִי — *And the name of his wife was Naomi.* For her actions were pleasant and sweet [the translation of Naomi being *pleasant*] (*Midrash*).

Not only was Elimelech well known, even his wife and two sons were שֵׁם אַנְשֵׁי — famous personages (*Malbim*).

שְׁנֵי־בָנָיו — *His two sons.* "Two" is mentioned because they were both equally great (*Rashba HaLevi*).

מַחְלוֹן וְכִלְיוֹן — *Machlon and Chilion.* The *Midrash* says that their names indicate שֶׁנִּמְחוּ וְכָלוּ מִן הָעוֹלָם, *they were blotted out and perished from the world.*

The *Talmud* enumerates them, along with Elimelech, as the leaders of that generation. They were all punished because they left Eretz Yisrael (*Bava Basra* 91a).

According to *Zohar Chadash*, he was called Machlon, שֶׁמָּחַל לוֹ הקב״ה לְאַחַר זְמַן, *because the Holy One, blessed is He, ultimately forgave him* [posthumously, by allowing יִבּוּם, *a levirate marriage*, to take place with his widow Ruth], שֶׁהָיָה מוֹחֶה, *because he protested* the injustices of his father. Chilion was so

named שֶׁנִּכְלֶה מִן הָעוֹלָם, *for he was utterly blotted out from the world.*

אֶפְרָתִים — *Ephrathites.* [This word, sometimes translated *Ephraimite* and sometimes *Ephrathite*, is variously interpreted by the Sages.]

The *Midrash* considers the word to be a title of honor, interpreting it to mean *courtiers, aristocrats.* It may be derived from the word אַפִּרְיוֹן, *a crown*, one who possesses the *crown* bequeathed by יַעֲקֹב אָבִינוּ, *our Patriarch Jacob*, at the time of his departure from the world ....

The word usually indicates a descendant of Ephraim, or a native of Ephrath, Bethlehem [see *Genesis* 35:19, 48:7]. The *Midrash* offers different interpretations because the word אֶפְרָתִים, *Ephrathites*, in our verse could not refer to the tribe of Ephraim since Elimelech and his sons were of the tribe of Judah. Also, the Sages did not define it as *Ephrathite, a native of Ephrath*, because if Bethlehem is referred to as Ephrath by the author of *Megillas Ruth*, then he should have used that name in verse 1 as well. Obviously, therefore, *Ephrathite* must be taken as a description of the family rather than as a reference to their city (*Torah Temimah; Gishmei Berachah*).

The *Targum*, translating אֶפְרָתִים, adds the word רַבָּנִין, *masters.*

I
3

יְהוּדָה וַיָּבֹאוּ שְׂדֵי־מוֹאָב וַיִּהְיוּ־שָׁם:

⟪ there. ⟨ and they ⟨ of Moab ⟨ to the ⟨ They ⟪ in Judah.
remained fields came

וַיָּמָת אֱלִימֶלֶךְ אִישׁ נָעֳמִי וַתִּשָּׁאֵר הִיא ₃

⟨ and she was left ⟪ of ⟨ the ⟨ Elimelech died, 3
Naomi; husband

According to *Rashi*: אֶפְרָתִים means *distinguished persons* .... See how important they were! Eglon, the king of Moab, married his daughter [Ruth] to Machlon, as the Master has expounded: Ruth was the daughter of Eglon.

Bethlehem was originally called Ephrath, and later given the name Bethlehem. Also, there was a very distinguished family in the tribe of Judah called אֶפְרָתִים, *Ephrathites*, because they descended from Ephrath [another name for Miriam, sister of Moses — (*Sotah* 11a)], the wife of Caleb [*I Chronicles* 2:19], a most distinguished lady (*Malbim*).

Pirkei DeRabbi Eliezer notes that throughout the Bible every great man who arose in Israel had the title Ephrathite attached to his name.

אֶפְרָתִים מִבֵּית לֶחֶם יְהוּדָה — *Ephrathites of Bethlehem in Judah.* Bethlehem is repeated in this verse as if to say that the sons, as *Ephrathites*, distinguished persons, were also held responsible for the sin of Elimelech's departure from Bethlehem; they should have protested!

... They were the most prominent citizens of the most prominent city in Eretz Yisrael (*Pri Chaim; Malbim*).

וַיִּהְיוּ־שָׁם — *And they remained there* [lit., *and they were there*].

Although it was their original intention only to *sojourn temporarily* in the fields of Moab, nevertheless, once they arrived they decided to settle permanently (*Malbim*).

They felt themselves drawn to the Moabites whom they resembled. They were mean and ungenerous like the Moabites who *did not meet Israel with bread and water on the way when they left Egypt* [compare *Deut.* 23:5] (*Meishiv Nefesh* quoting *Ruth Zuta*).

The word וַיִּהְיוּ, *they were*, rather than וַיֵּשְׁבוּ, *they settled*, is used to imply that they achieved a new status [הֲוָיָה] there: they felt no remorse that they had departed from Eretz Yisrael ... and for this reason they died (*Rav Yosef Yavetz*).

The *Targum* translates וַיִּהְיוּ שָׁם as: וַהֲווֹ תַּמָּן רוֹפִילִין, *they became officers there* [which, in the context of the traditional enmity between the Jews and Moab must be understood not as praise, but as condemnation; they stooped so low that they integrated themselves socially and militarily into the culture of Moab].

3. וַיָּמָת אֱלִימֶלֶךְ — *Elimelech died.* An untimely death (*Midrash*). This punishment was inflicted upon the family because they should have begged for mercy for their generation

פרק א

ד

וּשְׁנֵי בָנֶיהָ: ‏ ז **וַיִּשְׂאוּ לָהֶם נָשִׁים מְאֲבִיּוֹת**

‏《 who were 〈 wives 〈 for 〈 They 4 《 with her
Moabites, themselves took two sons.

and they did not do so (*Bava Basra* 91b). Even though one could perhaps rationalize that their departure from the Holy Land was necessary under the conditions of famine and need, they were still not guiltless. It was they who were responsible for the hunger because they did not pray for their generation (*Nachlas Yosef*).

The *Talmud*, giving Elimelech's ancestry, states: Elimelech, Salmah, Ploni Almoni, and the father of Naomi were all descendants of Nahshon son of Amminadab [prince of the tribe of Judah]. This teaches us that even זְכוּת אָבוֹת, *the merit of ancestors*, is of no avail when one leaves Eretz Yisrael for a foreign country (*Bava Basra* 91a).

אִישׁ נָעֳמִי — *The husband of Naomi.* Naomi is mentioned here in conjunction with Elimelech's death, notes the *Talmud*, because the death of a man is felt by no one as keenly and as deeply as by his wife (*Sanhedrin* 22b).

Elimelech, not Naomi, was punished, because, as the verse tells us, he was אִישׁ נָעֳמִי, *the husband of Naomi*, and she was subject to his authority. Therefore, the onus of the sin was thrust upon him (*Rashi, Malbim*).

[This great man, this פַּרְנָס הַדּוֹר (magnate of the generation), is described at his death merely as אִישׁ נָעֳמִי, *the husband of Naomi*. Only she grieved at his loss; to his people he had already died long before.]

וַתִּשָּׁאֵר הִיא וּשְׁנֵי בָנֶיהָ — *And she was left with her two sons.* She became like the שִׁיּוּרֵי מְנָחוֹת, *remnants of the meal offerings* [of little importance, now that her husband was dead] (*Midrash*).

As translated with the additions of the *Targum*: *And she was left* — a widow; *and her two sons* — orphans.

Had Elimelech's sons sinned only in leaving the Holy Land, the punishment of being orphaned would have been retribution enough. But they sinned further by marrying Moabite women [see next verse] (*Pri Chaim*).

[Some commentators, however, understand וַתִּשָּׁאֵר in the sense of *she remained* in a despised foreign land:] When her husband died, she should have seen it as a Divine warning to return to Eretz Yisrael. Instead, *she remained there with her two sons* (*Malbim*); as a result, her sons stayed on to marry Moabite women, and paid with their own lives (*Iggeres Shmuel*).

4. וַיִּשְׂאוּ לָהֶם נָשִׁים מְאֲבִיּוֹת — *They took for themselves wives who were Moabites.*

Shouldn't the sons have learned a lesson from their father's death and returned to Eretz Yisrael? What did they do? They married Moabite women without even having their wives undergo ritual purification and conversion (*Tanchuma, BeHar*).

I
4

שֵׁם הָאַחַת עָרְפָּה וְשֵׁם הַשֵּׁנִית רוּת

》 was 〈 of the 〈 and the 〈 was 〈 of one 〈 the
Ruth, second name Orpah, name

עֲבֵירָה גוֹרֶרֶת עֲבֵירָה — *One trans-gression leads to another* (*Simchas HaRegel*).

It should be noted that only after their father's death did the sons marry women who were not of their people, an indication that Elimelech, for all his faults, would not have allowed them to stoop so low (*Alshich*).

The common expression וַיִּשְׂאוּ, lit., *married*, is used rather than the legal term וַיִּקְחוּ, *took*, because the women were not ritually converted and were thus not legally married under Torah law (*Iggeres Shmuel; Malbim*).

The Torah's prohibition of marriage to a Moabite (even after ritual conversion) had within it the implication later expounded by the Sages that the ban extends only to a "Moabite but not to a Moabitess" [see *Deut.* 23:4]. Thus, their sin could be considered as of lesser magnitude. But Machlon and Chilion did not know that; in their own minds they *were* transgressing the law against Moabite marriage. Therefore their punishment was greater (*Kol Yehudah*).

The word לָהֶם, *for themselves*, implies that they married these women not לְשֵׁם שָׁמַיִם, *for the sake of heaven*, but to satisfy their own selfish, sensual desires ... and having married non-converted Moabite women, whatever offspring would have resulted from these unions would have been considered non-

Jewish (*Iggeres Shmuel*).

[There is an opinion (*Zohar Chadash* and *Ibn Ezra*), that Machlon and Chilion *did* subject their prospective brides to conversion and immersion, but the "fear of their husbands was upon them." (See *Overview* for a detailed explanation of this view, and its ramifications.)]

שֵׁם הָאַחַת עָרְפָּה — *The name of one was Orpah.* She was named Orpah because she ultimately turned her back [עֹרֶף, *the nape of her neck*] on her mother-in-law (*Midrash*).

וְשֵׁם הַשֵּׁנִית רוּת — *And the name of the second was Ruth.* She was named Ruth because she "saw" [רָאֲתָה — *considered well*] the words of her mother-in-law (*Midrash*).

According to the *Talmud*: Rav Yochanan said: Why was she called Ruth? — Because there issued from her David who *saturated* (רִוָּה) the Holy One, blessed is He, with hymns and prayers (*Bava Basra* 14b).

[The Torah contains 606 Commandments (in addition to the 7 Noachide Laws which are incumbent even upon non-Jews). The commentators note that this number, 606, is equal to the numerical value of the name רוּת, *Ruth*, the convert *par excellence*. This was the number of additional *mitzvos* she accepted upon her conversion.]

Esoterically speaking, the name Ruth [רות] is spelled with the letters

פרק א

ה-ו

וַיֵּשְׁבוּ שָׁם כְּעֶשֶׂר שָׁנִים: הוַיָּמֻתוּ גַם־

‹ and they lived › there › about ten › years. **5** ‹ They › likewise, ‹
died

---

of "turtledove" [תּוֹר]. Just as the turtledove is fit for sacrifice on the altar, so was Ruth fit for inclusion in the Assembly of God (*Zohar Chadash*).

[The Sages tell us that Machlon and Chilion, wealthy and distinguished, rose to such prominence while living in Moab that Eglon, king of Moab, offered them his daughters' hands in marriage.]

Ruth and Orpah were the daughters of Eglon, as it is written [*Judges* 3:19; (when Ehud came to Eglon to deliver God's message)] ... *and Ehud said: "I have a message from God to you." And [Eglon] arose from his throne.* The Holy One, blessed is He, said of him: *"You stood up from your throne in My honor, I will cause to emerge from you a descendant who will sit upon My throne"* (*Midrash*).

וַיֵּשְׁבוּ שָׁם כְּעֶשֶׂר שָׁנִים — *And they lived there about ten years* [lit., *they "sat" (dwelt) there about ten years*].

This confirms the view that they had given up all thoughts of returning to Eretz Yisrael (*Malbim*).

In verse 2 the words וַיִּהְיוּ שָׁם, *and they remained there*, is used; here, וַיֵּשְׁבוּ שָׁם, *and they lived there*, is used. Elimelech should have known better than to leave Eretz Yisrael. As soon as he "was" there he was punished. But the sons were helpless in the matter and could not overrule their father. They were not punished until וַיֵּשְׁבוּ שָׁם, *they dwelt there*, and tarried for so long (*Iggeres Shmuel*).

God waited all these years to give them the opportunity to repent (*Midrash Zuta*).

Having married princesses, they couldn't abandon them, nor could they return with them to Eretz Yisrael. They feared the Sages would have forced them to separate themselves from their Moabite wives, who, at the time, were still thought to be forbidden because the Sages had not yet ruled that a Moabitess was permitted. Therefore — divorce and return to Eretz Yisrael being impossible — God punished them with death (*Simchas HaRegel*).

כְּעֶשֶׂר שָׁנִים — *About ten years* [lit., *like ten years*]. The *Bach* explains why "like" ten years is used. The *Midrash* (on verse 1) states that before the famine, the Jews in Eretz Yisrael had looked upon Elimelech as one who could provide their sustenance for ten years. They placed all their trust in him, rather than in God. When the famine broke out, the miserly Elimelech left, and God caused his family to live away for a period *like ten years*, a length of time equal to the ten years for which the Jews had misplaced their trust in flesh and blood — until when these ten years were up, and the famine ended (*Meishiv Nefesh*).

5. וַיָּמֻתוּ גַם־שְׁנֵיהֶם — *They died likewise, the two of them.*

[God first punishes man, via warn-

I
5-6

שְׁנֵיהֶם מַחְלוֹן וְכִלְיוֹן וַתִּשָּׁאֵר הָאִשָּׁה

⟨ the ⟨ so there ⟪ and ⟨ Mahlon ⟨ the two
woman remained Chilion; of them,

מִשְּׁנֵי יְלָדֶיהָ וּמֵאִישָׁהּ: וַתָּקָם הִיא

⟨ she ⟨ She then **6** ⟪ and from ⟨ from her two children
got up, her husband.

ings, depriving him of his property, and only after that, if man does not repent, does God smite him in his person.]

"The Merciful One never begins His retribution by taking a human life .... And so it was with Machlon and Chilion also. First their horses, their asses, and their camels died, then Elimelech, and lastly the two sons" (Midrash).

After being stripped of their money and cattle the two of them גַּם, likewise, died (Rashi).

The word גַּם, likewise, indicates that just as the death of their father was punishment for having remained outside of Eretz Yisrael, so was their death in punishment for that sin (Iggeres Shmuel).

[Just as the death of Elimelech — in verse 3 — follows as punishment for וַיִּהְיוּ שָׁם, and they remained there, so does the death of the sons follow as punishment for וַיֵּשְׁבוּ שָׁם — and they lived there.]

Although [under certain conditions of great distress] one is permitted to emigrate, if one does, the act is not in conformity with the law of righteousness. Remember Machlon and Chilion! They were the two great men of their generation and they left Eretz Yisrael at a time of

great distress; nevertheless they incurred thereby the penalty of extinction (Rambam).

שְׁנֵיהֶם — The two of them. Because they were equally guilty (Pri Chaim).

מַחְלוֹן וְכִלְיוֹן — Machlon and Chilion. Note that they are no longer referred to as Ephrathites, as above in verse 2 [see Comm. there], nor are they identified as the husbands of Ruth and Orpah. They are stripped of their prestige: they are simply Machlon and Chilion (Alshich).

The verse repeats their names to emphasize that not only did they die physically, but because they were childless, their very names — Machlon and Chilion — died with them (Iggeres Shmuel).

וַתִּשָּׁאֵר הָאִשָּׁה מִשְּׁנֵי יְלָדֶיהָ וּמֵאִישָׁהּ — So there remained the woman from her two children and from her husband; she was left alone without her children or her husband. Her children are mentioned first because when one recounts past events one usually mentions the most recent first; or because of the greater anguish associated with the death of her children, who died young, whereas her husband died at an old age (Ibn Ezra).

The Midrash notes that before

פֶּרֶק א וְכַלֹּתֶיהָ וַתָּשָׁב מִשְׂדֵי מוֹאָב כִּי שָׁמְעָה
ו
‹ she had ‹ for ‹‹ of ‹ from ‹ to ‹ with her
heard Moab, the fields return daughters-in-law

punishing their persons, God first struck at their property, completely devastating and impoverishing them. Nevertheless, this verse tells us, Naomi did not anguish over the loss of her property, but over the loss of her children and husband (*Iggeres Shmuel*).

[After her husband's death Naomi was yet of some importance, but with her sons' death, that remaining prestige, too, left her.]

Rav Chaninah said: She was left as the remnants of the remnants [of the meal-offering and thus of no value whatsoever. See *Comm.* to verse 3 s.v. וַתִּשָׁאֵר, *And she was left*] (*Midrash*).

[Unlike verse 3 where they are called בָּנֶיהָ, *her sons*, here Machlon and Chilion are called יְלָדֶיהָ, *her children*, since they died like young children without their own offspring].

An excellent insight is offered in *Ima Shel Malchus*:

Naomi had many times asked herself by what merit she had survived. Had she not sinned as much as they? … Perhaps her sin was a greater one, and therefore her punishment too was greater …. It was she — of the whole family — who was left, desolate, to bear the burden of sorrow of the entire family ….

Naomi could not possibly have known, much less have dared to believe at the time, that she had been preserved through the kindness and

compassion of *HASHEM*, Who had allowed the spark of life of Elimelech's family to remain glowing in her … leading to the birth of King David.

6. וַתָּקָם הִיא וְכַלֹּתֶיהָ — *She then got up, she with her daughters-in-law.* The next verse tells us, in a seemingly redundant manner, וַתֵּצֵא מִן־הַמָּקוֹם, *she left from the place.* In this verse, therefore, וַתָּקָם, *she got up,* means: *she ''resolved'' to leave* (*Iggeres Shmuel; Ibn Ezra; Vilna Gaon*).

The resolve to *leave this ill-fated place* was shared equally by them all, because they surmised that their evil fortune was bound up with their present luckless abode (*Malbim*).

She was afraid that if they stayed there one more day they would all die (*Alshich*).

The *Besuras Eliyahu* interprets וַתָּקָם as *rising up from mourning;* as soon as the mourning period was over they resolved to leave.

The *Midrash* interprets וַתָּקָם in a spiritual sense: Fallen down, she now lifted herself up by returning to Eretz Yisrael (*Lekach Tov*).

(According to *Rashi*, however, וַתָּקָם, *she got up,* in this verse implies *actual* departure [see *Comm.* next verse].)

וַתָּשָׁב מִשְׂדֵי מוֹאָב — *To return from the fields of Moab.* The word וַתָּשָׁב [lit., *and she returned*] is singular to imply that although the three of them unanimously agreed that they

I
6

בִּשְׂדֵה מוֹאָב כִּי־פָקַד יהוה אֶת־עַמּוֹ

⟨ His people ⟨ HASHEM had ⟨ that ⟨ of Moab ⟨ in the fields
remembered

must leave their present luckless abode, at first it was Naomi alone who decided to leave Moab, her daughters-in-law concurring in that decision only later (*Malbim*).

כִּי שָׁמְעָה בִּשְׂדֵה מוֹאָב — *For she had heard in the fields of Moab.* She heard from peddlers making their rounds from city to city, says the *Midrash*. And what was it she heard? כִּי־פָקַד ה׳ אֶת־עַמּוֹ לָתֵת לָהֶם לֶחֶם ... *That HASHEM had remembered His people to give them food.* Now that the famine was over, Jewish peddlers resumed their rounds in Moab selling the produce of Eretz Yisrael. It was from these peddlers that she heard the good news. The *Midrash* reasons that she heard it from Jewish peddlers because the Moabites would never have invoked the Name of *HASHEM* (the proper Name of God) as the Cause of the famine and its removal. Also, as the *Midrash* states, God ended the famine for the sake of עַמּוֹ, *His people*; she was reassured that the cause of the famine [the lawlessness of the times (see *Comm.* to verse 1)], was remedied, the people having repented, and that the famine had permanently ended (*Malbim*).

Pri Chaim, on the other hand, analyzing the verse, comments that פָקַד ה׳ אֶת עַמּוֹ, *HASHEM had remembered His people*, is an exact quotation of what the peddlers were going around saying; and since עַמּוֹ,

His people, is in the third person — implying that the speaker excluded himself — we must say that it was Moabite peddlers who were acknowledging *HASHEM*'s ending of the famine in Eretz Yisrael.

Nachlas Yosef stresses the word עַמּוֹ, *His people* — the word was out that the Jews once again became *God's people*, having fully repented from their evil ways.

It should be noted that Naomi did not resolve to return home until she had the assurance that the famine was finally over, and that God had ended it for the sake of עַמּוֹ, *His people*, of which she, too, was part. For had He ended it for the sake of Eretz Yisrael, she could not be part of it, having forsaken the land. [The family's affront to the Land would have precluded their sharing in any prosperity granted for its sake. But a Jew remains a Jew even after having sinned; thus Naomi could share in abundance given for the sake of people] (*Alshich*).

According to the *Targum*: God gave the people food on account of the righteousness of the judge Ivtzan and the prayers of Boaz [who, according to the *Talmud*, was the same person].

A homiletical interpretation is offered by *Kol Yehudah*: At first, Naomi was afraid to return home during the famine lest the Jews take revenge against her by not

פרק א
ז-ח

לָתֵת לָהֶם לָחֶם: וַתֵּצֵא מִן־הַמָּקוֹם

⟨ the place ⟨ from ⟨ She left 7 ≪ food. ⟨ them ⟨ to give

אֲשֶׁר הָיְתָה־שָּׁמָּה וּשְׁתֵּי כַלֹּתֶיהָ עִמָּהּ

≪ were ⟨ and her two ⟨ there, ⟨ she had ⟨ that
with her; daughters-in-law been

וַתֵּלַכְנָה בַדֶּרֶךְ לָשׁוּב אֶל־אֶרֶץ יְהוּדָה:

≪ of Judah. ⟨ the land ⟨ to ⟨ to return ⟨ on the ⟨ and they
road set out

---

feeding her. She realized, however, that God, Who by warning against being vengeful, פָּקַד אֶת עַמּוֹ, *had* (in effect) *commanded His people* [פָּקַד, *remembered*, could also mean *commanded*], לָתֵת לָהֶם לָחֶם, *to give them* [Naomi and her family] *bread* just as Jews are commanded by the Torah to care for all unfortunates.

7. וַתֵּצֵא מִן־הַמָּקוֹם — *She left from the place. Rashi*, who holds that וַתָּקָם, *she got up*, in the previous verse denotes actual departure rather than a resolve to leave, queries: Her return home is already mentioned in the preceding verse; why does this verse speak of her departure? ....

[Her departure was particularly noticeable because:] The great person of a city is its brilliance, its distinction, its glory, and its praise. When he departs, its brilliance, its distinction, its glory, and its praise depart with him (*Midrash; Rashi*).

וּשְׁתֵּי כַלֹּתֶיהָ עִמָּהּ — *and her two daughters-in-law were with her.* The departure of the daughters-in-law was also particularly significant, as was Naomi's [see preceeding Comm.] (*Meishiv Nefesh*).

וַתֵּלַכְנָה — *And they set out* [lit., *they walked*]; they discussed הִלְכוֹת גֵּרִים, *the laws of proselytes*. [This interpretation is suggested by the seemingly redundant use of the word וַתֵּלַכְנָה, *they walked*, which has the same root as הֲלָכָה, *law.*] (*Midrash*).

בַּדֶּרֶךְ — *On the road.* The *Midrash* offers this explanation for the seemingly superfluous term בַּדֶּרֶךְ, *on the road:* The way was hard for them because they went barefoot; [nothing cushioned their bare feet from the road; such was the degree of their poverty] (*Torah Temimah*).

The words בַּדֶּרֶךְ לָשׁוּב, *on the road to return*, are superfluous; the verse could have read: *And they set out to the land of Judah.* The verse, as structured, teaches us that when our intentions are good, God rewards us every step of the way (*Kol Yehudah*).

לָשׁוּב — *To return.* This can only refer to Naomi who was *returning* to Eretz Yisrael. *Returning*, in this context, could not refer to Ruth or Orpah, who had never been in Eretz Yisrael (*Iggeres Shmuel*).

8. וַתֹּאמֶר נָעֳמִי — *Then Naomi said.* Naomi had assumed that her

I
7-8

וַתֹּאמֶר נָעֳמִי לִשְׁתֵּי כַלֹּתֶיהָ לֵכְנָה

⟨ *Go*, ⟨⟨   to her two   ⟨ Then Naomi said   **8**
daughters-in-law,

שֹׁבְנָה אִשָּׁה לְבֵית אִמָּהּ יַעַשׂ [יעשה כ']

⟨ *May He* ⟨⟨   of her   ⟨ to the   ⟨ each   ⟨ return,
deal   mother.   house   of you

daughters-in-law were merely accompanying her to Judah out of respect and courtesy, with the intention of returning to Moab afterward. She told them that this was unnecessary. Her maternal suggestion was that they should return to their mother's home, confident that God would reward them for having been good wives and dutiful daughters-in-law (*Malbim*).

לִשְׁתֵּי כַלֹּתֶיהָ — *To her two daughters-in-law.* The verse mentions *two* in order to make clear that Naomi showed no bias toward Ruth. Although she realized that Ruth's determination to convert was much stronger than Orpah's, she addressed them both in the same terms (*Meishiv Nefesh*).

Quite possibly, Naomi did not yet realize that Ruth's commitment was greater than Orpah's. She addressed them as equals in the hope that each would strengthen the other's resolve (*Rav Yosef Yavetz; Pri Chaim*).

לֵכְנָה שֹׁבְנָה — *Go, return.* She asked them to return home because she did not want to be embarrassed [by returning to Eretz Yisrael with Moabite daughters-in-law] (*Midrash Zuta*).

[The Sages rule that one must attempt to dissuade a would-be convert three times; this was the first time — the others are in verses 11 and 12.]

If Naomi's *only* intention was to fulfill the halachic requirement that a potential proselyte be discouraged, then the word שֹׁבְנָה, *return*, would have been sufficient. Since Naomi added לֵכְנָה, *go*, the Rabbis deduced that her intention was sincere, because she reflected that she, Elimelech's widow, was about to return to the Holy Land with non-Jewish daughters-in-law, and, as the *Midrash* tells us, she grew ashamed (*Midrash Zuta*).

According to *Alshich*, once they reached the *road to return to the land of Judah*, Naomi realized that they had not escorted her as a mere courtesy, but that their intention was to remain with her in Judah. She told them not to follow each other blindly, but, as individuals, to carefully consider the implications of conversion and to act out of a deep personal conviction. She said: "לֵכְנָה, *go* along with me, or שֹׁבְנָה, *return* to the house of your mother, but, whatever course you choose, may God repay your goodness, and may you find husbands."

יַעֲשֶׂה ה׳ עִמָּכֶם חֶסֶד — *May He deal*

פֶרֶק א   יהוה עִמָּכֶם חֶסֶד כַּאֲשֶׁר עֲשִׂיתֶם עִם־
ט-יא   — *HASHEM* — ⟩ with ⟩ kindly, ⟩ with ⟩ as ⟩ you have ⟩ with ⟩
                                        you   done

— *HASHEM may* — *with you kindly.*
The כְּתִיב, *k'siv* [the traditional spell-
ing], is יעשה [the simple future tense],
"He will *certainly* deal kindly with
you"] (*Midrash*).

[Our translation, of course, follows
the קְרִי, *kri* (the traditional *reading*)
יַעַשׂ, the wishful *may He do*. The jux-
taposition of *k'siv* and *kri* indicate
that, although Naomi said, "*May
He do,*" in the form of a prayer, she
was fully confident that God would,
indeed, reward their kindness.]

God does not withhold reward
from any creature! [God repays every
good deed appropriately; what special implication did Naomi's blessing
have?] Naomi's blessing must be understood as saying: Just as you both
have gone beyond what is expected
of you by doing חֶסֶד, *kindness*, so
may *HASHEM* not only reward you in
the usual manner, but may He also
go beyond the expected and do חֶסֶד,
kindness, with you (*Nachal Eshkol*).

Naomi's intention was, "Perhaps,
my daughters-in-law, you do not
part from me because you fear that
if you desert me now — leaving me
destitute — all your previous kindness to me will be nullified; instead
of being rewarded for the good you
have done for so many years, you
are afraid you will be punished for
the final lapse. Fear not. You may
return home to your mothers and
God will reward you nonetheless"
(*Iggeres Shmuel*).

כַּאֲשֶׁר עֲשִׂיתֶם עִם־הַמֵּתִים — *As you
have done with the deceased [ones]*,
by having been good to your husbands during their lifetimes, וְעִמָּדִי,
and with me (*Malbim*).

According to the *Midrash*: *As you
have done with the deceased [ones]*
— in that you [went beyond what
is *required* of a wife and] busied
yourselves with their shrouds; *and
with me* — in that you renounced
the marriage settlement to which
you were legally entitled.

The *Midrash* thus understands
the verse as referring to *posthumous*
kindness ["busying themselves with
their shrouds"]. Had Naomi referred
to kindness done during the lifetimes
of their husbands, she would have
said *with your husbands* instead
of *with the deceased [ones]* (*Torah
Temimah*).

Perhaps this is why Naomi addressed them in the Hebrew masculine gender [עִמָּכֶם, עֲשִׂיתֶם] as if to
say: Your posthumous kindness to
your husbands — in preparing their
shrouds and funeral — was not a
legal feminine obligation, but a masculine one (*Meishiv Nefesh*).

The *Targum* translates: The kindness you have done to your husbands
— *by refusing to remarry*; and to
me — *by feeding and sustaining me*.

9. [Naomi elaborates on her blessing
of the previous verse, specifying that
the "kindness" for which she prays
is that God reward them at long last

I
9-11

הַמֵּתִים וְעִמָּדִי: ט יִתֵּן יהוה לָכֶם וּמְצֶאןָ

⟨ that you ⟨ you ⟨ May HASHEM 9 ⟪ and ⟨ the deceased
may find grant with me! [ones]

מְנוּחָה אִשָּׁה בֵּית אִישָׁהּ וַתִּשַּׁק לָהֶן

⟪ them, ⟨ She ⟪ of her [new] ⟨ in the ⟨ each ⟨ contentment,
kissed husband. home woman

וַתִּשֶּׂאנָה קוֹלָן וַתִּבְכֶּינָה: י וַתֹּאמַרְנָה־לָּהּ

⟪ to ⟨ And they 10 ⟪ and they ⟨ their ⟨ and they
her, said wept. voice raised

כִּי־אִתָּךְ נָשׁוּב לְעַמֵּךְ: יא וַתֹּאמֶר נָעֳמִי

⟪ But Naomi said, 11 ⟪ to your ⟨ we shall ⟨ with ⟨ Rather,
people. return you

---

with domestic contentment.]

יִתֵּן ה' לָכֶם — *May HASHEM grant you*
[lit., *May HASHEM give to you*], over
and above what you rightfully deserve (*Malbim*).

Ibn Ezra adds the word בַּעַל, *a
husband.*

וּמְצֶאןָ מְנוּחָה — *That you may find
contentment*. The *k'siv* [traditional
written form] of the word is וּמְצֶאן,
without the suffix, ה. [Naomi foresaw that] "only one of you will find
rest; not both" (*Midrash*).

Although Naomi foresaw that
only Ruth was destined to be
blessed, she nevertheless addressed
them with the plural לָכֶם, to *you*,
out of respect for Orpah's feelings.
However the word וּמְצֶאןָ, *that you
may find*, is indistinguishable in its
spoken form with or without the
suffix ה (*Iggeres Shmuel*).

אִשָּׁה בֵּית אִישָׁהּ — *Each woman in
the home of her [new] husband* [lit.,
woman in the home of her man].
From Naomi's blessing, we see that

a woman has no contentment except
in her husband's house (*Midrash*).

Witnessing the unhappiness of
her daughters-in-law who became
widowed after being barren for ten
years, she wished them true domestic
contentment in the future (*Iggeres
Shmuel*).

וַתִּשַּׁק לָהֶן — *She kissed them*. A
parting embrace (*Malbim*).

וַתִּבְכֶּינָה — *And they wept*. [The
commentaries differ on whether the
daughters-in-law cried on account
of Naomi's imminent departure, or
whether all three cried while reflecting on their sad state. The *Zohar
Chadash* states that the spirits of
their dead husbands stirred within
them, evoking their tears.]

10. וַתֹּאמַרְנָה־לָּהּ — *And they said to
her*. Now, they told her for the first
time of their intention of returning
with her (*Malbim*).

לְעַמֵּךְ — *To your people*. At this
point they expressed a desire not

פרק א
יב-יג

שֹׁבְנָה בְנֹתַי לֵמָה תֵלַכְנָה עִמִּי הַעוֹד־לִי

⟨ Have I more ⟨⟨ with ⟨ should ⟨ Why ⟨⟨ my ⟨ Turn
me? you go daughters. back,

בָנִים בְּמֵעַי וְהָיוּ לָכֶם לַאֲנָשִׁים: יב שֹׁבְנָה

⟨ Turn 12 ⟨⟨ husbands? ⟨ for ⟨ who could ⟨ in my ⟨ sons
back, you become womb

בְנֹתַי לֵכְןָ כִּי זָקַנְתִּי מִהְיוֹת לְאִישׁ כִּי

⟨ Even ⟨⟨ to a ⟨ to become ⟨ I am ⟨ for ⟨⟨ go ⟨ my
if man. married too old along, daughters,

---

to accept the God of the Jews, but merely to settle among *your people* in Eretz Yisrael (*Malbim*).

According to *Alshich*, however, Naomi understood these words as an implicit declaration that they wished to convert. Otherwise their statement would have been self-contradictory: one cannot join the Jewish nation without accepting its God.

11. שֹׁבְנָה בְנֹתַי — *Turn back, my daughters.* [This was the second of Naomi's three attempts to dissuade the would-be converts; see verses 8 and 12.]

הַעוֹד־לִי בָנִים בְּמֵעַי — *Have I more sons in my womb?* Naomi was not seriously suggesting that her daughters-in-law wait for unborn sons to grow up and become their husbands! Rather, her statement was metaphorical: *Have I any grown-up sons whom I have been keeping hidden, out of your sight, in my womb, and whom I could instantly produce to become your husbands?* (*Malbim*).

וְהָיוּ לָכֶם לַאֲנָשִׁים — *Who could become for you husbands?* Could then a man marry the widow of

his brother [who became widowed] before he was born? [יבום, *levirate marriage* (see *Overview*), would not apply to a thus far unconceived child] (*Midrash*).

Since the law of levirate marriage could not apply, such a marriage would be forbidden by Torah law. Therefore, Naomi's words must be understood, not in the sense of יבום, *levirate marriage*, but rather as a loving gesture: "Had I more sons in my womb, I would gladly give them to you in place of your dead husbands" (*Ibn Ezra*).

12. שֹׁבְנָה בְנֹתַי לֵכְןָ — *Turn back, my daughters, go along.* Three times is it written שֹׁבְנָה, *turn back*, corresponding to the three times that a would-be convert is dissuaded. If he still persists, he is accepted (*Midrash*).

כִּי זָקַנְתִּי מִהְיוֹת לְאִישׁ — *For I am too old to become married to a man* and to bear children to be husbands to you (*Rashi*).

Naomi adds to her argument, "Even if you agreed to wait until I remarry, have children, and raise them to marriageable age, there are still two reasons why this is impos-

I

12-13

אָמַרְתִּי יֶשׁ־לִי תִקְוָה גַּם הָיִיתִי הַלַּיְלָה

⟨ tonight ⟨ I were to be ⟨ and ⟨⟨ hope!' ⟨ for ⟨ 'There ⟨⟨ I were
married even if me is to say,

לְאִישׁ וְגַם יָלַדְתִּי בָנִים: יֹג הֲלָהֵן ׀

⟨ — for them 13 ⟨⟨ sons ⟨ I were to ⟨ and ⟨⟨ to a man,
bear even if

sible — first, כִּי זָקַנְתִּי מִהְיוֹת לְאִישׁ, *for I am too old to become married to a man;* secondly, you could not bear to wait so long — הֲלָהֵן תְּשַׂבֵּרְנָה, *for them would you look with hope?"* (*Malbim*).

כִּי אָמַרְתִּי יֶשׁ־לִי תִקְוָה — *Even if I were to say, 'There is for me hope!'* [The *even* is not in the Hebrew, but the phrase is to be so understood according to the commentaries (e.g., *Rashi*).]

In a homiletic fashion *Rav Velvele Margolis* interprets the verse as reflecting the social ills of society and the rationale for delaying marriage. Many people, wanting to climb the social ladder, reject prospective suitors always hoping for someone better to come along. Thus, Naomi said: "I am too old to have a husband because I wanted to become the wife of someone comparable to Elimelech, important and aristocratic; therefore I delayed remarriage כִּי אָמַרְתִּי יֶשׁ לִי תִקְוָה, because I always said: *There is for me hope*, I will find someone better, more suitable for me" (*Ginzei Malchus*).

גַּם הָיִיתִי הַלַּיְלָה לְאִישׁ — *And even if I were to be married tonight to a man.* The *Malbim* explains: According to our Sages, Naomi said: "If I had a husband tonight I might have borne

sons" (*Midrash*). Now, according to the Sages, a woman who resigns herself to unmarried widowhood for ten years can no longer bear children afterward. Thus, the only two ways Naomi — ten years a widow — could have remained fruitful were if she had sustained the hope of remarriage throughout the period of widowhood; or if she would remarry *that very night*, the tenth anniversary of Elimelech's death.

Thus, we can translate the verse: *Turn back, my daughters, go along, for I am too old to become married to a man,* for having remained widowed ten years, I should, under normal circumstances, not be able to remarry and bear children. *But,* said Naomi, *I said 'There is for me hope'* — I sustained the hope of remarrying throughout the ten years of my widowhood, thus enabling me to have children even after this period — or on the other hand *if I were to be married tonight,* specifically *tonight,* the last night of the ten-year period, *I might have children* ... and so I ask you: *For then would you look with hope? etc.* (*Malbim*).

וְגַם יָלַדְתִּי בָנִים — *And even if I were to bear sons.* Or even if I had already given birth to children (*Rashi*).

[*Rashi* apparently understands

פֶּרֶק א   תְּשַׂבֵּרְנָה עַד אֲשֶׁר יִגְדָּלוּ הֲלָהֵן תֵּעָגֵנָה

יג

⟨ would you ⟨ For ⟨⟨ they were ⟨ when ⟨ until ⟨ would you
tie yourselves, them grown up? look with hope

לְבִלְתִּי הֱיוֹת לְאִישׁ אַל בְּנֹתַי כִּי־

⟨ For ⟨⟨ my ⟨ No, ⟨⟨ an [other] ⟨ marrying ⟨ not
daughters! man?

---

these words, not as the hypothetical result of *if I were to be married tonight*, but as an additional argument by Naomi: "Let us say I *had* given birth to sons ... *for them would you look with hope until when they were grown up?*"]

[The double use of גַם, *even*, in this verse implies Naomi's resignation to an almost futile situation.]

13. הֲלָהֵן תְּשַׂבֵּרְנָה — *For them would you look with hope* — for the hypothetical children to whom I might give birth? *(Iggeres Shmuel).*

הֲלָהֵן תֵּעָגֵנָה — *For them would you tie yourselves?* [The translation follows *Rashi* who holds that the root of תֵּעָגֵנָה is עוג, *to encircle, to constrict. Rashi* refutes those who translate the word as being related to עֲגוּנָה, *agunah* (a woman who is forbidden to marry because her husband is missing and she has no proof of his death). The root of that word is עגן. Thus if תֵּעָגֵנָה stemmed from עגן (with the suffix נה), there would be a double נ in the word, or at the very least, the single נ with a *dagesh* (נ) serving to take the place of the missing letter.]

In a lengthy grammatical discourse, the *Iggeres Shmuel* quotes the *Radak* as deriving the word from the root עגה, and translating

it as *delay*. The *Iggeres Shmuel* then refutes this translation, and insists that it is derived from עגן, as in עֲגוּנָה, *agunah*, which the Sages always use when referring to a married woman living without her husband. Therefore, explains the *Iggeres Shmuel*, the ג, *gimmel*, is vocalized with a *tzerei* (גֵ), for were the word derived from the root עגה, the ג, *gimmel*, would be vocalized with a *segel* (גֶ).

The *Iggeres Shmuel* thus translates: *Would you remain as agunahs* — in memory of your dead husbands?

The *Talmud* translates the word as coming from the Hebrew עגן, *an anchor* — *would you remain anchored ... ? (Bava Basra* 73a).

לְבִלְתִּי הֱיוֹת לְאִישׁ — *Not marrying an [other] man?* [lit., *and not be to a man?*] Would you delay and remain tied down, waiting for these children to grow up — with the end result that לְבִלְתִּי הֱיוֹת לְאִישׁ, *you will never marry anyone because you will be too old to have husbands?* No, my daughters! ... *(Iggeres Shmuel).*

אַל בְּנֹתַי — *No, my daughters!* Do not come with me *(Ibn Ezra).*

The *Midrash* quotes Naomi as saying, אַלְלַי בְּנוֹתַי, *woe is to me, my daughters* ... [Had she meant

I
13

מַר־לִי מְאֹד מִכֶּם כִּי־יָצְאָה בִי יַד־

⟨ has the ⟨ against ⟨ gone ⟨ although ⟨⟨ on your ⟨ exceed- ⟨ to ⟨ bitter
hand   me   forth   account; ingly   me   it is

---

an absolute negation, an order that they not accompany her based on the irrefutable logic cited earlier, she would have said לֹא. The word אַל, on the other hand, indicates an entreaty (*Torah Temimah*).]

כִּי־מַר־לִי מְאֹד מִכֶּם — *For bitter it is to me exceedingly on your account.* [The translation follows the majority of the commentaries and the *Midrash*, which renders: *on your account.*]

Naomi blamed her bitterness and the tragedies of her sons' deaths on their marriage to gentile women, rather than to their leaving Eretz Yisrael because that had been done at the command of their father (*Binyan Ariel*).

Although she had attempted to discourage them by insisting that there were no more unborn sons in her womb, she made it clear that she would not have allowed her children to marry Ruth and Orpah in any case (*Simchas HaRegel*).

The *Chida*, in his above-mentioned *Simchas HaRegel*, offers an alternate interpretation of מִכֶּם: Naomi felt that her sons had been placed in an impossible situation by their marriages to the Moabite princesses. Machlon and Chilion could not divorce or desert them because of the political repercussions. They could not return to Eretz Yisrael with Moabite wives. Naomi reasoned that her sons had no alternative but to re-main in Moab *because of them.* As a result, God had punished her sons.

Other commentaries interpret מִכֶּם — *more than you, I am more embittered than you* [for I have suffered more tragedies than you] (*Rav Arama; Iggeres Shmuel; Malbim*).

The *Vilna Gaon* interprets the phrase: I am greatly distressed witnessing your plight, כִּי־יָצְאָה בִי יַד־ה', *although gone forth against me has the hand of* HASHEM, I am more concerned with *your* anguish.

According to the *Bach*, מִכֶּם is not "additive" but "causitive," *I am bittered because of you* — seeing your bereavement, and remembering that because of you my sons died makes me bitter.

כִּי־יָצְאָה בִי יַד־ה' — *Although gone forth against me has the hand of* HASHEM Against me, against my sons, and against my husband (*Midrash*).

Whatever God could possibly have done to me, He has already done (*Malbim*).

יָצְאָה — *Gone forth* [lit., *went out*] is used because God's wrath was so severe in this case that it *went out* beyond the bounds of its usual temperance (*Iggeres Shmuel*).

יַד־ה' — *Has the hand of* HASHEM, *affliction.* The reference to "hand" is anthropomorphic; speaking in human terms (*Ibn Ezra*).

The *Iggeres Shmuel* offers a

פֶּרֶק א **יד-טו** ‹‹ of HASHEM. › They 14 ‹ raised up › their voice ‹ and they wept ‹‹ again.

יד: וַתִּשֶּׂנָה קוֹלָן וַתִּבְכֶּינָה עוֹד יהוה:

‹ clung ‹ but Ruth ‹‹ her mother-in-law, ‹ Orpah kissed

וַתִּשַּׁק עָרְפָּה לַחֲמוֹתָהּ וְרוּת דָּבְקָה

novel interpretation: Naomi told her daughters-in-law not to think that she blamed them for her sons' deaths; אַל בְּנוֹתַי, no, my daughters, do not think *that my bitterness is because of you.* Definitely not! *The hand of God has gone forth against* me — in retribution for *my own sins.''*

14. The *Alshich* paraphrases verses 11-14:

Naomi, realizing that they wanted to convert and go to Eretz Yisrael, called them בְּנוֹתַי, *my daughters,* and said: ''If you desire to serve HASHEM, you can do that in Moab. If you wonder whom you could marry in Moab — all of them being idol worshipers — then realize that no Jew will marry you, because you are Moabites [and the law permitting marriage to female Moabites was not yet promulgated]. Don't rely on me for husbands; I am too old for marriage. Even if I were to marry, even tonight, who can say that I will give birth? If I do give birth, I might bear only daughters! And even if I were to have sons, would you wait for them?

''You might reply that you are content to accompany me to Eretz Yisrael with no thought of remarriage. No, my daughters: My state of bitterness is for you. I cannot bear to see you in such a troubled state, for the hand of God has gone forth against *me;* you

are sinless. It was for my sins that God has been punishing me, and you have been bearing my iniquity.''

When Orpah and Ruth heard this, they cried. Orpah kissed her mother-in-law; but in Ruth's *clinging* to her, Naomi realized a רוּחַ קְדוּשָׁה, *a spirit of holiness (Alshich).*

וַתִּשֶּׂנָה קוֹלָן וַתִּבְכֶּינָה עוֹד — *They raised up their voice and wept again.* There is an א, *aleph,* missing [from ותשנה] teaching that תָּשֵׁשׁ כֹּחָן, *their strength diminished,* as, weeping, they went on their way (*Midrash*).

The word וַתִּשֶּׂאנָה — with an א, *aleph,* as in verse 9 — means *they raised up.* Here, since וַתִּשֶּׂנָה omits the א, *aleph,* the *Midrash* homiletically links the word to תשש, *to be weak.* The verse indicates that they wept continuously throughout their conversation with Naomi until even their strength to cry was weakened (*Iggeres Shmuel*).

וַתִּשַּׁק עָרְפָּה לַחֲמוֹתָהּ — *Orpah kissed her mother-in-law.* [The kiss was their parting. No words. Only a kiss. Scripture divulges no more, but the pain was intense. As Naomi watched Orpah walk toward Moab, she knew that the last vestige of her son Chilion was lost to her forever.]

וְרוּת דָּבְקָה בָּהּ — *But Ruth clung to her.* Ruth, too, remained silent.

I

14-15

בָּה: טו וַתֹּאמֶר הִנֵּה שָׁבָה יְבִמְתֵּךְ אֶל־

⟨ to ⟨ your sister-in-law ⟨ Indeed, ⟨⟨ So she **15** ⟨⟨ to
has returned said, her.

עַמָּהּ וְאֶל־אֱלֹהֶיהָ שׁוּבִי אַחֲרֵי יְבִמְתֵּךְ:

⟨⟨ your sister- ⟨ following ⟨ go ⟨⟨ her god; ⟨ and to ⟨ her
in-law. back people

Her eyes showed her devotion to Naomi: her eyes and her refusal to go. But Naomi could not understand: Wasn't Orpah right? (*Ima Shel Malchus*).

"Ruth and Orpah were of royal lineage, descended from Eglon king of Moab (*Nazir* 23b); it was a heroic sacrifice to forsake their country to accompany the impoverished Naomi. There, on a country road in the fields of Moab, *was enacted one of the great scenes of history.* Three times did Naomi urge Ruth and Orpah to desist from their kindliness and turn back. They refused to yield, but on the third time, Orpah weakened and returned to her land and her people. Ruth persisted in her resolve to go with Naomi .... Generations later, David, the descendant of Ruth, faced Goliath, the descendant of Orpah, on the battlefield" (*Behold a People*).

15. הִנֵּה שָׁבָה יְבִמְתֵּךְ — *Indeed, your sister-in-law has returned.* [Orpah's departure is not stated, but it is inferred from her "farewell" kiss in the previous verse.]

The accent in Hebrew, notes *Rashi*, is under the שׁ of שָׁבָה, indicating that it is simple past tense, *she returned*, unlike the same word [in *Esther* 2:14] where there the ac-

cent is under the בּ and the tense is imperfect: וּבַבֹּקֶר הִיא שָׁבָה, *and in the morning she would return.*

אֶל־עַמָּהּ וְאֶל־אֱלֹהֶיהָ — *To her people and to her god. Rashba HaLevi* understands לְעַמֵּךְ, *to your people,* in verse 10 as indicating their desire to convert. In contrast, he notes, the expression *returned to her people and to her god* in this verse reveals that she renounced her previous intention to embrace Judaism.

[The *Ibn Ezra* and *Zohar Chadash,* in keeping with their interpretation that Ruth and Orpah had already converted when they got married (see *Comm.* to v. 4), deduce from this verse that Orpah now *returned* to her old faith. (See *Overview* for full exposition of this interpretation).]

שׁוּבִי אַחֲרֵי יְבִמְתֵּךְ — *Go back following your sister-in-law.* Naomi said: Your sister-in-law accompanied me because she was ashamed to leave. Now she finally succumbed and returned home. I grant you the same opportunity to depart gracefully and follow her (*Iggeres Shmuel*).

Naomi simply said, *Go back following your sister-in-law;* she carefully refrained from adding *to her god* (*Alshich*).

פרק א
טז-יז

טז וַתֹּאמֶר רוּת אַל־תִּפְגְּעִי־בִי לְעָזְבֵךְ
16 But Ruth said, ⟨⟨ Do not ⟩⟩ urge ⟨ me ⟨ to leave you, ⟩

לָשׁוּב מֵאַחֲרָיִךְ כִּי אֶל־אֲשֶׁר תֵּלְכִי
to turn ⟨ back ⟩ from going after you. ⟨⟨ For ⟩ to ⟨ wherever ⟨ you go ⟩

אֵלֵךְ וּבַאֲשֶׁר תָּלִינִי אָלִין עַמֵּךְ עַמִּי
I will go; ⟨⟨ where ⟨ you lodge ⟨ I will lodge; ⟨⟨ your people, ⟨ are my people, ⟩⟩

16. אַל־תִּפְגְּעִי־בִי — *Do not urge me.* Do not persist so diligently in trying to dissuade me from joining you. Don't offer me excuses לְעָזְבֵךְ, *to leave you,* לָשׁוּב מֵאַחֲרָיִךְ, *to turn back from going after you,* in your return to Judaism — for no matter what, I am determined to convert (*Iggeres Shmuel*).

Better that my conversion should be at your hands than at those of another (*Midrash*).

The *Midrash* [understanding תִּפְגְּעִי as a form of פגע, *misfortune*] translates: Do not turn your misfortune against me — do not seek to turn me away by reciting your misfortunes to me (*Yefei Anaf*); do not court misfortune through me, by repulsing me (*Anaf Yosef*); do not sin and incur punishment by dissuading me from converting (*Torah Temimah*).

כִּי אֶל־אֲשֶׁר תֵּלְכִי אֵלֵךְ — *For to wherever you go, I will go.* [From this, the Sages infer,] if one desired to become a proselyte, he be acquainted with the various punishments [for neglect of the commandments], so that if he wishes to withdraw, let him do so (*Yevamos* 47b). (Or, following the approach of the *Zohar Chadash/Ibn Ezra* — that Ruth and Orpah had already converted upon marrying Machlon and Chilion [see *Overview*] — Naomi was testing Ruth's resolve and commitment, now that her husband was dead, by acquainting her with the additional commandments.) From Ruth's responses we can deduce what Naomi must have told her ...

When Naomi heard Ruth's absolute resolve to convert, she began to reveal the laws to her, saying: "My daughter, Jewish girls do not go to gentile theaters and circuses" [which had a well-deserved reputation for lewdness]; to which she replied: *Wherever you go, I will go* (*Midrash*). ...

Do not ascribe to me a motive different from your own. It is my desire, also, to live in Eretz Yisrael so that I may fulfill the *mitzvos* that the Torah associates with that land (*Malbim*).

וּבַאֲשֶׁר תָּלִינִי אָלִין — *Where you lodge, I will lodge.* "We are forbidden יִחוּד, seclusion between man and woman!" — *Where you lodge,* Ruth responded, *I will lodge* (*Yevamos* 47b).

I
16-17

וֵאלֹהַיִךְ אֱלֹהָי: ¹⁷ בַּאֲשֶׁר תָּמוּתִי אָמוּת

⟨ I will die, ⟨ you die ⟨ where 17 ⟨⟨ is my God; ⟨ and your God

וְשָׁם אֶקָּבֵר כֹּה יַעֲשֶׂה יהוה לִי וְכֹה

⟨ and ⟨ to ⟨ may HASHEM do ⟨ Thus ⟨⟨ I will be ⟨ and
  thus   me,   buried.   there

יוֹסִיף כִּי הַמָּוֶת יַפְרִיד בֵּינִי וּבֵינֵךְ:

⟨⟨ and ⟨ between ⟨ will ⟨ [only] ⟨ for ⟨⟨ may He
between you. me   separate   death   do more

"My daughter, Jewish girls do not live in a house which has no *mezuzah*," — to which Ruth responded: *Where you lodge, I will lodge (Midrash)*. "I do not expect luxuries; *I am prepared to be a mere lodger* because there is only one object in my going" [as follows:] (*Malbim*).

עַמֵּךְ עַמִּי — *Your people are my people*. "I will never forsake the Torah of the Jews and the Oneness of God" (*Ibn Ezra*).

[Naomi said:] "We have been given 613 Commandments!" Ruth answered, *Your people shall be my people*" [I am now part of your people and I accept the *mitzvos*] (*Yevamos* 47b).

וֵאלֹהַיִךְ אֱלֹהָי — *And Your God is my God*. "We are forbidden idolatry!" Said Ruth, *Your God is my God* (*Yevamos* 47b).

This refers to the acceptance of all the *mitzvos*, for, by accepting the sovereignty of God, one accepts all of His commandments. ... Another interpretation: "*Your God is my God* ... Who will repay me the reward of my labor" (*Midrash*).

17. בַּאֲשֶׁר תָּמוּתִי אָמוּת — *Where you die, I will die.* [According to the *Talmud* and *Midrash*, Naomi enumerated the four forms of capital punishment to which Ruth responded; By *whatever mode you die, I will die*; I am prepared to face death for capital offenses; *and there I will be buried.*]

She expressed her innermost desire to die, the same מוֹת יְשָׁרִים, *death of the upright*, as would Naomi (*Malbim*).

"I want to die in Eretz Yisrael," Ruth declared (*Zos Nechemasi*).

וְשָׁם אֶקָּבֵר — *And there I will be buried.* For our Sages tell us that he who is buried in Eretz Yisrael is likened to one who is buried under the altar (*Zos Nechemasi*).

כֹּה יַעֲשֶׂה ה' לִי וְכֹה יוֹסִיף — *Thus may HASHEM do to me — and thus may He do more.* [Ruth emphasized her loyalty to the Jews by invoking God's Name, in this formula of an oath which is common in the Bible. Usually, however, the Name אֱלֹקִים, *God of Judgment*, is used in such a context.]

Ruth insisted that she would willingly follow Naomi in her beliefs,

פרק א
יח-כב

יח וַתֵּ֕רֶא כִּי־מִתְאַמֶּ֥צֶת הִ֖יא לָלֶ֣כֶת אִתָּ֑הּ
‹‹ with her, ‹ to go ‹ she was determined ‹ that ‹ When she saw 18

וַתֶּחְדַּ֖ל לְדַבֵּ֥ר אֵלֶֽיהָ: יט וַתֵּלַ֣כְנָה שְׁתֵּיהֶם֙
‹ the two of them ‹ They went, 19 ‹‹ with her. ‹ arguing ‹ she stopped

where she went, and where she slept. But death is out of one's hands. She prayed, therefore, that she would die near enough to Naomi to be buried alongside her (*Iggeres Shmuel*).

This was the crux of Ruth's plea: "My main reason for following you was I realized that as close as we are in life, if I remain in my heathen state we will be separated in death — you will return to HASHEM, and I will wallow amid idolaters" (*Malbim*).

18. מִתְאַמֶּצֶת הִיא לָלֶכֶת — *She was determined to go.* The verb אמץ suggests moral strength and determination (*Malbim*).

[Once Ruth's genuine convictions were demonstrated beyond any doubt, Naomi stopped dissuading her.]

According to *Zos Nechemasi*, this verse refers to Naomi: when Naomi perceived that God had not stricken her down like her husband and children, she realized that she was endowed with a special strength לָלֶכֶת אִתָּהּ, *to accompany her* [Ruth] and that she should be the instrument for bringing Ruth into the fold. Everything that God had wrought was in preparation for this event; Naomi then stopped arguing with Ruth.

וַתֶּחְדַּל לְדַבֵּר אֵלֶיהָ — *She stopped arguing with her* [lit., *she stopped "talking" to her*].

From this verse the Rabbis (*Yevamos* 47b) deduced that a convert is not to be persuaded or dissuaded too much (*Rashi*).

19. וַתֵּלַכְנָה שְׁתֵּיהֶם — *They went, the two of them.*

See how precious proselytes are to God! Once she decided to convert, Scripture ranked her equally with Naomi (*Midrash; Rashi*).

שְׁתֵּיהֶם, *the two of them*, is mentioned to stress the determination of Ruth, who, although she was leaving her home, birthplace, and kindred, marched on with the same strength of soul and purpose as Naomi. Also, *they went, the two of them;* just the two of them alone. They didn't even wait for a caravan (*Iggeres Shmuel*).

The *Alshich* deduces from the fact that שְׁתֵּיהֶם, *the two of them*, ends with the masculine ם instead of the feminine ן, that the two were afraid to travel the dangerous roads of Moab alone and they disguised themselves as men, עַד בּוֹאָנָה בֵּית לֶחֶם, *until they came to Bethlehem,* at which time they discarded their disguises.

I
18-20

עַד־בּוֹאָנָה בֵּית לֶחֶם וַיְהִי כְּבוֹאָנָה

‹ when they arrived ‹ And it came to pass, 《 to Bethlehem. ‹ they came ‹ until

בֵּית לֶחֶם וַתֵּהֹם כָּל־הָעִיר עֲלֵיהֶן

《 over them, ‹ city ‹ was the entire ‹ in a tumult ‹ in Bethlehem,

וַתֹּאמַרְנָה הֲזֹאת נָעֳמִי: כּ וַתֹּאמֶר אֲלֵיהֶן

《 to them, ‹ She said **20** 《 Naomi? ‹ Is this ‹ and the women said,

---

עַד־בּוֹאָנָה בֵּית לֶחֶם — *Until they came to Bethlehem.* [The journey to Bethlehem was a profound emotional experience for Naomi. She recalled the scenery and paths that had once been her own and which she and Elimelech had renounced ten years earlier.]

וַתֵּהֹם כָּל־הָעִיר עֲלֵיהֶן — *In a tumult was the entire city over them.* The fact that *the entire city* learned of their return so quickly, notes the *Iggeres Shmuel*, indicates that the townsfolk were gathered together. The *Midrash* offers several reasons for such an assembly:

That day was the reaping of the *Omer* [the measure of the barley which was offered on the second day of Passover], and all the inhabitants of the surrounding towns assembled to watch the ceremony; the wife of Boaz died on that day, and a multitude of Jews assembled to pay their respects. Just then Ruth entered with Naomi. Thus, one [the wife of Boaz] was taken and the other [Ruth] entered (*Midrash*).

Naomi had always gone about surrounded with servants, and now, when the townsfolk gathered to-

gether to see two women — alone, hungry, and barefoot — the pitiful sight threw all the citizens into a state of tumult and flurry (*Malbim*).

וַתֹּאמַרְנָה הֲזֹאת נָעֳמִי — *And [the women] said, "Is this Naomi?"* [The women is not explicit in the Hebrew but it is to be inferred because תֹּאמַרְנָה, *they said,* is in the feminine form.]

The afflicted Naomi had so changed in appearance from her past glory that her former neighbors could hardly recognize her (*Alshich*).

When they first appeared, the *entire city was in a tumult* at their very arrival, but upon closer scrutiny of Naomi's appearance, it was *the women* who addressed her (*Gishmei Berachah*).

"Is this the one whose actions were fitting and נְעִימִים, *pleasant?* In the past, she used to go in a covered carriage, and now she walks barefoot; in the past, she wore a cloak of fine wool, and now she is clothed in rags; in the past, her appearance was full from food and drink, now it is shrunken from hunger — *is this Naomi?"* (*Midrash*).

Did you see what befell her for leaving Eretz Yisrael? (*Rashi*).

אַל־תִּקְרֶאנָה לִי נָעֳמִי קְרֶאןָ לִי מָרָא

‹ Mara ‹ me ‹ call ‹‹ Naomi ‹ me ‹ call ‹ Do not
[Embittered   [Pleasant
One],   One];

כִּי־הֵמַר שַׁדַּי לִי מְאֹד: כא אֲנִי מְלֵאָה

‹ was full ‹ I   21 ‹‹ exceed- ‹ with ‹ has the ‹ dealt ‹ for
                      ingly.   me Almighty bitterly

הָלַכְתִּי וְרֵיקָם הֱשִׁיבַנִי יהוה לָמָּה

‹ Why ‹‹   has HASHEM   ‹ but empty ‹ when I
          brought me back.   went away,

תִּקְרֶאנָה לִי נָעֳמִי וַיהוה עָנָה בִי וְשַׁדַּי

‹ and ‹‹ against ‹ has ‹ when ‹‹ Naomi, ‹ me ‹ should you call
the   me, borne HASHEM
Almighty   witness

20. אַל־תִּקְרֶאנָה לִי נָעֳמִי קְרֶאןָ לִי מָרָא — *Do not call me Naomi [Pleasant One]; call me Mara [Embittered One].* Naomi said, "Don't think that I was righteous and my deed pleasant, and that God punished me unjustly. No! *Call me 'Embittered One' because my deeds were bitter, and God justly dealt bitterly with me"* (*Alshich*).

Also, by calling me "Naomi" you are reminding me of my former glory and thus making my pain even worse (*Pri Chaim*).

מָרָא — *Mara* ends with an *aleph*, א, instead of the usual *hei*, ה, to accentuate the extent of her bitterness. There are two other instances of words usually ending in a *hei* that are spelled with an *aleph*, in both cases to strengthen the connotation: *Numbers* 11:20, זָרָא for זָרֶה — *very loathsome;* and *Daniel* 11:44, חֵמָא for חֵמָה, great anger (*Rabbeinu Bachya*).

21. אֲנִי מְלֵאָה הָלַכְתִּי — *I was full when I went away.* "I went out full

with sons and daughters!" Another interpretation: "I was pregnant" (*Midrash*).

Full — with wealth and children (*Rashi; Ibn Ezra*).

וְרֵיקָם הֱשִׁיבַנִי ה׳ — *But empty has HASHEM brought me back* [widowed, childless, and poverty-stricken].

לָמָּה תִקְרֶאנָה לִי נָעֳמִי — *Why should you call me Naomi.* How can you call me a name describing good fortune — a name which, in retrospect, I was never really entitled to — seeing how afflicted I have become! (*Malbim*).

וַה׳ עָנָה בִי — *When HASHEM has borne witness against me* [lit., *and HASHEM answered in me*].

He testified against me that I sinned against Him (*Rashi*).

"You see from the gravity of my punishment how severely I sinned against God, for the punishment bears witness to the extent of my evil ways. To you, my sin was leaving Eretz Yisrael during a famine — an action

I
21-22

הֵרַע־לִי: כב וַתָּשָׁב נָעֳמִי וְרוּת הַמּוֹאֲבִיָּה

‹ the Moabite, ‹ with Ruth ‹ And so **22** ❮❮ upon ‹ has
Naomi returned, me! brought
misfortune

כַּלָּתָהּ עִמָּהּ הַשָּׁבָה מִשְּׂדֵי מוֹאָב וְהֵמָּה

‹ They ❮❮ of Moab. ‹ from ‹ who ‹ with ‹ her daughter-
the fields returned her, in-law,

בָּאוּ בֵּית לֶחֶם בִּתְחִלַּת קְצִיר שְׂעֹרִים:

❮❮ of barley. ‹ of the ‹ at the ‹ to Bethlehem ‹ came
harvest beginning

which might be justified. But HASHEM,
Who knows our innermost intentions,
knew that we left to avoid feeding the
poor and that we stayed overlong, in
Moab" (Rashba Ha-Levi).

וְשַׁדַּי הֵרַע־לִי — And the Almighty
has brought misfortune upon me!
[lit., And the Almighty did bad to
me.]

Here Naomi refers to God as שַׁדַּי,
(Shaddai) Almighty God, the Name
which indicates that, despite His infinite power, He is the God שֶׁאוֹמֵר
[דַּי] לְצָרוֹתַי דַּי, Who says, enough of
my suffering. Although He took my
husband and sons, He stopped short
of taking my life, limiting His punishment to having הֵרַע לִי, brought
misfortune upon me (Alshich).

22. הַשָּׁבָה מִשְּׂדֵי מוֹאָב — Who returned from the fields of Moab.

The subject of who returned is
not clear: According to Ibn Ezra it
refers to Naomi; Iggeres Shmuel
comments that it refers to Ruth
despite the fact that she could not
have returned, having never been
in Eretz Yisrael. Ruth entered Eretz
Yisrael with the same burning desire
as did Naomi, so Scripture describes

it as she returned — as if she had
lived there before and it had been
her birthplace.

"People pointed to her [Ruth]
saying: This is the first one who
returned from the fields of Moab"
(Yerushalmi, Yevamos 8:3), i.e., she
is the first Moabite woman who שָׁבָה,
repented, and converted to Judaism.
With her, the law of "Moabite not
Moabitess" [see Overview] was pro-
mulgated (Torah Temimah).

Quite possibly no other Moabite
woman had ever converted before,
because it would have been her
impression that she would not be
permitted to marry a Jew; Ruth's
sincerity was so great, however, that
she converted without caring if she
could ever remarry (Iggeres Shmuel).

[The Midrash seems to imply that
the subject is Naomi: This is the
one who returned from the fields
of Moab! (People pointed a finger
at Naomi, identifying her as the one
who returned from Moab (Iggeres
Shmuel).]

בִּתְחִלַּת קְצִיר שְׂעֹרִים — At the beginning of the harvest of barley. The
verse refers to the Omer harvest [on

פרק ב   ב   א וּלְנָעֳמִי מוֹדָע [מידע כ'] לְאִישָׁהּ אִישׁ
א-ב   1 [2] 〉 Naomi had 〉 a relative 〈 through her 〉 a man
                                              husband,

גִּבּוֹר חַיִל מִמִּשְׁפַּחַת אֱלִימֶלֶךְ וּשְׁמוֹ
of 〉 capability, 〉〉 from the family 〈 of Elimelech, 〉〉 whose 〉
great   name

Passover] (*Midrash; Rashi*).

This chronological detail serves as an introduction to the next chapter. It tells us that it was already the harvest season and too late to plant new crops in the fields belonging to the family of Elimelech. Hence they were poverty-stricken (*Malbim*).

II.

1. וּלְנָעֳמִי מוֹדָע — *Naomi had a relative* [*moda*]. The word *moda* means *kinsman, relative* (*Midrash*) — a familiar relative (*Ibn Ezra*).

He was the son of Elimelech's brother (*Rashi*).

Although Boaz was a close relative, Naomi avoided him even in her dire need. She did not ask him for support because she still felt shame at having deserted her people during the famine, while Boaz stayed on and supported them. In addition, she was aware that Boaz was angry that she had brought a Moabite girl back with her. He avoided them both until God brought Ruth to his fields [verse 3] and he realized how virtuous she was (*Alshich*).

Scripture tells us of the strength of these two women. Even though she had a rich relative, Naomi did not thrust herself upon him; and Ruth, the daughter of the king of Moab, was not too proud to shoulder the burden of support for herself and her mother-in-law (*Alkabetz*).

On the other hand, it should be mentioned that according to the Sages, Boaz's wife died on the day that Naomi and Ruth returned to Bethlehem (see *Comm.* 1:19 s.v. וַתֵּהֹם). Boaz, involved with the funeral and mourning, could not give them a proper welcome. When Ruth chanced upon his field, on the day he returned from mourning, he recognized her rare qualities. Seeing her glean, he assumed that she would not avail herself of charity, preferring to maintain herself with her own hands. Also, as a widower, he did not want to be suspected of ulterior motives regarding Ruth, so he refrained from overt acts of kindness toward her. As a result of his restraint in regard to Ruth, Naomi also did not benefit from his beneficence (*Rav Arama; Iggeres Shmuel*).

אִישׁ גִּבּוֹר חַיִל — *A man of great capability* [often translated *a mighty man of valor*. *Rashi* translates (*Exodus* 18:21): "Men of means, who need not flatter or show partiality."]

A man endowed with the highest

II
1-2

בְּעַז: וַתֹּאמֶר רוּת הַמּוֹאֲבִיָּה אֶל־נָעֳמִי

《 Naomi, 〈 to 〈 the Moabite 〈 Ruth 〈 Said 2 《 was Boaz.

אֵלְכָה־נָּא הַשָּׂדֶה וַאֲלַקֳטָה בַשִּׁבֳּלִים

《 among the [left- 〈 and I 《 to the field, 〈 if you 〈 Let me over] ears of grain, will glean please, go out,

אַחַר אֲשֶׁר אֶמְצָא־חֵן בְּעֵינָיו וַתֹּאמֶר

〈 And she 《 in his 〈 favor 〈 I shall find 〈 someone 〈 behind said eyes. whom

human qualities, including magnanimity and dislike of ill-gotten gains (*Malbim*).

וּשְׁמוֹ בֹּעַז — *Whose name was Boaz.* In the case of wicked men, their names are given before the word שֵׁם, *name*, as it says: גָּלְיַת שְׁמוֹ, *Goliath was his name;* נָבָל שְׁמוֹ, *Nabal was his name;* שֶׁבַע בֶּן בִּכְרִי שְׁמוֹ, *Sheva son of Bichri was his name.* But the names of the righteous are preceded by the word שֵׁם, *name*, as it says: וּשְׁמוֹ קִישׁ, *his name was Kish;* וּשְׁמוֹ שָׁאוּל, *his name was Saul;* וּשְׁמוֹ יִשָׁי, *his name was Jesse;* וּשְׁמוֹ מָרְדְּכַי, *his name was Mordechai;* וּשְׁמוֹ אֶלְקָנָה, *his name was Elkanah;* וּשְׁמוֹ בֹּעַז, *his name was Boaz.* They thus resemble their Creator of Whom it is written [*Exodus* 6:3]: וּשְׁמִי ה׳, *But [with] My Name HASHEM [I did not make Myself known to them]* (*Midrash*).

Our Sages said (*Bava Basra* 91a) that Boaz was the judge Ivtzan [see *Comm.* to 1:1] (*Ibn Ezra*).

2. וַתֹּאמֶר רוּת הַמּוֹאֲבִיָּה — *Said Ruth the Moabite.* Scripture praises the righteousness of Ruth, who, according to the Sages, was the daughter of Eglon, king of Moab. The verse

stresses the noble character of this princess who offered to glean like a common pauper to spare her mother-in-law the indignity of *her* going out and being subject to the humiliating gaze of those who knew her in her former affluence (*Malbim*).

אֵלְכָה־נָּא הַשָּׂדֶה — *Let me go out, if you please, to the field,* to the safety of the field; not to vineyards or orchards where poor people must be concerned with the danger of climbing trees in order to glean forgotten fruits (*Malbim*).

וַאֲלַקֳטָה בַשִּׁבֳּלִים — *And I will glean among the [leftover] ears of grain.* She limited herself to לֶקֶט, *gleaning* [the ears of grain that *fell* from the hands of harvesters, to which the poor were entitled — *Lev.* 19:9; 13:22; *Deut.* 29:19], because fields for *gleaning* were plentiful and she would not have to compete fiercely with the other poor, unlike the competition for פֵּאָה, *Pe'ah* [see ibid.], which was much more severe (*Malbim*).

אַחַר אֲשֶׁר אֶמְצָא־חֵן בְּעֵינָיו — *Behind someone whom I shall find favor in his eyes,* where the owner will

פֶּרֶק ב ג-ד

לָהּ לְכִי בִתִּי: ‹‹ וַתֵּלֶךְ וַתָּבוֹא וַתְּלַקֵּט

‹ to her, ‹‹ Go, ‹ my daughter. ‹‹3 So she went; ‹‹ and she came ‹ and she gleaned

בַּשָּׂדֶה אַחֲרֵי הַקֹּצְרִים וַיִּקֶר מִקְרֶהָ

‹ in the field ‹ behind ‹‹ the harvesters, ‹‹ and it happened that she came

permit me to glean and not scold me (Rashi).

אַחַר, "After I find favor in his eyes" (Targum); "I will not glean in a field until I am sure the owner allows it and that I won't be embarrassed by the other gleaners" (Malbim).

She stressed that she will glean אַחַר, after, in back of, as a gesture of modesty (Simchas HaRegel).

לְכִי בִתִּי — Go, my daughter. It is not that I hold you in low esteem that I permit you to so degrade yourself by gleaning like a common pauper. I permit you only because of the circumstances and our dire needs which demand it (Iggeres Shmuel).

Even had you been בִּתִּי, my own daughter, I would have let you go (Alshich).

[Naomi obviously consented very reluctantly, remembering only too painfully her former wealth and the circumstances which brought her to such depths, and which now forced her daughter-in-law to descend to pauperdom by gleaning to provide for their basic sustenance.]

The term בִּתִּי, my daughter, in this particular instance is not necessarily an indication of Ruth's youth.

According to Rabbinic tradition, she was then forty years of age (Midrash).

3. וַתֵּלֶךְ וַתָּבוֹא — So she went; and she came. She repeatedly went and came until she found decent people to accompany (Shabbos 113b).

The Midrash interprets this to mean that she went back and forth to "mark off," to familiarize herself, with the country lanes, so as not to lose her way on her return (Rashi).

According to Malbim, the proximity of these verbs suggest that as soon as she left she arrived, indicating that the field of Boaz to which she went was very near her home.

Rav Alkabetz sees in these words what must have been a brief account of her daily schedule: she would go and return daily until the harvest was over.

Rav Arama interprets it simply: she went — she left her home, and she came — she arrived at the field.

וַתְּלַקֵּט בַּשָּׂדֶה אַחֲרֵי הַקֹּצְרִים — And she gleaned in the field behind the harvesters. Although it was morning, the time when other poor people were involved in the more productive gathering of פֵּאָה, Pe'ah

II
3-4

חֶלְקַת הַשָּׂדֶה לְבֹעַז אֲשֶׁר מִמִּשְׁפַּחַת

⟨ from the family ⟨ who ⟨⟨ [belonging] ⟨ of the field ⟨ to the part
was   to Boaz,

אֱלִימֶלֶךְ: ₄ וְהִנֵּה־בֹעַז בָּא מִבֵּית לֶחֶם

⟨⟨ from Bethlehem. ⟨ came ⟨ Boaz ⟨ And then, 4 ⟨⟨ of Elimelech.

[see *Leviticus* 19:9-10; *Deut.* 24:19], Ruth limited herself to לֶקֶט [*leket*], *gleaning*, and she was directly *behind the harvesters*, because there was no one else *gleaning* at the time (*Malbim*).

She limited her gleaning to the grain the harvesters left *behind* them — that which they definitely and undoubtedly discarded; also, she stayed in back of them out of modesty, so no one would glance at her (*Rav Gakkun*).

וַיִּקֶר מִקְרֶהָ — *And it happened that she came.* [Alternate translation, *Her fate made her happen upon*, is in consonance with the profound philosophy of *Rav S.R. Hirsch* as expressed in his *Commentary* on *Genesis* 24:12:] "Nothing is farther from the Jewish concept of מִקְרֶה [*happening*] than the idea of "chance" with which it is associated. Rather, it refers to those moments of one's life that he himself did not direct but which directed him; they were only events which were not expected, not reckoned on, not intended, but which, all the more, could be the most intentional messages sent by the One Who directs and brings about all things."

The *Malbim* notes that the fact that she was gleaning in the field of Boaz would seem to be nothing more

than coincidence. The verse stresses, however, that it was מִקְרֶה, "*her*" *fate*, the apparent coincidence was Divinely arranged with *her* benefit in mind. By "chancing" upon the field of Boaz, she was implementing the Heavenly plan to build the royal house of Israel.

אֲשֶׁר מִמִּשְׁפַּחַת אֱלִימֶלֶךְ — *Who was from the family of Elimelech,* who — prophetically — would prove ready to exercise his right as גּוֹאֵל, *redeemer,* and would יַבְּמָהּ, *marry her,* and ultimately father the Davidic dynasty (*Malbim*).

4. וְהִנֵּה־בֹעַז בָּא — *And then, Boaz came.* He had returned to his field after the completion of the mourning period for his wife (*Iggeres Shmuel*).

The word וְהִנֵּה, *and then,* suggests something unusual. Boaz's coming to the field was unusual, and it was the guiding hand of Divine Providence that led him there on that particular day in order to meet Ruth. Also, Boaz is credited by the Sages with originating the custom of greeting one's neighbor in the Name of *Hashem* so as to instill into the hearts of that lawless generation [see *Comm.* 1:1] the all-pervading presence of God as the Source of mankind's welfare. The custom was introduced that day with the sanction of the Sages in

פרק ב

ה-ו

וַיֹּאמֶר לַקּוֹצְרִים יהוה עִמָּכֶם וַיֹּאמְרוּ

⟨ And they ⟩ ⟨⟨ be with ⟩ ⟨ HASHEM ⟨⟨ to the ⟨ He said
answered   you!   harvesters,

לוֹ יְבָרֶכְךָ יהוה: ה וַיֹּאמֶר בֹּעַז לְנַעֲרוֹ

⟨ to his ⟩ ⟨ Boaz then said 5 ⟨⟨ May HASHEM ⟨⟨ him,
worker   bless you!

הַנִּצָּב עַל-הַקּוֹצְרִים לְמִי הַנַּעֲרָה הַזֹּאת:

⟨⟨ that girl? ⟩ ⟨ To whom ⟨⟨ the ⟨ over ⟨ who was
belongs   harvesters,   supervising

Bethlehem (*Malbim*), and with the intimated approval of the Heavenly *Beis Din* (*Midrash*).

יְבָרֶכְךָ ה' — *May HASHEM bless you!* May He bless you with an abundant harvest! (*Ibn Ezra*).

Boaz had just been widowed and the Sages consider הַשָּׁרוּי בְּלֹא אִשָּׁה, *one who dwells without a wife,* as שָׁרוּי בְּלֹא בְּרָכָה, *one who dwells without "blessing."* They greeted him, therefore, יְבָרֶכְךָ ה', "May HASHEM 'bless' you with a worthy wife" (*Iggeres Shmuel*).

Rav Alkabetz observes that the workers did not *initiate* the greeting because one does not greet a mourner; he greeted first and they responded.

5. לְמִי הַנַּעֲרָה הַזֹּאת — *To whom belongs that girl?* Asking, is she fit to enter the Assembly of HASHEM?

The *Talmud* asks: Was it then Boaz's practice to inquire about young girls? [Surely he didn't inquire about *every* girl gleaning in the fields!] Rav Elazar answered: Her [halachic] knowledge and exemplary conduct caught his attention. She would glean two ears [of grain that fell from the harvesters' hands] but she would not glean three [in accordance with the law in *Mishnah Pe'ah* 6:5] (*Shabbos* 113b).

When he noticed her modesty, he inquired about her. She would stand while gleaning the standing ears and sit while gleaning the fallen ears; the other women hitched up their skirts, and she kept hers down; the other women jested with the harvesters, while she remained reserved; the other women gathered from *between* the sheaves, while she gathered only from that which was definitely abandoned (*Midrash*).

According to the *Malbim* who commented [verse 3] that Ruth was the only woman gleaning in the field at the time, her presence was obvious and Boaz readily noticed her. He assumed that she was related to one of the harvesters who had cleared the field of the other paupers so she could glean alone. This aroused his curiosity and he inquired about her identity.

Some commentators feel that Boaz was interested in finding out

II
5-6

וַיַּעַן הַנַּעַר הַנִּצָּב עַל־הַקּוֹצְרִים וַיֹּאמַר

《 and said, 《 the harvesters, 〈 over 〈 who was 〈 the 〈 Replied 6
supervising worker

נַעֲרָה מוֹאֲבִיָּה הִיא הַשָּׁבָה עִם־

〈 with 〈 who returned 《 is she, 〈 A Moabite girl

if she was married or single, but he was ashamed to pose the question explicitly lest he be suspected of harboring unseemly thoughts about her. Instead he asked seemingly innocent questions about the identity of a stranger who was obviously new to Bethlehem, confident that the reply would supply the information he sought (*Iggeres Shmuel*).

The *Dubno Maggid* points out that just as Ruth's *coincidental choice* of Boaz's field [verse 3] and Boaz's unusual visit to his field on that particular day were acts of Divine Providence, so, too, was his notice of her and his inquiry about her upon his arrival — *immediately after he greeted his men and before even asking about the progress of the harvest* — also an act of Divine Providence.

6. וַיַּעַן הַנַּעַר הַנִּצָּב עַל־הַקּוֹצְרִים — *Replied the worker who was supervising over the harvesters.* His position as supervisor and trusted employee is repeated to emphasize that he responded to Boaz's inquiry in a most familiar and intimate manner [see *Midrash* further] (*Nachal Eshkol*).

נַעֲרָה מוֹאֲבִיָּה הִיא — *A Moabite girl is she* — "and yet you say her conduct is praiseworthy and modest? Her mother-in-law instructed

her well" (*Midrash*). "Her good manners are not her own," the supervisor responded. "Her seemingly modest behavior was drilled into her by her mother-in-law" (*Torah Temimah*).

The supervisor tried, by many means, to dissuade Boaz from showing interest in the girl. He replied that she is a נַעֲרָה, *a girl*, and was too young for Boaz [who was eighty years old at the time! Despite the fact that, according to the *Midrash*, she was forty years old, her beauty was that of a young girl]. Additionally, she was מוֹאֲבִיָּה, *a Moabite*, and as such not permitted in marriage (for the law of "Moabite not Moabitess" was not yet widely known [see *Overview*]). The supervisor also suggested that she was still *a Moabite* at heart: her conversion had not been sincerely motivated out of love of God or desire to "find shelter under His wings," but rather out of love for Naomi (*Iggeres Shmuel*).

"Also," the supervisor added, "her luck is bad — she buried her husband and is destitute" (*Zos Nechemasi*).

The supervisor said: "Furthermore (even if her marriage to a Jew were permitted), are there no *Jewish* girls for someone as important as Boaz to marry? — Girls *not* brought up amid the miserliness of the Moabites?" (*Rashba HaLevi*).

פרק ב
ז-ח

נָעֳמִי מִשְּׂדֵי מוֹאָב: וַתֹּאמֶר אֲלַקֳטָה־

⟨ 'I will glean, ⟨⟨ She said, 7 ⟨⟨ of Moab. ⟨ from ⟨ Naomi
the fields

נָּא וְאָסַפְתִּי בָעֳמָרִים אַחֲרֵי הַקּוֹצְרִים

⟨⟨ the ⟨ behind ⟨ among ⟨ and gather ⟨ if you
harvesters.' the sheaves please,

וַתָּבוֹא וַתַּעֲמוֹד מֵאָז הַבֹּקֶר וְעַד־עַתָּה

⟨⟨ now; ⟨ until ⟨ the ⟨ since ⟨ and has ⟨ So she
morning been standing came,

Alshich notes that the supervisor probably did not dare verbalize these gibes at Ruth to his master; the propriety of the master-servant relationship would not have allowed it. Rather, from the wording and tone of the supervisor's response Boaz inferred his displeasure.

הַשָּׁבָה עִם־נָעֳמִי מִשְּׂדֵי מוֹאָב — Who returned with Naomi from the fields of Moab. According to the Malbim's interpretation of the episode, the supervisor responded: "Don't wonder why I allow a foreign Moabite woman to glean in your field. She is the one who returned with Naomi; she converted, and as a Jew is entitled to glean."

The Iggeres Shmuel stresses the positive in the overseer's response: She is a Moabite girl — she is young and capable of childbearing; a Moabitess — female, and thus not under the ban of "Moabite"; who returned with Naomi — the sincerity of her conversion is beyond reproach, for she returned with an impoverished Naomi, leaving her country and royal ancestry behind.

7. וַתֹּאמֶר — She said. [This is a continuation of the supervisor's response to Boaz.]

אֲלַקֳטָה־נָּא — I will glean, if you please, the leket [gleaning] of the sheaves (Rashi).

Note how even though gleaning was a legal right granted by the Torah to the impoverished, for which no permission is required, Ruth nevertheless displayed good manners and modesty by first asking permission (Iggeres Shmuel).

וְאָסַפְתִּי בָעֳמָרִים אַחֲרֵי הַקּוֹצְרִים — And [I will] gather among the sheaves ["forgotten" stalks] behind the harvesters, the שִׁכְחָה, a stalk overlooked or "forgotten" by the harvesters (Rashi).

A different interpretation:
I don't want charity; I'll even pay you for the privilege of gleaning by helping the harvesters gather the sheaves (Iggeres Shmuel).

וַתָּבוֹא וַתַּעֲמוֹד — So she came and has been standing. Diligently involved with her needs (Ibn Ezra).

She has been working all along until this very moment, just prior to your arrival (Malbim).

II
7-8

זֶה שִׁבְתָּהּ הַבַּיִת מְעָט: חוַיֹּאמֶר בֹּעַז

⟨ Then Boaz said   **8** ⟪ a short   ⟨ in the   ⟨ when ⟨ [except]
while.   hut   she sat that [time]

אֶל־רוּת הֲלוֹא שָׁמַעַתְּ בִּתִּי אַל־תֵּלְכִי

⟨ go   ⟨ Do ⟪ my   ⟨   Hear me well,   ⟪ Ruth, ⟨ to
not daughter.

זֶה שִׁבְתָּהּ הַבַּיִת מְעָט — *[Except] that [time] when she sat in the hut a short while.* [The translation of the very obscure Hebrew follows *Ibn Ezra* and *Malbim*.]

According to the *Midrash:* "She gathered a quantity — barely enough for two — for her who was in the house [Naomi] since she was waiting for it." [The language of the *Midrash*, too, is obscure. The above rendering follows *Mattanos Kehunah*.] The *Torah Temimah* comments that according to the *Midrash*, the supervisor misunderstood the question, and feared that Boaz was angry with him for allowing this stranger to enter the field. He defended himself by saying that she gleaned only a small amount and gave it to Naomi who had remained home, and for whom there was no other form of sustenance.

8. וַיֹּאמֶר בֹּעַז — *Then Boaz said.* [Having heard that the girl is Naomi's daughter-in-law, he displayed special interest in her, but apparently did not reveal that he was a relative.]

הֲלוֹא שָׁמַעַתְּ בִּתִּי — *Hear me well, my daughter* [lit., *have you not heard, my daughter?*].

Boaz said: "You heard me discussing you with my supervisor. Don't think I inquired about you because

of any displeasure at your being here. To the contrary! I insist that you stay on and glean in my fields exclusively …" (*Iggeres Shmuel*).

According to *Pri Chaim* (who holds that the supervisor spoke positively about Ruth): "You have surely heard, my daughter, what the supervisor said about you and how, impressed with your modest ways, he allowed you to glean here."

בִּתִּי — *My daughter.* [A natural way for an elderly man to address a woman much younger than he. It also suggests that he would now treat her in a paternal fashion. (See *Comm.* end of verse 2, s.v. בִּתִּי.)]

A question arises:

Is this the same righteous Boaz lauded by the Sages? Ruth and Naomi were his closest kin; he should have offered them his home and supported them in dignity and comfort rather than just allowing Ruth the "privilege" of exercising a pauper's legal right to glean the harvest!

As soon as Boaz met Ruth he was told of her modest behavior and he was greatly impressed. But she was a foreigner and he wanted to assure himself, firsthand, of her integrity, so he put her to the test. Had her conversion been insincere and had it been motivated by the knowledge that her relative, Boaz, would treat

פֶּרֶק ב לִלְקֹט בְּשָׂדֶה אַחֵר וְגַם לֹא תַעֲבוּרִי

ט-י

⟨ go away ⟩ ⟨ do not ⟩ and
also ⟨⟨ of anyone
else, ⟨ in the field ⟩ ⟨ to glean

מִזֶּה וְכֹה תִדְבָּקִין עִם־נַעֲרֹתָי: ט עֵינַיִךְ

⟨ Your eyes 9 ⟩⟨ my female
workers. ⟨ to ⟩ ⟨ stay close ⟩ ⟨ but
here ⟨⟨ from
here,

בַּשָּׂדֶה אֲשֶׁר־יִקְצֹרוּן וְהָלַכְתְּ אַחֲרֵיהֶן

⟨⟨ after them. ⟨ and go ⟩⟨ they are
harvesting, ⟨ which ⟨ on the field

her royally, her reaction to his offer would have revealed her as a fraud. Instead she reacted superbly, like the righteous person she truly was [see also *Comm.* on 2:1] (*Rav Arama*).

אַל־תֵּלְכִי לִלְקֹט בְּשָׂדֶה אַחֵר — *Do not go to glean in the field of anyone else.* You may not be welcome by the owner (*Malbim*).

Boaz said: "A poor person leaves one field for another for two reasons: the crop is exhausted, or the inhospitality of the owner forces him to leave. Neither reason applies here, therefore: Do *not go to glean in another field ...*" (*Pri Chaim*).

The *Midrash*, interpreting the verse on a more lofty plane, explains *field* allegorically: "Do not go to glean in another 'spiritual' field — *You shall have no other gods before Me*" [*Exodus* 20:3].

וְגַם לֹא־תַעֲבוּרִי מִזֶּה — *And also, do not go away from here.* Even to another one of my own fields (*Malbim*).

Reside here and don't return home until the harvest is over (*Rav Arama*).

וְכֹה תִדְבָּקִין עִם־נַעֲרֹתָי — *But here stay close to my female workers.* Stay on the side of my field where the girls

are working; not on the other side with the men (*Malbim*).

9. עֵינַיִךְ בַשָּׂדֶה — *Your eyes [should be] on the field.* Keep your eyes on the field that the girls are harvesting (*Malbim*).

Boaz recognized Ruth as a צִדְקָנִית, *a righteous woman,* whose עַיִן טוֹב, *generous eye* [antonym of עַיִן הָרָע, *evil eye*], will cause blessing to descend upon the object of her generosity, as Scripture says: טוֹב עַיִן הוּא יְבֹרָךְ, *He who has a generous eye shall bring blessing* [lit., *shall be blessed*] (*Proverbs* 22:9). Knowing that Ruth would be a source of blessing to whatever field provided her sustenance, Boaz asked her to *keep her eyes on the field during the harvest* so that a blessing would descend on the crop (*Iggeres Shmuel*).

Your eyes [should be] on the field — and as soon as it is harvested be the first to glean: Boaz was planning to tell his men to deliberately discard sheaves for Ruth to glean [verse 16], and he wanted to make sure that she would benefit from his largesse by being on the scene first (*Kol Yaakov*).

וְהָלַכְתְּ אַחֲרֵיהֶן — *And go after them.* [אַחֲרֵיהֶן is feminine], thus meaning

II
9-10

הֲלוֹא צִוִּיתִי אֶת־הַנְּעָרִים לְבִלְתִּי נָגְעֵךְ
》 to touch 〈   not   〈 the male workers 〈 I have 〈 Indeed,
you.   ordered

וְצָמִת וְהָלַכְתְּ אֶל־הַכֵּלִים וְשָׁתִית
〈 and drink   〈   the jugs   〈 to 〈   you   〈 Should you
                                    should go   get thirsty,

מֵאֲשֶׁר יִשְׁאֲבוּן הַנְּעָרִים: וַתִּפֹּל עַל־
〈 on 〈 She fell 10 》   the workers draw.   〈 from what

פָּנֶיהָ וַתִּשְׁתַּחוּ אָרְצָה וַתֹּאמֶר אֵלָיו
》to him, 〈 and she said》to the ground, 〈 bowing down 〈 her face,

follow the female workers. [They
will harvest, and you will glean after
them] (*Malbim*).

לְבִלְתִּי נָגְעֵךְ — *Not to touch you.*
Even if you are all alone in the field
(*Rashba HaLevi*).

[נָגְעֵךְ, *touch you,* can also be understood in the more simple sense:
not to interfere with you.]

They have been so commanded
by the Torah: וְאָהַבְתָּ אֶת הַגֵּר, *love
the stranger* [*Deut.* 10:19] (*Midrash
Lekach Tov*).

The *Midrash,* which has been allegorically explaining this verse as
an admonition by Boaz for Ruth to
be faithful to her new religion [see
Comm. end of verse 8], translates
לְבִלְתִּי נָגְעֵךְ, *they will not discourage
you.*

וְהָלַכְתְּ אֶל־הַכֵּלִים — *You should go
to the jugs.* If you get thirsty, don't
hesitate to drink from the jugs of
water fetched by the young men
(*Rashi*).

Go yourself, and don't have the
young men bring it to you. The less

you associate with them, the better
(*Rav Yavetz*).

מֵאֲשֶׁר יִשְׁאֲבוּן הַנְּעָרִים — *From what
the workers draw.* And don't worry
that the men might be angry; I already warned them לְבִלְתִּי נָגְעֵךְ, *not
to bother you* (*Iggeres Shmuel*).

The well with the good drinking
water was far from the fields and
laborious to fetch from. Therefore,
the men who brought the water
would keep it for themselves. The
poor would have to drink inferior
water drawn from closer wells. Boaz
told Ruth that if she became thirsty
she should not hesitate to drink from
the men's jugs, as they had been
instructed by him personally not to
interfere with her (*Malbim*).

10. וַתִּפֹּל עַל־פָּנֶיהָ וַתִּשְׁתַּחוּ אָרְצָה —
*She fell on her face, bowing down
to the ground.* In humble gratitude
for his graciousness and cordiality
toward her (*Alshich*).

At the same time she bowed down
and praised God for His beneficence
(*Meishiv Nefesh*).

פרק ב
יא-יב

מַדּוּעַ מָצָאתִי חֵן בְּעֵינֶיךָ לְהַכִּירֵנִי
‹‹ that you should ‹ in your ‹ favor ‹ have I found ‹ Why
take note of me, eyes,

וְאָנֹכִי נָכְרִיָּה: יא וַיַּעַן בֹּעַז וַיֹּאמֶר לָה
‹‹ to and said ‹ Boaz replied **11** ‹‹ am a ‹ though I
her, foreigner?

הֻגֵּד הֻגַּד לִי כֹּל אֲשֶׁר־עָשִׂית אֶת־
‹ for ‹ you have ‹ that ‹ all ‹ to me ‹ It was fully
done reported

חֲמוֹתֵךְ אַחֲרֵי מוֹת אִישֵׁךְ וַתַּעַזְבִי אָבִיךְ
‹ your ‹ that you ‹‹ of your ‹ the ‹ after ‹ your mother-
father left husband; death in-law

מַדּוּעַ ... וְאָנֹכִי נָכְרִיָּה — *Why ... though I am a foreigner?* What did you see in me that made you take special notice and inquire about me though I am a נָכְרִיָּה, *an ordinary stranger?* Many other women who glean here also are strangers, but no one pays any special attention to them (*Iggeres Shmuel*).

According to *Pri Chaim*, Ruth was not aware that Boaz was a relative. Her question was prompted by the fact that she thought it unusual for a stranger to be showered with such attention.

The *Targum* translates: "How is it that I have found favor in your eyes? I am of a foreign nation, a daughter of Moab, a nation not fit to enter into קְהַל ה', the Assembly of HASHEM."

11. [Boaz responds that he has heard of her extraordinary and magnanimous deeds in the exemplary way she treated her mother-in-law, and her leaving home and family to embrace Judaism.]

הֻגֵּד הֻגַּד לִי — *It was fully reported to me.* The verb הגד is doubled for emphasis. Your deeds are so widely discussed that *I have been hearing about them in the house and in the fields*, from all sides (*Midrash*).

Ruth considered herself unworthy of Boaz's attention and she sincerely wanted him to explain the reason for his unexpected kindness; therefore, she posed the question to him. He responded that she — for her goodness — deserves much more kindness than he is capable of performing for her, and that whatever he did for her was minuscule compared to the rewards which would be bestowed upon her from God [see next verse] (*Alshich; Rashba HaLevi*).

כֹּל אֲשֶׁר־עָשִׂית אֶת־חֲמוֹתֵךְ — *All that you have done for your mother-in-law.* Boaz told Ruth that his favorable attitude to her was a result of two things: First, despite the fact that a woman usually has ill feelings toward her mother-in-law, Ruth treated Naomi in an exemplary

II
11-12

וְאִמֵּךְ וְאֶרֶץ מוֹלַדְתֵּךְ וַתֵּלְכִי אֶל־

⟨ to ⟨ and went ⟪ of your birth ⟨ and the ⟨ and your
land mother

עַם אֲשֶׁר לֹא־יָדַעַתְּ תְּמוֹל שִׁלְשֹׁם:

⟪ or the day ⟨ yesterday ⟨ you had not ⟨ whom ⟨ a
before that. known people

יב יְשַׁלֵּם יהוה פָּעֳלֵךְ וּתְהִי מַשְׂכֻּרְתֵּךְ

⟨ and may your ⟪ your ⟨ May HASHEM repay 12
reward be actions,

manner — especially after Naomi became widowed and forlorn — thus demonstrating a rare nobility of character; and secondly, for having left her parents and homeland to convert, etc. (*Malbim*).

אַחֲרֵי מוֹת אִישֵׁךְ — *After the death of your husband*, and certainly during his lifetime (*Midrash*).

וַתַּעַזְבִי אָבִיךְ וְאִמֵּךְ וְאֶרֶץ מוֹלַדְתֵּךְ — *That you left your father and your mother and the land of your birth.* Your conversion is remarkable because, in the face of coercion to remain in Moab, you freely left your parents' home and the country of your birth and, with no material considerations, you came to a strange country (*Alshich*).

אֲשֶׁר לֹא־יָדַעַתְּ תְּמוֹל שִׁלְשֹׁם — *Whom you had not known yesterday or the day before that.* Boaz said, "The law permitting female Moabite converts to marry Jews was popularized only in the last few days, and you could not possibly have been aware of it when you converted. Therefore, you could only have been motivated by the purest religious motivations with no ulterior motives" (*Rashba HaLevi*).

12. יְשַׁלֵּם ה' פָּעֳלֵךְ — *May HASHEM repay your actions.* [lit., *HASHEM will repay your actions*]. The verse may be interpreted either as a prayer for Divine reward or as a promise of it. One who performs acts of חֶסֶד, *kindness*, with the poor is likened to one who lends money to God, and He assuredly repays all His debts (*Iggeres Shmuel*).

The *Malbim* differentiates between פּוֹעֵל, an artisan who is paid for a specific project, e.g. a tailor for a garment, and שׂוֹכֵר, a salaried employee who is paid for a period of time regardless of actual production.

Thus Boaz said: "For the kindness you have shown your mother-in-law, HASHEM *will reward your actions* [פָּעֳלֵךְ] as an artisan is rewarded for whatever handiwork he has actually produced. But for accepting the Torah and the service of God as a שׂוֹכֵר, *an employee*, of HASHEM, so to speak, you have come under God's wings — under His perpetual protection and care — you will be paid your 'salary' [מַשְׂכֻּרְתֵּךְ] fully and regularly" (*Malbim*).

Only God can reward you, for no human act is capable of rewarding

פרק ב
יג-יד

שְׁלֵמָה מֵעִם יהוה אֱלֹהֵי יִשְׂרָאֵל אֲשֶׁר־
‹ Whom ‹‹ of Israel, ‹ the God ‹ HASHEM, ‹ from ‹ complete

בָּאת לַחֲסוֹת תַּחַת־כְּנָפָיו: יג וַתֹּאמֶר
‹‹ Then she 13 ‹‹ His wings. ‹ under ‹ to seek ‹ you have
said,   refuge   come

you commensurate with your deed (*Rav Arama*).

וּתְהִי מַשְׂכֻּרְתֵּךְ שְׁלֵמָה — *And may your reward be complete* [lit., *and your payment will be complete*]. The *Iggeres Shmuel* interprets this verse as follows: HASHEM *will definitely reward your actions* in this world; *and your repayment will be full*, boundless, *from* HASHEM, *the God of Israel*, in the World to Come when you will bask directly in His radiance. And all of this will be in *reward for* having converted with a sincere heart, to *seek shelter under His wings* ....

The *Iggeres Shmuel* further comments that Ruth's merits might be greater than those of Abraham. Of Abraham's merits, the Sages sometimes note that תָּמָה זְכוּת אָבוֹת, *the merit of the Patriarchs* [which act as a shield] *is exhausted* (*Shabbos* 55a); but of Ruth's merit Boaz blessed her that it be שְׁלֵמָה, *complete*, or eternally undiminishable. Abraham left his father's house only in response to God's call, לֶךְ לְךָ, *Go for yourself* [*Genesis* 12:1], but Ruth left on her own initiative — without a Divine call, and despite the dissuasion of her mother-in-law — in order to come under the wings of HASHEM.

אֲשֶׁר־בָּאת לַחֲסוֹת תַּחַת־כְּנָפָיו — *Whom you have come to seek refuge under His wings*. [Commenting on

the anthropomorphic reference to the ''wings'' of God, the Midrash enumerates the many anthropomorphic references to ''wings'' in תנ"ך, Scripture:]

Rav Abin said: We gather from Scripture that there are wings to the earth (*Isaiah* 24:16); wings to the sun (*Malachi* 3:20); wings to the חַיּוֹת, *celestial beings* (*Ezekiel* 3:13); wings to the כְּרוּבִים, *cherubim* (*I Kings* 8:7); wings to the שְׂרָפִים, *seraphim* (*Isaiah* 6:2) ....

Come and see how great is the power of צַדִּיקִים, *the righteous*, and the power of צְדָקָה, *righteousness and charity*, and how great the power of גּוֹמְלֵי חֶסֶד, *those who do kindly deeds*, for they find shelter neither in the shadow of the morning, nor of the sun, the *chayos*, the *cherubim*, or the *seraphim*, but *under the wings of Him at Whose word the world was created* (*Midrash*).

Boaz wished her that she should never have to rely on flesh and blood for sustenance, but on Hashem alone (*Zos Nechemasi*).

The *Dubno Maggid* elaborates, in his *Kol Yaakov*, on the concept of reward for performing *mitzvos*, and sums up that the highest reward for any *mitzvah* is the satisfaction of the performance of that *mitzvah* which is a reward and incentive unto itself. Thus, Boaz told Ruth: Have no fear,

II
13-14

אֶמְצָא־חֵ֣ן בְּעֵינֶ֤יךָ אֲדֹנִי֙ כִּ֣י נִֽחַמְתָּ֔נִי

‹‹ you have ‹ because ‹‹ my lord, ‹ in your ‹ favor ‹ May I [con-
comforted me, eyes, tinue to] find

וְכִ֥י דִבַּ֖רְתָּ עַל־לֵ֣ב שִׁפְחָתֶ֑ךָ וְאָנֹכִ֕י

‹ though I ‹‹ of your ‹ the ‹ to ‹ you have ‹ and
maidservant, heart spoken because

לֹ֣א אֶֽהְיֶ֔ה כְּאַחַ֖ת שִׁפְחֹתֶֽךָ: ¹⁴ וַיֹּ֩אמֶר֩

‹ Say **14** ‹‹ of your ‹ as one ‹ am not
maidservants. [even as worthy]

my daughter, Hashem will repay your actions; but may you reach a level of righteousness sufficient to appreciate that the most "complete reward" from HASHEM, *the God of Israel*, is the very fact *that you have been inspired to seek shelter under His wings* (also *Vilna Gaon*).

Boaz's blessing was that in addition to rewarding Ruth for the performance of every *mitzvah* she would perform, God should also additionally reward her for the crucial decision upon which all her future good deeds ultimately hinged: the decision to "come under His wings" (*Chida*, quoting his father).

13. אֶמְצָא־חֵן בְּעֵינֶיךָ אֲדֹנִי — *May I [continue to] find favor in your eyes.* [The word *continue* is not in the Hebrew but is so understood by the commentators.]

After he told her his reasons for favoring her, she expressed hope that she will continue to find favor in his sight (*Malbim*).

כִּי נִֽחַמְתָּנִי — *Because you have comforted me*, by your promise of care and Divine compassion (*Vilna Gaon; Malbim*).

The *Targum* adds: and declared me fit to enter the congregation of HASHEM.

Even if Boaz were to do nothing for her, his words of comfort were sufficient to win her gratitude (*Alshich*).

וְכִי דִבַּרְתָּ עַל־לֵב שִׁפְחָתֶךָ — *And because you have spoken to the heart of your maidservant* words which are receptive to the heart (*Rashi on Genesis* 50:21).

Not merely אֶל לֵב, to *the heart*, but עַל לֵב [lit., *upon the heart*], so that that your words prevailed over my feelings (*Rav S.R. Hirsch*, ibid.).

שִׁפְחָתֶךָ — *Your maidservant.* [A deferential term used in Scripture by women when addressing gentlemen (comp. עַבְדְּךָ, *your servant*, used by men).]

וְאָנֹכִי לֹא אֶהְיֶה כְּאַחַת שִׁפְחֹתֶךָ — *Though I am not [even as worthy] as one of your maidservants.* [This translation follows *Rashi* and *Malbim*. Literally, *And I will not be as one of your maidservants.*]

Ibn Ezra seems to translate: I am not even worthy enough to be as one of your maidservants.

You have indeed comforted me by

פרק ב

טו

לָהֹ בֹעַז לְעֵת הָאֹכֶל גֹּשִׁי הֲלֹם וְאָבַלְתְּ

⟨ and eat ⟨ here ⟨ Come ⟨⟨ for eating, ⟨ at the ⟨ did ⟨ to her
over time Boaz

מִן־הַלֶּחֶם וְטָבַלְתְּ פִּתֵּךְ בַּחֹמֶץ וַתֵּשֶׁב

⟨ So she ⟨⟨ in the ⟨ your ⟨ and dip ⟨⟨ the bread, ⟨ of
sat vinegar. morsel

מִצַּד הַקֹּצְרִים וַיִּצְבָּט־לָהֹ קָלִי וַתֹּאבַל

⟨ and ⟨⟨ some ⟨ her ⟨ He ⟨⟨ the harvesters. ⟨ beside
she ate roasted handed
grain,

your kind words, for I have never considered myself to be as worthy in your eyes as one of your maidservants (*Iggeres Shmuel*).

A different approach is taken by *Mashal Umelitzah*: Ruth heard Boaz's promise to her of Divine reward for her good actions. She answered him: Thank you, my lord, for your attempt to comfort me with promises of reward, but it is unnecessary, *I am not like one of your maidservants* who perform good deeds for the sake of reward; my intentions are only לְשֵׁם שָׁמַיִם, *for the sake of Heaven*.

14. לְעֵת הָאֹכֶל — *At the time for eating.* By this time their conversation had stretched so long that dinner was being served (*Alshich*).

He did not invite her earlier because he was afraid she would demur; he waited until everyone except her was eating, and then he invited her (*Iggeres Shmuel*).

גֹּשִׁי הֲלֹם — *Come over here*, to Boaz's table (*Pri Chaim*).

According to the *Midrash*: Approach to royalty [prophetically intimating to her that kings would one day descend from her] (*Midrash*).

וְאָבַלְתְּ מִן־הַלֶּחֶם — *And eat of the bread*, the bread of the harvesters (*Midrash*). Share our meal with us (*Alshich*).

וְטָבַלְתְּ פִּתֵּךְ בַּחֹמֶץ — *And dip your morsel in the vinegar.* To refresh yourself from the heat (*Ibn Ezra*).

Harvesters use vinegar to allay the thirst, cool the body, and stimulate the digestive system. Boaz was afraid that, as a princess, Ruth was not accustomed to spending so many hours in the sun. He suggested vinegar to avoid sunstroke (*Rav Alkabetz*).

וַתֵּשֶׁב מִצַּד הַקֹּצְרִים — *So she sat beside the harvesters.* Not in front of them, so they should not glance at her; not in back of them, so she should not watch them; but alongside them (*Alshich; Midrash*).

Boaz invited her to גֹּשִׁי הֲלֹם, *come over here*, and sit with him at the head of the table, but obviously she modestly preferred to station herself *beside the harvesters* (*Malbim*).

וַיִּצְבָּט־לָהֹ קָלִי — *He handed her some roasted grain* [Boaz to Ruth]. This

II
15

וַתִּשְׁבַּע וַתִּתַר: טו וַתָּקָם לְלַקֵּט וַיְצַו בֹּעַז

‹ and Boaz ‹‹ to ‹ Then she **15** ‹‹ and left ‹ and was
ordered glean, got up some over. satisfied,

אֶת־נְעָרָיו לֵאמֹר גַּם בֵּין הָעֳמָרִים

‹ the sheaves ‹ between ‹ Even ‹‹ saying, ‹ his workers,

---

is the only place in Scripture where this word (וַיִּצְבָּט, *and he handed*) occurs (*Rashi; Ibn Ezra*).

Seeing that she was *sitting beside the harvesters* and that she modestly refrained from taking any food, Boaz himself handed the food to her like a gracious host (*Iggeres Shmuel*).

The verse teaches us that if a man is about to perform a good deed, he should do it with all his heart. For had Boaz known that Scripture would record of him, *he handed her parched grain*, he would have fed her fatted calves ....

In the past when a man performed a good deed the prophet recorded it, but nowadays when a man performs a good deed who records it? Elijah records it and the Messiah and the Holy One, Blessed is He, affix His seal to it (*Midrash*).

וַתֹּאכַל וַתִּשְׂבַּע וַתִּתַר — *And she ate and was satisfied, and left some over.*

According to the *Midrash* [connecting the word קָלִי, *parched grain*, with קָלִיל, *a little*], Boaz gave her just a "pinch of parched grain between his two fingers," and Ruth's stomach was blessed for she was satisfied with such a small morsel and even had some left over.

Other commentaries (*Ralbag, Malbim, Rav Alkabetz*), however,

interpret this verse that Boaz displayed unusual generosity: he graciously prepared her a portion so abundant that she ate her fill and still had a great deal left over.

Alshich notes that this was the first filling meal she had eaten in a long while.

15. וַתָּקָם לְלַקֵּט — *Then she got up to glean.* Having eaten, she returned to her task with increased vigor (*Alshich*).

וַיְצַו בֹּעַז אֶת־נְעָרָיו — *And Boaz ordered his workers.* Boaz's invitation to Ruth was meant as a signal to her that he was ready to support her at his table. He assumed that she would no longer wish to demean herself by gleaning in the fields like a common pauper. But when he saw that she was determined to continue gleaning, he acquiesced to her wishes. Simultaneously, however, he informed his employees that he expected them to treat her especially well (*Pri Chaim*).

גַּם בֵּין הָעֳמָרִים תְּלַקֵּט — *Even between the sheaves let her glean.* "Even if she gleaned from between the sheaves — which the poor are not legally entitled to — nevertheless," Boaz ordered, "*do not embarrass her*" (*Ralbag*).

פֶּרֶק ב
טז-יט

תְּלַקֵּט וְלֹא תַכְלִימוּהָ: טז וְגַם שֹׁל־תָּשֹׁלּוּ
‹ deliberately ‹ And 16 « embarrass her. ‹ do not « let her
drop some even   glean;

לָהּ מִן־הַצְּבָתִים וַעֲזַבְתֶּם וְלִקְטָה וְלֹא
‹ do « so she can ‹ and leave ‹ the bundles ‹ from ‹ for
not glean them;   them   her

תִגְעֲרוּ־בָהּ: יז וַתְּלַקֵּט בַּשָּׂדֶה עַד־
‹ until ‹ in the field ‹ So she gleaned 17 « her. ‹ rebuke

הָעָרֶב וַתַּחְבֹּט אֵת אֲשֶׁר־לִקֵּטָה וַיְהִי
‹ and « she had ‹ which ‹ that ‹ She beat out « the
it was gleaned,   evening.

וְלֹא תַכְלִימוּהָ — *Do not embarrass
her.* [Quietly encourage her, and be
sympathetic to her situation.]

16. שֹׁל־תָּשֹׁלּוּ לָהּ מִן־הַצְּבָתִים — *Deliberately drop some for her from the
bundles.* Pretend you forgot them
(*Rashi*). [He knew that her pride
would not permit her to take charity]:
Rav Yochanan used to deliberately
drop coins in order that Rav Shimon
bar Abba (who was extremely poor)
might "find" them. Rav Yehudah
used to leave lentils about in order
that Rav Shimon ben Chalafta might
acquire them (*Midrash*).

Rav Alkabetz stresses the word
לָהּ, *for her,* to indicate that Boaz
made it clear that when they deliberately pulled out stalks and "forgot"
them, the stalks should be dropped
where Ruth could reach them before
anyone else.

וְלֹא תִגְעֲרוּ־בָהּ — *Do not rebuke her.*
[Even though you might not understand my intent, and my request
causes you extra work, don't vent
your anger at her.]

With this Boaz explicitly stated his
noble intention to fully sustain her
(*Malbim*).

She is a convert, and thus deserving of our compassion (*Nachal
Eshkol*).

17. וַתְּלַקֵּט בַּשָּׂדֶה עַד־הָעָרֶב — *So she
gleaned in the field until the eve-
ning.* The verse stresses *gleaned* because although the harvesters were
deliberately dropping large amounts
for her as Boaz ordered, Ruth limited herself to the meager gleanings
she was entitled to by law [a maximum of two stalks at a time], and
avoided Boaz's charity. Nevertheless,
the verse tells us, her efforts were
greatly blessed, because she worked
hard and managed to gather over an
ephah of barley (*Iggeres Shmuel*).

For this reason she had to glean *until the evening;* had she availed herself of Boaz's charity she could have
finished much earlier (*Ibn Yachya*).

וַתַּחְבֹּט אֵת אֲשֶׁר־לִקֵּטָה — *She beat
out that which she had gleaned,* to
make it easier to carry. The burden

II
16-19

יח וַתִּשָּׂא֙ וַתָּב֣וֹא הָעִ֔יר כְּאֵיפָ֣ה שְׂעֹרִ֑ים

‹ to the ‹ and she ‹ She **18** ‹‹ of barley. ‹ about an
city. came carried [it] ephah

וַתֵּ֥רֶא חֲמוֹתָ֖הּ אֵ֣ת אֲשֶׁר־לִקֵּ֑טָה וַתּוֹצֵ֗א

‹ and she ‹‹ she had ‹ which ‹ that ‹ Her mother-in-law saw
took out gleaned,

וַתִּתֶּן־לָ֔הּ אֵ֥ת אֲשֶׁר־הוֹתִ֖רָה מִשָּׂבְעָֽהּ׃

‹‹ after she was ‹ she had ‹ which ‹ that ‹ her ‹ and gave
satisfied. left over

יט וַתֹּאמֶר֩ לָ֨הּ חֲמוֹתָ֜הּ אֵיפֹ֨ה לִקַּ֤טְתְּ

‹ did you ‹ Where ‹‹ did her ‹ to her ‹ Say **19**
glean mother-in-law,

of carrying home the ears still attached to the stalks would have been too much for her (*Midrash Lekach Tov*).

The *Iggeres Shmuel* also suggests that Ruth was afraid to travel the roads alone. Had she not beaten the ears from the stalks, she would have had to make two or three trips carrying stalks. This she wanted to avoid.

וַיְהִי כְּאֵיפָה שְׂעֹרִים — *And it was about an ephah of barley.* Very heavy to carry (*Ibn Ezra*).

An *ephah* equals three *seahs* [see *Exodus* 17:36 where an *ephah* equals ten *omers*. (An *omer* is a day's food for one person.) Thus, Ruth's yield from her first day of gleaning was sufficient to feed Naomi and herself for five days — a rather impressive amount].

18. וַתִּשָּׂא וַתָּבוֹא הָעִיר — *She carried [it] and she came to the city.* She went directly home without stopping or detouring (*Midrash Lekach Tov*).

She went to Naomi that day to ask

permission to accept Boaz's invitation and remain henceforth with his female workers (*Rav Arama*).

וַתֵּרֶא חֲמוֹתָהּ אֵת אֲשֶׁר־לִקֵּטָה — *Her mother-in-law saw that which she had gleaned.* Ruth had worked so quickly that darkness had not yet descended, and Naomi was still able to see Ruth approaching by daylight (*Iggeres Shmuel*).

Ruth did not go about pompously displaying her gleanings; her mother-in-law looked into her packages to see (*Rav Alkabetz*).

אֵת אֲשֶׁר־הוֹתִרָה מִשָּׂבְעָהּ — *That which she had left over after she was satisfied.* Iggeres Shmuel stresses *she* was satisfied — someone else might have eaten more; Ruth purposely left food for her mother-in-law.

19. אֵיפֹה לִקַּטְתְּ הַיּוֹם — *Where did you glean today?* Seeing such an abundant load, Naomi knew that the gleaning had to have been done in the field of a particularly friendly owner (*Alkabetz*).

פֶּרֶק ב   הַיּוֹם ׀ וְאָנָה עָשִׂית יְהִי מַכִּירֵךְ בָּרוּךְ

‹ be blessed. › ‹ May the one who took notice of you › ‹ did you work? › ‹ And where › ‹ today?

וַתַּגֶּד לַחֲמוֹתָהּ אֵת אֲשֶׁר־עָשְׂתָה עִמּוֹ

‹ with him, › ‹ she had worked › ‹ whom › ‹ the one › ‹ her mother-in-law › ‹ So she told

---

וְאָנָה עָשִׂית — *And where did you work?* Besides the gleanings, Ruth also brought back leftovers from the afternoon meal to which Boaz had invited her. Naomi therefore asked, *"Where did you glean today,* yielding such a large produce; *and where did you work,* even bringing back leftover food?" (*Iggeres Shmuel*).

The quality of the leftovers made it obvious that Ruth could not have merely spent the day gleaning, but must have performed some extra work to have earned so sumptuous a meal; on the other hand, the sheer abundance of her gleanings bespoke a full day of toil in the field. Therefore, in bewilderment, Naomi asked her both questions: *"Where did you glean today and where did you work? — a kind person must have befriended you"* (*Malbim*).

The *Iggeres Shmuel* notes that it was unusual for the gleaners to beat the stalks while still in the field; usually the landowner would not allow it, and they would have to carry the stalks home and beat them there. Seeing Ruth coming home with beaten grain, Naomi was prompted to ask her: *"Where did you work?* Which owner was kind enough to allow you to beat the stalks in his field?"

יְהִי מַכִּירֵךְ בָּרוּךְ — *May the one who took notice of you be blessed.* May blessing alight upon the head of the field-owner who so generously permitted you to glean in his field! (*Rashi*).

I hope that this man's intentions are blessed and that it was not lust which prompted him to be so extraordinarily kind to you (*Iggeres Shmuel*).

An alternate interpretation: Naomi said: "The large amount you gleaned in one day is quite impressive; how did you manage it? — יְהִי מַכִּירֵךְ בָּרוּךְ! I am certain that the *man who will come to know you* some day as his wife *will indeed be blessed* — having such an industrious wife as you!" (*Vilna Gaon*).

Ruth modestly *told her mother-in-law all that had occurred* — that it was not her zeal which allowed her to glean so much. but the kindness of Boaz (*Alshich*).

וַתַּגֶּד לַחֲמוֹתָהּ — *So she told her mother-in-law.* וַתַּגֶּד, *told,* has a harsher connotation than וַתֹּאמֶר, *said.* Ruth was angered by Naomi's suggestion that the landowner's intentions were not honorable, so she detailed all that had happened and revealed his name (*Iggeres Shmuel*).

Ruth explained that the special

II
20

וַתֹּאמֶר שֵׁם הָאִישׁ אֲשֶׁר עָשִׂיתִי עִמּוֹ

‹ with ‹ I worked ‹ whom ‹ of the man ‹ The ‹‹ and said,
him   name

הַיּוֹם בְּעַז: וַתֹּאמֶר נָעֳמִי לְכַלָּתָהּ

‹‹ to her ‹ Naomi said 20 ‹‹ is Boaz. ‹ today
daughter-in-law,

בָּרוּךְ הוּא לַיהוָֹה אֲשֶׁר לֹא־עָזַב חַסְדּוֹ

‹ His ‹ aban- ‹ has ‹ Who ‹‹ by HASHEM, ‹ be he ‹ Blessed
kindness doned not

אֶת־הַחַיִּים וְאֶת־הַמֵּתִים וַתֹּאמֶר לָהּ

‹ to her ‹ And said ‹‹ the dead! ‹ and with ‹ the living ‹ with

---

kindness was not for any labor performed by her, but rather because
the landowner was impressed with
the stories circulating about her
(*Malbim*).

שֵׁם הָאִישׁ ... בְּעַז — *The name of the
man ... is Boaz.* As the judge of
Israel, Boaz was greatly impressed
with the rumors about my special relationship with you and my conversion, so he rewarded me with extra
food (*Malbim*).

[Apparently, Ruth was making a
simple revelation, still not aware that
Boaz was related to them. Naomi, however, was especially delighted at hearing Boaz's name. She felt that Boaz,
as a cousin and as a recent widower,
might feel obligated to enter into a
levirate marriage with Ruth, thus
perpetuating the name of Machlon.]

אֲשֶׁר עָשִׂיתִי עִמּוֹ — *Whom I worked
with him.* The *Midrash* comments
in a homiletical fashion: The verse
does not read אֲשֶׁר עָשָׂה עִמָּדִי, *who
has wrought for me;* but אֲשֶׁר עָשִׂיתִי
עִמּוֹ, *I have wrought for him.* This

teaches us that יוֹתֵר מֵאֲשֶׁר בַּעַל הַבַּיִת
עוֹשֶׂה עִם הֶעָנִי, *more than the householder does for the poor man,* עוֹשֶׂה
הֶעָנִי עִם בַּעַל הַבַּיִת, *the poor man does
for the householder* [the householder
benefits more — spiritually — from
the charity he dispenses than the
poor man gains — temporally —
from the charity he receives from the
householder].

20. בָּרוּךְ הוּא לַה׳ — *Blessed be he by
HASHEM.* When Naomi heard that
the man was Boaz, she said: "This
righteous man has no need of *my*
blessing. בָּרוּךְ הוּא לַה׳, *He is blessed
of HASHEM.*"

[In the preceding verse she merely
blessed him. Now that he was identified as Boaz, she blessed him in God's
Name.]

אֲשֶׁר לֹא־עָזַב חַסְדּוֹ אֶת־הַחַיִּים וְאֶת־הַמֵּתִים
— *Who has not abandoned His
kindness with the living and with
the dead.* [There is a difference of
opinion among the commentators
whether the subject of this am-
biguous phrase is God or Boaz. The

פרק ב
כא

נָעֳמִי קָרוֹב לָנוּ הָאִישׁ מִגֹּאֲלֵנוּ הוּא:
‹‹ is he. ‹ one of our ‹‹ is the ‹ of ours ‹ A ‹‹ did
redeeming kinsmen man; relative Naomi,

כא וַתֹּאמֶר רוּת הַמּוֹאֲבִיָּה גַּם ׀ כִּי־אָמַר
‹ he ‹ in ‹ All the ‹‹ the Moabite, ‹ Ruth ‹ Said 21
said that more so

אֵלַי עִם־הַנְּעָרִים אֲשֶׁר־לִי תִּדְבָּקִין
‹‹ you should ‹ I have ‹ that ‹ the workers ‹ 'With ‹‹ to me,
stay close,

translation follows the views that the subject is God.]

Thus, Naomi blessed him: *May he be blessed by HASHEM Who has not abandoned His kindness with the living* — in this world; *and with the dead* — in the World to Come (*Iggeres Shmuel*).

Alternatively the subject of the phrase may be Boaz, in which case Naomi blessed Boaz who always sought to do kindness with the living and the dead. The kindness he did with the living (Ruth and Naomi) is obvious; the *kindness he did with the dead* is the gratification that the dead receive beyond the grave when benefits are bestowed upon their living relatives (*Iggeres Shmuel*).

With the living — by sustaining us; *and with the dead* — for he will ultimately perform יבום, *levirate marriage*, with you and he will thus do kindness to the memory of your dead husband (*Alshich; Pri Chaim*).

According to *Rav Arama*, Naomi said: "I have been wondering all along how this man, famous for his kindness, has ignored us since our arrival here. But now, seeing *that he has not abandoned his kind-*

ness with us, the living, or with the memory of our dead husbands, I truly bless him."

קָרוֹב לָנוּ הָאִישׁ מִגֹּאֲלֵנוּ הוּא — *A relative of ours is the man; one of our redeeming kinsmen is he.* The גּוֹאֵל, *redeemer,* is the next of kin who is obligated to redeem the property which his impoverished relative was compelled to sell (see *Leviticus* 25:25).

"I no longer question this man's motives — he is our close relative and he is fulfilling the verse — מִבְּשָׂרְךָ לֹא תִתְעַלָּם, *do not hide yourself from your own flesh*" [*Isaiah* 58:7] (*Ibn Yachya*).

The *Iggeres Shmuel* quotes a homiletic interpretation: מִגֹּאֲלֵנוּ הוּא — from him will eventually descend our Redeemer, a reference to the Messiah.

21. גַּם כִּי־אָמַר אֵלַי — *All the more so in that he said to me.* You blessed him for what he did on my behalf. He deserves your additional blessing for having also invited me to *stay close to the workers* (*Rav Yavetz*).

Rav Yehudah Ibn Shushan notes that at first Ruth did not mention Boaz's offer for her to stay with his

II

21

עַד אִם־כִּלּוּ אֵת כָּל־הַקָּצִיר אֲשֶׁר־לִי:

《 *I* 〈 *that* 〈 *the harvest* 〈 *all* 〈 *they have* 〈 *when* 〈 *until*
have.' *finished*

maidens for fear that Naomi might suspect Boaz of dishonorable, ulterior motives. Once Naomi revealed that Boaz was a close kinsman, however, Ruth was reassured that Boaz was sincere, so she confidently related his additional kind offer.

עִם־הַנְּעָרִים אֲשֶׁר־לִי תִּדְבָּקִין — *With the workers that I have you should stay close* [lit., *cleave to my young men;* our translation follows *Rav Alkabetz;* see below].

[There is a great discrepancy here between Boaz's actual words (*stay close to my female workers* — verse 8), and Ruth's version (*stay close to my young men*). Various interpretations are offered:

The *Midrash,* noting that in this verse her title *Moabite* was restored, comments: In truth she was still *a Moabite,* for Boaz said to her, "*Stay close to my female workers,*" while she said, "*to my young men ....*"

The *Torah Temimah* explains the *Midrash* in two possible ways: *She was still a Moabite* — and still imbued with the immorality of her upbringing. At the very least, it was very indelicate of her to describe Boaz as asking her to keep company with his young *men.* Scripture refers to her as a Moabite, as an implied rebuke as if to say, "Spoken like a descendant of the nation that was born in incest." Or, as a Moabite, Ruth was not intimately familiar with the Hebrew differentiation between the masculine and feminine forms. In the Moabite language, like English, most nouns do not have separate male and female forms. Ruth mistakenly used the masculine form without intending to be suggestive, because, as the *Midrash* interprets, *she was a Moabite!* Naomi tactfully corrected her mistake [next verse].

Rav Alkabetz feels that Ruth simply used נְעָרִים as a general term for *workers* without making a distinction between male and female workers.

The *Simchas HaRegel* suggests that Ruth had become aware of the recently publicized law permitting her, as a female Moabite, to "enter the Assembly of God." She was, of course, anxious to tell this to her mother-in-law, but, out of modesty, she alluded to it by hinting that Boaz told her she could now *stay close to one of his young men,* for she is henceforth permitted to marry an Israelite. [See comment of *Simchas HaRegel* next verse.]

The *Besuras Eliyahu* notes, that in any case, the phrase גַּם כִּי־אָמַר אֵלַי, *All the more so, in that he said to me,* is obscure. He suggests that Ruth's intention was to convey the idea to Naomi that she held Boaz and his men in such high esteem that she remarked, "I would listen to him, אֵלַי, גַּם כִּי־אָמַר אֵלַי, *even if her were to tell me* עִם־הַנְּעָרִים אֲשֶׁר־לִי תִּדְבָּקִין, 'stay close to my young *men.*' "

פרק ב כב וַתֹּאמֶר נָעֳמִי אֶל־רוּת כַּלָּתָהּ טוֹב
כב-כג
‹ It is ‹‹ her daughter- ‹ Ruth ‹ to ‹ Naomi ‹ Said 22
best, in-law,

פרק ג בִּתִּי כִּי תֵצְאִי עִם־נַעֲרוֹתָיו וְלֹא יִפְגְּעוּ־
א
‹ mistreat ‹ so that ‹‹ his female ‹ with ‹ you go ‹ that ‹ my
[they] not workers, out daughter,

בָךְ בְּשָׂדֶה אַחֵר: כג וַתִּדְבַּק בְּנַעֲרוֹת בֹּעַז
‹ of ‹ to the female ‹ So she 23 ‹‹ of some- ‹ in the ‹ you
Boaz workers stayed close one else. field

לְלַקֵּט עַד־כְּלוֹת קְצִיר־הַשְּׂעֹרִים וּקְצִיר
‹ and the ‹ of the ‹ of the ‹ the ‹ until ‹‹ to glean,
harvest barley harvest completion

22. אֶל־רוּת כַּלָּתָהּ טוֹב בִּתִּי — *To Ruth, her daughter-in-law, "It is best, my daughter ...."* [Note how Naomi's motherly response is accented in this verse by the contrasting use of *daughter-in-law* and *daughter*.]

According to the interpretation of *Simchas HaRegel* [see his *comm.* end of previous verse], Naomi answered: "Fine, I am overjoyed to learn that you are now permitted to marry within the fold. As for the practical matter of how to respond to Boaz, yes, you may stay with his female workers."

כִּי תֵצְאִי עִם־נַעֲרוֹתָיו — *That you go out with his female workers.* I am sure that if Boaz invited you to associate with his young men he knows them well and they are צַדִּיקִים, *righteous,* and above reproach. Nevertheless, my motherly advice is *go out with his female workers* (*Rashba HaLevi*).

וְלֹא יִפְגְּעוּ־בָךְ בְּשָׂדֶה אַחֵר — *So that [they] not mistreat you in the field of someone else* [lit., *and they will not mistreat you in another field*].

[Boaz had cautioned his men

against molesting her in any way (verse 16) and Ruth was thus safe in Boaz's fields; she had no such assurances in other fields.]

[It is perhaps possible to translate וַיִּפְגַּע, *be met,* thus, *so that you will not be met in another field* and appear to be כְּפוּיָה טוֹב, *ungracious* of his hospitality.]

The *Malbim* adds: and come under suspicion.

23. וַתִּדְבַּק בְּנַעֲרוֹת בֹּעַז לְלַקֵּט — *So she stayed close to the female workers of Boaz to glean.* Most commentators feel that she spent the entire harvest period with Boaz's female workers away from Naomi.

According to *Iggeres Shmuel,* the verse specifies *to glean* — only during gleaning time; Ruth stayed close to the female workers only during the day, when she gleaned. She did not sleep away from Naomi for the duration of the harvest; she went home every night so as not to leave her mother-in-law alone.

עַד־כְּלוֹת קְצִיר הַשְּׂעֹרִים וּקְצִיר הַחִטִּים —

II 22-23
III 1

הַחִטִּים וַתֵּשֶׁב אֶת־חֲמוֹתָהּ: ג א וַתֹּאמֶר

‹ Say 1 [3] ‹‹ her mother- ‹ with ‹ [Then] she ‹‹ of the
in-law. stayed [at home] wheat.

Until the completion of the harvest of the barley and the harvest of the wheat. A total period of three months (*Midrash*).

The *Malbim* notes that this period of time is equal to the יְמֵי הַבְחָנָה, the ninety-day waiting period a new convert must wait before she can marry. After this period was up, she began considering יִבּוּם, *levirate remarriage.*

וַתֵּשֶׁב אֶת־חֲמוֹתָהּ — *[Then] she stayed [at home] with her mother-in-law.* Although the verse mentions that Ruth *stayed close* [וַתִּדְבַּק] to the

female workers, nevertheless, her deep love for and *clinging to* [compare 1:14] Naomi never subsided. As soon as the harvest was over she resumed living with her mother-in-law, because Ruth's love for Naomi surpassed all other considerations (*Iggeres Shmuel; Malbim*).

Also, the verse ends with וַתֵּשֶׁב אֶת־חֲמוֹתָהּ, *she stayed with her mother-in-law*, to emphasize that although Ruth was away in the fields gleaning, her thoughts were with Naomi *as if she were living with her* (*Iggeres Shmuel*).

III.
Prefatory Remarks

[When reading this chapter, we must attempt to approach it by comprehending fully the purity and innocence with which the Sages — in the context of Biblical times — understood the episode as being fully לְשֵׁם שָׁמַיִם, *for the sake of Heaven*. Two women sacrificed themselves for the sake of the tribe of Judah — declares the *Yalkut Shimoni* — Tamar and Ruth:

During the harvest, while Ruth spent her time gleaning in Boaz's field and had at least limited access to him, Naomi dreamt and hoped that Boaz would bestir himself and "redeem" Ruth, thus perpetuating Machlon's memory. But now the harvest was over and Boaz had made no such move. The future prospect of Ruth's meeting Boaz was remote, and Naomi feared that since Boaz had not taken the initiative when Ruth was so at hand, he could hardly be expected to respond to more conventional suggestions of marriage when Ruth was out of sight. For all they knew, Boaz might even be offended at the mere suggestion of his marrying Ruth. After all, Naomi was destitute, Ruth was of foreign, Moabite stock, and Boaz was a man of substance, the Judge and leader of the generation. Could she expect to approach him and simply ask him to redeem and marry this girl?

Naomi became convinced that the condition of stalemate could not continue. Things had to be brought to a head one way or the other.

It must be remembered that the prohibition of יִחוּד פְּנוּיָה, the seclusion of a man with an unmarried woman — later forbidden by the court of King David — had not yet been proclaimed. Naomi therefore decided that the best course of action — however daring and unconventional — was for Ruth herself to approach Boaz under the most intimate and personal circumstances and remind him of his responsibility to the family of his dead uncle, Elimelech. In a personal confrontation — convinced that her motives were sincere — his compassion for her bitter plight might be evoked. (See *Overview*.) — M.Z.]

פרק ג
ב-ג

לָהּ נָעֳמִי חֲמוֹתָהּ בִּתִּי הֲלֹא אֲבַקֶּשׁ־

‹ I seek ‹ indeed, ‹ My ⟪ her mother- ‹ did ‹ to her
daughter, in-law, Naomi,

לָךְ מָנוֹחַ אֲשֶׁר יִיטַב־לָךְ: בּ וְעַתָּה הֲלֹא

‹ indeed, Now, 2⟪ for ‹ will be ‹ that ‹ content- ‹ for
you. best ment, you

1. וַתֹּאמֶר לָהּ נָעֳמִי חֲמוֹתָהּ — *Say to her did Naomi, her mother-in-law.* Naomi and Ruth both interpreted Boaz's actions toward Ruth in his field as if he was considering marriage with her. They waited until the harvest was over and Boaz was free of business worries. Still, he made no move in that direction. Noami therefore sought out ways to expedite the matter. She was convinced that a direct action was needed (*Kol Yehudah; Akeidas Yitzchak*).

בִּתִּי — *My daughter.* [The word בִּתִּי, *my daughter*, is treated differently throughout the Book, according to its context; see *Comm.* on 2:2; 2:8; and 2:22.] In this case, the *Commentaries* observe, *my daughter* is stressed because human nature is such that when one's daughter-in-law is left widowed, the mother-in-law begrudges her remarriage. However, when a daughter is widowed, her mother encourages quick remarriage. Therefore, Naomi addressed Ruth as follows:

"Although I am your mother-in-law, I feel as if you are my own daughter, and I seek only the very best security in marriage for you, that it may go well with you. If you counter: Boaz is an old man [he was 80 at the time! (*Midrash*)] and

how 'good' could such a marriage be? — Yes! Earthly pleasures might not be plentiful, but the Heavenly reward for being married to such a צַדִּיק, *righteous man*, as he — and the righteous children that would result from such a marriage — is abundant!" (*Nachal Eshkol; Iggeres Shmuel*).

הֲלֹא אֲבַקֶּשׁ־לָךְ מָנוֹחַ — *Indeed, I seek for you contentment* [lit., *shall I not find "rest" for you?*]. A woman has no contentment [*rest*] until she marries (*Rashi*) [compare Naomi's blessing in 1:9, וּמְצֶאןָ מְנוּחָה, *that you may find contentment*].

On an esoteric level, the *Zohar Chadash* explains the use of the term *rest* as a synonym for marriage: The first husband's "spirit" continues to stir within his widow's body until she remarries and replaces it with a new spirit. Naomi, therefore, suggested to Ruth that she must seek to quiet the spiritual turmoil within herself — the remnants of Machlon — by marriage, to as near a kin as possible and thereby find *rest*.

אֲשֶׁר יִיטַב־לָךְ — *That will be best for you.* I am not concerned with the memory of my son; your welfare is foremost in my mind (*Meishiv Nefesh*).

III
2-3

בֹּעַז מֹדַעְתָּנוּ אֲשֶׁר הָיִית אֶת־נַעֲרוֹתָיו

⟨ his female ⟨ with ⟨ you ⟨ the one ⟨ our relative, ⟨ Boaz,
workers were that

הִנֵּה־הוּא זֹרֶה אֶת־גֹּרֶן הַשְּׂעֹרִים

⟨ [full] of barley ⟨ the threshing ⟨ is ⟨ he ⟨ — indeed,
floor winnowing

הַלָּיְלָה: ₃וְרָחַצְתְּ ׀ וָסַכְתְּ וְשַׂמְתְּ [נ״א ושמתי כ׳]

⟨ put ⟨ and apply ⟨ So bathe 3 ⟨⟨ tonight.
[fragrant] oil,

[The phrase may also be interpreted in the spiritual sense: "Your marriage to this צַדִּיק, *righteous man*, though he is old, will bring you spiritual happiness. The *Talmud* interprets לְמַעַן יִיטַב לָךְ, *and so that it will be good for you* [*Deut.* 5:16] — "in the World to Come" (*Kiddushin* 39b).]

[The word יִיטַב which we have translated "*it*" *will be best*, can also be translated "*he*" *may do good.* The "*he*" could conceivably apply to the new husband who will "*treat you well.*"]

2. הֲלֹא בֹעַז מֹדַעְתָּנוּ אֲשֶׁר הָיִית אֶת־נַעֲרוֹתָיו — *Indeed, Boaz, our relative, the one that you were with his female workers.* Naomi, afraid that Ruth would possibly have a negative attitude toward marrying this octogenarian, enumerates his qualities: "His name *Boaz* is known and familiar to all; *he is our relative*, from the same aristocratic family as your late husband, and he is a 'redeemer' of ours; you are personally familiar with his righteousness and kindnesses since *you were with his female workers* ..." (*Iggeres Shmuel*).

הָיִית אֶת־נַעֲרוֹתָיו — *You were with his female workers.* [A reference to verses 22 and 23 of the preceding chapter.]

הַלָּיְלָה — *Tonight.* [Naomi was certain that Boaz would spend the night there because] the generation was crime ridden, and he would sleep at the threshing floor to guard his grain from thieves (*Rashi*).

Now that the harvest was over, and it was the most productive one in many years, Naomi knew that Boaz would certainly be well disposed toward taking a new wife to share his good fortune (*Meishiv Nefesh*).

The *Malbim* comments that there must have been workers at the threshing floor during working hours. If any of them were to see Ruth going to the threshing floor that particular night, they would assume she was going to visit the girls with whom she had worked previously, and to rejoice with her relative Boaz over his abundant harvest.

3. וְרָחַצְתְּ — *So bathe* [lit., *wash*]. Since the verse does not specify hands or face, but simply *bathe*, in a general sense, and since Naomi would not have to instruct Ruth to do such a basic thing, the *Midrash*

פרק ג
ד-ה
שִׂמְלֹתַיִךְ [שמלתך כ'] עָלַיִךְ וְיָרַדְתְּ [וירדתי כ']
‹ and go   ‹ on   ‹ your [fine]
  down   yourself,   garments

הַגֹּרֶן אַל-תִּוָּדְעִי לָאִישׁ עַד כַּלֹּתוֹ
‹ he has   ‹ until   ‹ to the   ‹ make   ‹ but   ‹‹ to the
  finished   man   yourself   do not   threshing
                                   known   floor,

interprets this verse in the spiritual sense: וְרָחַצְתְּ, *wash yourself*, "clean yourself from your idolatry" [take a ritual bath] (*Torah Temimah*).

The *Bach* quotes a *Midrash HaNe'elam* that a convert is not free of the remnant of his impurity until three months following conversion. The three months were now ended [see *Comm.* to verse 1], and Naomi thus instructed her to take a ritual bath and cleanse herself entirely.

Rav Breuer notes that Naomi specified these Sabbath-like preparations to ready Ruth for her holy mission because she was preparing for a solemn, holy occasion.

וָסַכְתְּ — *And apply [fragrant] oil*, perfume — as was the custom of Jewish nobility, both men and women (*Ibn Ezra*).

The *Midrash* interprets: *anoint yourself with good deeds and righteous conduct*.

וְשַׂמְתְּ שִׂמְלֹתַיִךְ עָלַיִךְ — *Put your [fine] garments on yourself*. Was she then naked? It must refer to Sabbath garments. It was from this verse that Rav Chaninah said: A man should have two sets of garments, one for weekdays and one for Sabbath (*Yerushalmi Pe'ah* 8:6).

According to the *Akeidas Yitzchak* and *Malbim*, Naomi did not advise Ruth to go down to the threshing floor *wearing* her Sabbath finery. The verse says וְשַׂמְתְּ, *put*, not וְלָבַשְׁתְּ, *wear*, *dress*. Rather, Naomi advised Ruth to *put her [fine] garments on her*; take along her Sabbath clothes and change into them at the threshing floor after everyone else was gone and she was in hiding.

The *k'siv* [traditional spelling] of the word is in first person: וְשַׂמְתִּי, *I will dress you*, to imply that Naomi intimated, "My זְכוּיוֹת, *merits*, will enhance your appearance" (*Shoresh Yishai*).

וְיָרַדְתְּ הַגֹּרֶן — *And go down to the threshing floor*. [The *k'siv* is first person: וירדתי, *I will go down*, which the *Midrash* interprets: "My merits will descend with you" — "through my merits the plan will work, and Boaz will not be angry with you" (*Nachal Eshkol*).

Go down is used, because the threshing floor was situated below the city (*Midrash*).

אַל-תִּוָּדְעִי לָאִישׁ — *But do not make yourself known to the man*. "The" man — to Boaz (*Rashi*).

III
4-5

לֶאֱכֹל וְלִשְׁתּוֹת: דּוִיהִי בְשָׁכְבוֹ וְיָדַעַתְּ

⟨ you should ⟨⟨ that when ⟨ And it **4** ⟨⟨ and drinking. ⟨ eating
note   he lies down, shall be

אֶת־הַמָּקוֹם אֲשֶׁר יִשְׁכַּב־שָׁם וּבָאת

⟨ and you ⟨⟨ there, ⟨ he lies ⟨ in which ⟨ the place
should   down
go over,

וְגִלִּית מַרְגְּלֹתָיו וְשָׁכָבְתְּ [ושכבתי כ׳] וְהוּא

⟨ He   ⟨⟨ and you should ⟨ his feet, ⟨ you should
lie down.   uncover

יַגִּיד לָךְ אֵת אֲשֶׁר תַּעֲשִׂין: הוַתֹּאמֶר

⟨ She   **5** ⟨⟨ you ⟨ which ⟨ that ⟨ you ⟨ will tell
replied   should do.

Remain hidden (*Ralbag*), and the workers will assume that you left before them (*Malbim*).

4. וִיהִי בְשָׁכְבוֹ — *And it shall be that when he lies down.* When you see him preparing to retire, note his sleeping place. Then later, in the dark of night when he is fast asleep, you can easily locate him (*Targum; Iggeres Shmuel*).

וְגִלִּית מַרְגְּלֹתָיו — *You should uncover his feet.* The *Malbim* suggests that Naomi was proposing a method of reminding Boaz, as a redeemer, of his moral obligation to marry Ruth. A brother who refuses to enter into יִבּוּם, *a levirate marriage*, undergoes a ceremony of *chalitzah* which involves the removal of his shoe [see *Deut.* 25:5-10]. For Naomi to directly suggest that Boaz marry Ruth would have been a gross impropriety. Therefore she asked Ruth to *uncover his feet*, a gesture reminiscent of

chalitzah, in the hope that it would make Boaz aware of his moral obligation to her.

וְשָׁכָבְתְּ — *And you should lie down.* [Here, too, the *k'siv* (traditional spelling) of the imperative verb *lie down* is written as if it were a first-person verb — וְשָׁכַבְתִּי, *I will lie down*, as if to say that Naomi's merit will accompany her (see preceding verse), and Naomi thus identified herself with the deed.]

וְהוּא יַגִּיד לָךְ אֵת אֲשֶׁר תַּעֲשִׂין — *He will tell that which you should do.* Whether you or he should undertake to approach a closer redeemer (*Malbim*).

The *Besuras Eliyahu* takes הוּא, *he*, to refer to God. Naomi said: "I can't possibly know what Boaz will say or how you should respond. Follow my directions and God will inspire you to say the right thing."

פרק ג אֵלֶיהָ כָּל אֲשֶׁר־תֹּאמְרִי אֵלַי [אֵלַי ק' ולא כ']
ו-ח
‹ to me ‹ you say ‹ that ‹ All ‹‹ to her,

אֶעֱשֶׂה: וַתֵּרֶד הַגֹּרֶן וַתַּעַשׂ כְּכֹל אֲשֶׁר־
‹ that ‹ in accord- ‹ and ‹‹ to the ‹ So she 6 ‹‹ I will do.
ance with she did threshing went
everything floor, down

צִוַּתָּה חֲמוֹתָהּ: וַיֹּאכַל בֹּעַז וַיֵּשְׁתְּ
‹‹ and ‹ Boaz ate 7 ‹‹ did her ‹ instruct
drank, mother-in-law. her

5. כָּל אֲשֶׁר־תֹּאמְרִי [אֵלַי] אֶעֱשֶׂה — *All that you say to me I will do.* The word אֵלַי, *to me*, is read, but it does not appear in the written Hebrew text. This, and all textual readings, as transmitted by the *Soferim*, are Halachah from Moses at Sinai (*Nedarim* 37b). [This means that the "contradiction" between the written and read versions is apparent but not real. Each is valid; the discrepancy is to teach us the deeper meaning implied in the text. The *Commentaries* offer several interpretations:]

The absence of אֵלַי, *to me*, in the Hebrew suggests that Ruth cast her whole dependence upon Naomi, and removed *herself* from all decision making. Ruth vowed to do not only what Naomi had *specifically instructed her* to do, but even what she only *alluded* to, indirectly through speaking to others. Moreover, "even those instructions which were not אֵלַי, *to me*, for my own benefit, I will still do" (*Iggeres Shmuel*).

According to *Akeidas Yitzchak*, אֵלַי, *to me*, is read but not written

to convey that although the advice seemed improper *to her*, nevertheless Ruth would obey because Naomi had given it.

M'lo HaOmer suggests that the omitted אֵלַי demonstrates the extent to which Ruth left matters בִּידֵי שָׁמַיִם, *in the hands of Heaven* — as if she excluded *herself*, and had no personal stake in their resolution; she left everything to God's beneficence.

"Although you tell me that Boaz will instruct me, I will first consult you, and *all that you say to me I will do*" (*Alshich; Malbim*).

6. וַתֵּרֶד הַגֹּרֶן וַתַּעַשׂ כְּכֹל אֲשֶׁר־צִוַּתָּה חֲמוֹתָהּ — *So she went down to the threshing floor and she did in accordance with everything that instruct her did her mother-in-law.* Ruth didn't follow her bidding in every detail. She feared that by going to the threshing floor perfumed and festively attired she would attract curious glances, making it impossible to carry out her mission discreetly. Therefore, the verse tells us first וַתֵּרֶד הַגֹּרֶן, *she went down to the threshing floor* — and then *she did in accordance with*

III
6-8

וַיִּיטַב לִבּוֹ וַיָּבֹא לִשְׁכַּב בִּקְצֵה הָעֲרֵמָה

‹‹ of the   ‹ at the   ‹ to lie   ‹ He went ‹‹ was his ‹   and
[grain] heap,   edge   down   heart.   merry

וַתָּבֹא בַלָּט וַתְּגַל מַרְגְּלֹתָיו וַתִּשְׁכָּב:

‹‹ and she   ‹   his feet,   ‹ and she ‹ stealthily, ‹ and she
lay down.   uncovered   came

ח וַיְהִי בַּחֲצִי הַלַּיְלָה וַיֶּחֱרַד הָאִישׁ

‹ that the man trembled, ‹ of the night ‹ in the   ‹ It   **8**
middle   happened

---

everything that instruct her did her mother-in-law. Only after arriving at the threshing floor did Ruth follow Naomi's bidding by perfuming and dressing in her best finery (*Rashi;* see *Malbim* verse 3).

אֲשֶׁר־צִוְּתָה חֲמוֹתָהּ — *That instruct her did her mother-in-law.* Although Ruth didn't quite understand or fully agree with the plan, she did it blindly and respectfully, *because her mother-in-law instructed her* (*Besuras Eliyahu*).

7. וַיִּיטַב לִבּוֹ — *And merry was his heart.* Having recited the blessing after meals (*Midrash*) and having added a special prayer thanking God for heeding his prayers and putting an end to the famine [see *Comm.* 1:6] (*Targum*).

His heart was merry — because he studied Torah (*Rashi*).

The Sages note the difference between a צַדִּיק, *righteous man,* and a רָשָׁע, *wicked man.* Boaz's *heart was merry,* and the presence of a pure, beautiful, and festively attired woman was a great temptation. Nevertheless, he mastered his impulses and did nothing in the least immoral. Of the wicked Ahasuerus, on the other hand, we find that when *his heart was merry* [*Esther* 1:10] he ordered his queen to appear before his guests unclothed (*Iggeres Shmuel*).

בִּקְצֵה הָעֲרֵמָה — *At the edge of the [grain] heap.* To guard his grain from that immoral generation (*Midrash*) [see *Comm.* verse 2, s.v. הַלַּיְלָה, *tonight*]. Also, because they are so scrupulous about earning their money honestly, the righteous are zealous about their property (*Sotah* 12a).

וַתָּבֹא בַלָּט — *And she came stealthily,* בְּנַחַת, *quietly* (*Rashi*). Radak derives the word from לוּט, *wrapped,* and translates: *She came with her face covered.*

8. בַּחֲצִי הַלַּיְלָה — *In the middle of the night,* when he got up to study Torah ... (*Iggeres Shmuel*).

וַיֶּחֱרַד הָאִישׁ — *That the man trembled.* He could easily have cursed her but God put it in his heart to bless her, as it is said [verse 10]: בְּרוּכָה

פרק ג וַיֶּחֱרַד וְהִנֵּה אִשָּׁה שֹׁכֶבֶת מַרְגְּלֹתָיו:
ט-י
‹‹ at his feet. **‹** lying **‹** a **‹** and there **‹‹** and turned
woman was about;

ט וַיֹּאמֶר מִי־אָתְּ וַתֹּאמֶר אָנֹכִי רוּת
‹ am **‹** I **‹‹** And she **‹‹** are **‹** Who **‹‹** He asked, **9**
Ruth, answered, you?

אַתְּ לַה׳, *Blessed be you by* HASHEM
(*Midrash*).

וַיֶּחֱרַד — *And turned about.* [See *Ibn
Ezra*; according to *Rashi*:] He thought
she was a demon and he wanted to
scream, so she held him back.

The *Talmud*, deriving the word
from לֶפֶת, *turnip*, translates: His
skin hardened like a turnip [as from
fright] (*Sanhedrin* 19b).

וְהִנֵּה אִשָּׁה — *And there was a woman.* Purest of women (*Midrash*).

He touched her head and realized
it was a woman (*Rashi*).

Perhaps she whispered: "Don't
be afraid!" and he recognized it as a
woman's voice, or he distinguished
a womanly form by the light of the
moon (*Ibn Ezra*).

How few words are used to express the fear Boaz must have felt
during this incident! The leader of
that generation, involved all his life
in elevating the morals of his people,
spends a night at his threshing floor
to guard against robbers in that lawless generation, wakes up in the middle of the night, and finds a woman
lying at his feet! What audacity she
must have had; how embarrassing
for him, what an awkward position
to be put into!

Under normal circumstances he

should have cursed her and banished
her for her unseemly act. But the
sincerity of Ruth and the determination of Naomi caused Providence to
inspire Boaz with a compassion for
Ruth. Recognizing her sincerity, he
did not curse her; instead he blessed
her. This is but another one of the
many miracles wrought for the Jews
in the middle of the night throughout their history.

As interpreted by the Sages, this
is the incident King David referred
to when generations later he would
get up at midnight and recount all
the miracles wrought for the Jews
throughout history: חֲצוֹת לַיְלָה — *At
midnight I arise to thank You for
Your judgments that are righteous*
(*Psalms* 119:62). And among the miracles he recounted was the miracle wrought for his great-grandpar-
ents, that midnight on the threshing
floor. As the *Midrash* states: "*And
the righteousness which you have
wrought for my great-grandfather
and great-grandmother*, for had
Boaz hastily cursed her but once,
from where would I have come?"
(*Nachalas Yosef*).

9. וַיֹּאמֶר מִי־אָתְּ — *He asked "Who
are you?"* "A woman," she an-
swered. "Married or unmarried?" She
answered, "Unmarried" (*Midrash*).

III
9-10

אֲמָתֶ֔ךָ וּפָרַשְׂתָּ֤ כְנָפֶ֨ךָ֙ עַל־אֲמָ֣תְךָ֔ כִּ֥י גֹאֵ֖ל

⟨ [the] ⟨ for ⟨⟨ your hand- ⟨ over ⟨ your ⟨ You should ⟨⟨ your hand-
redeemer maiden; wing spread maiden.

אָ֑תָּה: ,וַיֹּ֗אמֶר בְּרוּכָ֨ה אַ֤תְּ לַיהוה֙ בִּתִּ֔י

⟨⟨ my ⟨ by ⟨ be you ⟨ Blessed ⟨⟨ And he **10** ⟨⟨ are you.
daughter; HASHEM, said,

וּפָרַשְׂתָּ כְנָפֶךָ עַל־אֲמָתֶךָ — *You should spread your wing over your handmaiden.*

The "wing" is a metaphor borrowed from birds, who shield each other with their wings during mating. Therefore it is used as a symbol of marriage (*Malbim*).

Most commentators, however, understand the word in the sense of "corner" of a garment: *place the corner of your garment over me as a token of marriage* (*Rashi*).

Take me as your wife, with a proper wedding ceremony (*Iggeres Shmuel*).

"Cursed be the wicked," says the *Midrash* [noting the difference between the behavior of Ruth and others]. In the case of Potiphar's wife and Joseph it is said [*Gen. 39:7*]: *"Lie with me,"* but here Ruth said: *"Spread your wing over your handmaiden."*

כִּי גֹאֵל אָתָּה — *For [the] redeemer are you,* and, as such, it is incumbent upon you to redeem the estate of my husband in accordance with *Lev.* 25. Ruth explained to Boaz that she and her mother-in-law are forced to sell their inheritance, and as a redeemer, it is his obligation to buy the property so that it would remain in the family. She then made an additional request: "Take possession of me, too, so that the name of the deceased will be perpetuated on his property. If you marry me, people will say: 'She was the wife of Machlon,' whenever I visit the field" (*Rashi*).

"And it is your duty to 'redeem' the soul of Machlon and marry me …" (*Alshich*).

The Bach states, esoterically, that she hinted: "Only from both of us together will the Davidic dynasty descend, not from only one of us."

10. בְּרוּכָה אַתְּ לַה' בִּתִּי — *Blessed be you by HASHEM, my daughter.* [The Sages stress Boaz's righteousness and superhuman self-control. He recognized her mission as a difficult one and wholly devoted לְשֵׁם שָׁמַיִם, *for the sake of Heaven.* No evil thoughts came to his mind. He was moved, and he blessed her.]

He might easily have cursed her, but God put it in his heart to bless her (*Midrash*).

Boaz compared this incident in his mind with the incidents of Lot's daughters, and Judah and Tamar. He said, "You, my daughter, are more blessed than Lot's daughters and Tamar, because your actions do not involve serious prohibitions such as theirs did" (*Kol Yehudah*).

פרק ג
יא-יג

הֵיטַבְתְּ חַסְדֵּךְ הָאַחֲרוֹן מִן־הָרִאשׁוֹן
《 the first, 〈 than 〈 with your latest act of kindness 〈 you have done a greater good

לְבִלְתִּי־לֶכֶת אַחֲרֵי הַבַּחוּרִים אִם־דַּל
〈 poor 〈 whether 《 the young men, 〈 after 〈 going 〈 in not

וְאִם־עָשִׁיר: יא וְעַתָּה בִּתִּי אַל־תִּירְאִי
《 fear. 〈 do not 〈 my daughter, 〈 And now, 11 《 rich. 〈 or whether

כֹּל אֲשֶׁר־תֹּאמְרִי אֶעֱשֶׂה־לָּךְ כִּי יוֹדֵעַ
《 they know 〈 for 《 for you; 〈 I will do 〈 you say, 〈 that 〈 All

כָּל־שַׁעַר עַמִּי כִּי אֵשֶׁת חַיִל אָתְּ:
《 are you. 〈 a capable woman 〈 that 《 of my people — 〈 [the men in] 〈 — all the gate

הֵיטַבְתְּ חַסְדֵּךְ הָאַחֲרוֹן מִן־הָרִאשׁוֹן — You have done a greater good with your latest act of kindness than the first. For a woman in the prime of life to give up the opportunity to marry a young man in favor of marrying a very old one is a great sacrifice. Yet you are prepared to do this solely to perpetuate the name of your late husband. This, your latest act of kindness, is even greater than your earlier kindness to your mother-in-law. [According to Bach it is also greater than the kindness you did your soul by embracing Judaism ...] (Ralbag; Rav Arama; Iggeres Shmuel; Alshich).

לְבִלְתִּי־לֶכֶת אַחֲרֵי הַבַּחוּרִים — In not going after the young men. With your beauty you could have whomever you want, and yet you honor your husband's memory by choosing me, though I am old, because I am a close relative (Ibn Ezra; Malbim).

אִם־דַּל וְאִם־עָשִׁיר — Whether poor or whether rich. Rav Shmuel bar Isaac said: A woman usually prefers a poor young man to an old rich man (Midrash).

11. כֹּל אֲשֶׁר־תֹּאמְרִי אֶעֱשֶׂה־לָּךְ — All that you say, I will do for you. Boaz reassured her that he was not merely putting her off with soothing words (Meishiv Nefesh).

"I will even do anything you request of me in the future, but at the moment we face an obstacle: there is a redeemer closer than I" (Iggeres Shmuel).

Knowing he could not marry her immediately, he reassured her in this way because he did not want her to be discouraged for having approached him (Alshich).

כִּי יוֹדֵעַ כָּל־שַׁעַר עַמִּי — For they know — all [the men in] the gate of my people [lit., the gate of my people knows — those who assemble at the

III
11-13

יבוְעַתָּה כִּי אָמְנָם כִּי [אם כ' ולא ק'] גֹּאֵל

⟨ a redeemer   ⟨ that ⟨ it is true ⟨ while ⟨ Now, 12

אָנֹכִי וְגַם יֵשׁ גֹּאֵל קָרוֹב מִמֶּנִּי: יג *לִינִי ׀

⟨ Stay   13 ⟪ than I. ⟨ who is more ⟨ a re- ⟨ is ⟨ there ⟪ am I,
                      closely related deemer   also

* ל' רבתי [נ"א נ' רבתי]

gate, the gathering point of the city].

Those who sit at the gate of the Great Sanhedrin (*Targum*).

It now became manifestly clear to Boaz why the law of *Moabite not Moabitess* "happened" to be the topic of discussion of the Sanhedrin and was "revealed" to them immediately prior to Ruth's arrival (*Nachal Eshkol*).

Boaz said: My intentions are compatible with yours. But don't worry, even though you think that the wise men at the gate will try to dissuade me, saying it is below my dignity to marry a Moabite girl, have no fear. "The people at the gate *know* you are a worthy woman" (*Malbim*).

The *Iggeres Shmuel* offers a different interpretation of these verses: "*Do not fear, my daughter; I want to marry you. And things will probably work out. 'I' will be the one to do whatever you say. Only I and the people of my gate [the Sanhedrin] are aware that as a female Moabite you are now permitted to me; everyone else thinks you are still prohibited. The other redeemer definitely does not know the law and he will demur, but, in the event he does decide to redeem you, then it is for the best. I promise you, however, that if he does not accept the responsibility of redeeming you with a good heart, I myself will redeem you.*"

כִּי אֵשֶׁת חַיִל אָתְּ — *That a capable woman are you* — and fit for a גִּבּוֹר, חַיִל, *man of great capability* [2:1, Boaz] (*Midrash Lekach Tov*).

12. כִּי גֹאֵל אָנֹכִי — *That a redeemer am I.* The written text has כִּי אִם גֹאֵל אָנֹכִי, *For if a redeemer am I*; but according to the *Masorah* the word אִם, *if*, is כְּתִיב וְלֹא קְרִי, *written but not read*: This occurs several times in Scripture and is a Halachah from Moses at Sinai (*Nedarim* 37b) [see *Comm.* beginning of verse 5].

The word אִם is not read because it implies uncertainty, while in fact there *was* definitely another גּוֹאֵל (*Midrash Lekach Tov; Rashi*).

Commenting on why אִם is written, *Rav Alkabetz* suggests that it implies a doubt that Boaz left unstated. Boaz was impressed by Ruth's noble act and was flattered at the suggestion that he "redeem" Ruth and raise up the memory of her husband, but he was doubtful whether he could function in that capacity and have children due to his advanced age [he was eighty!].

וְגַם יֵשׁ גֹּאֵל קָרוֹב מִמֶּנִּי — *There also is a redeemer who is more closely related than I.* A brother of Elimelech; whereas Boaz was only a nephew [see *Comm.* next verse] (*Rashi*).

[Boaz did not believe that the closer redeemer would exercise his right,

פֶּרֶק ג הַלַּיְלָה וְהָיָה בַבֹּקֶר אִם־יִגְאָלֵךְ טוֹב
יד-טו

‹ fine, ‹ he will redeem you, ‹ if ‹ in the morning, ‹ then it shall be ‹‹ the night,

יִגְאָל וְאִם־לֹא יַחְפֹּץ לְגָאֳלֵךְ וּגְאַלְתִּיךְ

‹ then I will redeem you ‹ to redeem you, ‹ he does not want ‹ But if ‹‹ let him redeem.

אָנֹכִי חַי־יהוה שִׁכְבִי עַד־הַבֹּקֶר:

‹‹ the morning. ‹ until ‹ Lie down ‹‹ as HASHEM lives! ‹ — I [will] —

but he was obliged to first consult him and give him the opportunity of doing so.]

13. לִינִי הַלַּיְלָה — *Stay the night.* Without a husband (*Rashi*).

"This night you will spend without a husband, but you will not be without a husband for another night" (*Midrash*).

When Ruth heard, now for the first time, that there was a redeemer closer than Boaz, she grew discouraged and got up to leave. Boaz then asked her not to lose heart, but to remain the night, and then he swore to her that he is quite ready to marry her if the other redeemer would not (*Rav Alkabetz*).

[The *Minchas Shai* observes that in some texts the ל, *lamed*, of לִינִי is enlarged, in some the נ, *nun*, is enlarged, and in many manuscripts neither is enlarged.]

אִם־יִגְאָלֵךְ טוֹב יִגְאָל — *If he will redeem you, fine, let him redeem.* The *Midrash* states that Salmon, Tov, and Elimelech were brothers. Many commentators [e.g., *Alshich, Bach, Rav Arama, Malbim*] maintain therefore that the word טוֹב, *Tov*, is

the name of the closer redeemer, the *Ploni Almoni* referred to later. According to their interpretation, the verse translates thus: אִם־יִגְאָלֵךְ טוֹב, *if Tov will redeem you*, יִגְאָל, *let him redeem ....*

Ibn Ezra, however, disagrees: If Scripture here identifies the redeemer as Tov, why should he be referred to as *Ploni Almoni* later? Rather the meaning is: *If he will redeem you, fine,* he is a good man, etc.

The redeemer was not learned, and Boaz knew that if, by some chance, he would agree to redeem, it would be the result of shame, not of conviction. Therefore, the translation is: If he will redeem you from the goodness of his heart, let him redeem; if he does not so desire, then I will redeem (*Shoresh Yishai*).

חַי־ה' — *As HASHEM lives!* [a Biblical form of oath]. Ruth accused him of paying lip service to her request, so he jumped up and swore to her that he was sincere. Some Sages say he was addressing his יֵצֶר הָרַע, *evil inclination* (*Rashi*).

שִׁכְבִי עַד־הַבֹּקֶר — *Lie down until the*

III
14-15

יד וַתִּשְׁכַּב מַרְגְּלוֹתָיו [מרגלותו כ׳] עַד־
‹ until ‹ at his feet ‹ So she lay **14**

הַבֹּקֶר וַתָּקָם בְּטֶרֶם [בטרום כ׳] יַכִּיר אִישׁ
‹ one man could ‹ before ‹ and she ‹‹ the
recognize got up morning,

אֶת־רֵעֵהוּ וַיֹּאמֶר אַל־יִוָּדַע כִּי־בָאָה
‹ come ‹ that ‹ be ‹ Let it ‹‹ for [Boaz] ‹‹ his friend,
known not said,

הָאִשָּׁה הַגֹּרֶן: טו וַיֹּאמֶר הָבִי הַמִּטְפַּחַת
‹ the shawl ‹ Give ‹‹ And **15** ‹‹ to the ‹ did the
me he said, threshing woman
floor.

אֲשֶׁר־עָלַיִךְ וְאֶחֳזִי־בָהּ וַתֹּאחֶז בָּהּ
‹‹ it, ‹ She held ‹‹ it. ‹ and hold ‹ is upon you ‹ that

---

morning — early in the morning, so you can leave at the crack of dawn and not be discovered (*Iggeres Shmuel*).

14. וַתִּשְׁכַּב מַרְגְּלוֹתָיו עַד־הַבֹּקֶר — *So she lay at his feet until the morning.* [Some commentators see in the fact that מַרְגְּלוֹתָיו is spelled defectively, חָסֵר (it should be spelled מַרְגְּלוֹתָיו, with a *yud*), that she did not lie close to his feet. Instead, out of modesty, she moved away.]

בְּטֶרֶם יַכִּיר אִישׁ אֶת־רֵעֵהוּ — *Before one man could recognize his friend.* The word בְּטֶרֶם, *before,* is spelled here with a superfluous ו, *vav,* teaching that she spent six hours with him, the numerical equivalent of the letter ו, *vav* (*Midrash*); and we can further appreciate from this length of time the extent of their self-control (*Torah Temimah*).

וַיֹּאמֶר אַל־יִוָּדַע כִּי־בָאָה הָאִשָּׁה הַגֹּרֶן — *For [Boaz] said, "Let it not be known that come did the woman to the threshing floor."* The *Midrash* comments that he was addressing himself to God: All that night Boaz lay stretched out upon his face and prayed, "Lord of the Universe, it is revealed and known to You that I did not touch her; so may it be Your will that it not be known that the woman came *into* the threshing floor, that the name of Heaven be not profaned through me."

He wasn't concerned for his own reputation; he was known as a צַדִּיק, *a righteous man,* and he was old — he would not be accused of unbecoming conduct. It was Ruth's reputation he was concerned with; after all, *she* went out in the middle of the night! He therefore specified *that it not be known that the*

פרק ג
טז-יח

וַיָּ֣מׇד שֵׁשׁ־שְׂעֹרִים֮ וַיָּ֣שֶׁת עָלֶ֔יהָ וַיָּבֹ֖א

〉 then he 〈〈 on her; 〈 and set it 〈 [measures 〈 six 〈 and he mea-
went   of] barley,   sured out

הָעִ֑יר: טז וַתָּבוֹא֙ אֶל־חֲמוֹתָ֔הּ וַתֹּ֖אמֶר מִי־

〉 How 〈〈 who said, 〈 her mother- 〈 to 〈 She 16 〈〈 into
is it   in-law,   came   the city.

woman *came to the threshing floor*
(*Alshich*).

15. וַיָּמׇד שֵׁשׁ־שְׂעֹרִים — *And he mea-*
sured out six [measures of] barley
[lit., *and he measured six barleys*].
The exact measure is not stated. The
Talmud discusses this: What are
"*six barleys*"? Shall we translate it
literally [six grains of barley]? But
would [the magnanimous] Boaz give
only six grains? On the other hand,
if it means six *se'ahs* [the measure
usually used on the field and in the
threshing floor (*Rashi*)], a woman
cannot carry such a heavy weight!
Rather he symbolically alluded to
her [by giving her a token six barley grains] that six righteous men
— each possessing six outstanding
virtues — are destined to descend
from this marriage: David, the Messiah, Daniel, Hananiah, Mishael, and
Azariah (*Sanhedrin* 93a-b).

Rav Einhorn, in his Commentary
to the Midrash, points out that since
it says *measured* and later וַיָּשֶׁת עָלֶיהָ,
he set it on her, it must refer to a
quantity larger than six grains! He
resolves the apparent contradiction
by suggesting that first he gave her
the symbolic six grains, then he measured out a larger quantity which
she carried home.

The *Malbim* maintains that שֵׁשׁ
does not mean *six* in this verse but
that *shesh* was a standard measure,
one-sixth of a *se'ah*. Half a *shesh*
is considered enough for one meal
for one person. Thus, Boaz gave
her enough to provide a meal for
herself and Naomi. The implication
of this gesture was that by the time
that meal was finished she would be
"redeemed" and would not have to
worry about the next meal.

According to *Rav Alkabetz*, the
reason he gave her the barley [in addition to having given it as a gift for
Naomi, as Ruth states in verse 17]
was so that if anyone would see her
leaving the threshing floor early in
the morning, he would assume that
she was carrying home barley gleanings.

וַיָּבֹא הָעִיר — *Then he went into the*
city. Surely it should have stated that
she went into the city, yet it says,
he went into the city. This teaches
that he accompanied her lest she be
molested (*Midrash*).

16. וַתָּבוֹא אֶל־חֲמוֹתָהּ — *She came*
to her mother-in-law. [Imagine the
anxiety Naomi must have experienced through the night, waiting for
Ruth and wondering whether her
hazardous plan had succeeded.]

III
16-18

אַתְּ בִּתִּי וַתַּגֶּד־לָהּ אֵת כָּל־אֲשֶׁר

⟨ that ⟨ all ⟨ her ⟨ So she told ⟪ my daughter? ⟨ with you,

עָשָׂה־לָהּ הָאִישׁ: ‹יז› וַתֹּאמֶר שֵׁשׁ־הַשְּׂעֹרִים

⟨ of barley ⟨ The six ⟪ And 17⟪ the man had done
[measures] she said, for her.

הָאֵלֶּה נָתַן לִי כִּי אָמַר אֵלַי [אלי ק' ולא כ']

⟪ to me, ⟨ he said ⟨ for ⟪ me, ⟨ he ⟨ that
gave are these,

אַל־תָּבוֹאִי רֵיקָם אֶל־חֲמוֹתֵךְ: ‹יח› וַתֹּאמֶר

⟪ Then 18⟪ your mother- ⟨ to ⟨ empty- ⟨ go ⟨ 'Do not
she said, in-law.' handed

מִי־אַתְּ בִּתִּי — *How is it with you, my daughter?* [lit., *who are you, my daughter?*]. The translation follows the *Midrash*: Did she then not recognize her? Yes, but she meant: "Are you still unmarried or are you a married woman?" She answered, "Unmarried," *and she told her all that the man had done for her*. *Midrash Lekach Tov* offers the above commentary, and also suggests that perhaps it was still dark and Naomi did not recognize her.

אֵת כָּל־אֲשֶׁר עָשָׂה־לָהּ הָאִישׁ — *All that the man had done for her.* The question demanded more than a yes or no answer. Ruth went into elaborate detail so Naomi would know exactly where matters stood (*Alshich*).

17. [אלי] כִּי אָמַר — *For he said to me.* [The word אֵלַי, *to me*, is read, but it does not appear in the written Hebrew text. This is Halachah from Moses at Sinai (*Nedarim* 37b); see *Comm.* on 2:5.]

By omitting אֵלַי, *to me*, Ruth in-timated that Boaz, in his modesty, did not even look directly at her during their conversation (*Iggeres Shmuel*).

אַל־תָּבוֹאִי רֵיקָם אֶל־חֲמוֹתֵךְ — *Do not go empty-handed to your mother-in-law.* It is not recorded that Boaz actually told her this. However, the large amount of grain he had given her could not have been intended for Ruth alone, so Ruth stretched the truth a bit for the sake of שְׁלוֹם בַּיִת, *domestic tranquility*, and to flatter her lonely, widowed mother-in-law. Perhaps this is why אֵלַי is not writ-ten, because in actuality Boaz had not said it; she, in her wisdom, added it on her own (*Iggeres Shmuel*).

Ruth also wanted to impress upon her mother-in-law that the barley was intended for her, and not as a gift to Ruth for loose conduct on the threshing floor (*Rav Alkabetz*). Nor did she want Naomi to think that it was a farewell gift and that Boaz had forsaken them (*Ibn Shushan*).

פרק ד
א-ב

שְׁבִי בִתִּי עַד אֲשֶׁר תֵּדְעִין אֵיךְ
⟨ how ⟩ ⟨ you will know ⟩ ⟨ when ⟩ ⟨ until ⟩ ⟨ my daughter, ⟩ ⟨ Sit [and wait], ⟩

יִפֹּל דָּבָר כִּי לֹא יִשְׁקֹט הָאִישׁ כִּי־אִם־
⟨ rather ⟩ ⟨ but ⟩ the man will not rest ⟨ for ⟨⟨ the matter will be determined,

כִּלָּה הַדָּבָר הַיּֽוֹם: ד ₁ וּבֹעַז עָלָה הַשַּׁעַר
⟨⟨ to the [city] gate, ⟩ ⟨ went up ⟩ ⟨ Boaz ⟩ 1 [4] ⟨⟨ today. ⟩ ⟨ the matter ⟩ ⟨ he will settle

וַיֵּשֶׁב שָׁם וְהִנֵּה הַגֹּאֵל עֹבֵר אֲשֶׁר
⟨ the one of whom ⟨⟨ passed by, ⟩ ⟨ the redeemer ⟩ ⟨ Just then, ⟨⟨ there. ⟩ ⟨ and sat down

18. וַתֹּאמֶר שְׁבִי בִתִּי — *Then she said, "Sit [and wait], my daughter,"* be prepared (*Alshich*).

We can do nothing but wait. We have done ours, God will now do His (*Zos Nechemasi*).

אֵיךְ יִפֹּל דָּבָר — *How the matter will be determined.* If your destined husband is Boaz or Tov (*Zos Nechemasi*).

Since all decrees issue from Heaven (*Ibn Ezra*).

כִּי אִם־כִּלָּה הַדָּבָר הַיּוֹם — *But rather he will settle the matter today.* Rav Huna said in the name of Rav Shmuel bar Yitzchak: The yes of the righteous is yes, and their no, no (*Midrash*). [If Boaz said he will act on the matter, rest assured he will not delay.]

IV.

1. וּבֹעַז עָלָה הַשַּׁעַר — *Boaz went up to the [city] gate.* To fulfill his promise to Ruth [3:13] (*Zos Nechemasi*).

Boaz was the head of the Sanhedrin, and in that capacity he stationed himself there (*Iggeres Shmuel*).

[The gate, like the gates around the Old City of Jerusalem today, was a fairly large edifice. The Sanhedrin convened there, Torah was taught, and disputes settled.]

וַיֵּשֶׁב שָׁם — *And sat down there.*

Knowing that there was nothing more he could do, and confident that God would arrange something for him (*Iggeres Shmuel*).

וְהִנֵּה הַגֹּאֵל עֹבֵר — *Just then, the redeemer passed by.* The *Midrash*, noting the striking coincidence of the redeemer's passing by just at that very moment, asks: "Was he waiting behind the gate? Rav Shmuel bar Nachman answered: Had he been at the opposite end of the earth God would have caused him to fly, so to speak, to be there, in order to relieve

IV
1-2

דְּבֶר־בֹּעַז וַיֹּאמֶר סוּרָה שְׁבָה־פֹּה פְּלֹנִי

⟨ *Ploni* ⟨ *here,* ⟨ *sit down* ⟨ *Turn aside,* ⟨⟨ He said, ⟨⟨ Boaz had spoken.

אַלְמֹנִי וַיָּסַר וַיֵּשֵׁב: ²וַיִּקַּח עֲשָׂרָה

⟨ *ten* ⟨ He then ² took ⟨⟨ *and he sat down.* ⟨ *So he turned aside.* ⟨⟨ *Almoni.*

אֲנָשִׁים מִזִּקְנֵי הָעִיר וַיֹּאמֶר שְׁבוּ־פֹּה

⟨⟨ *here,* ⟨ *Sit* ⟨⟨ *and said,* ⟨ of the city, ⟨ of the elders ⟨ *men*

---

the righteous Boaz of the anxiety of waiting ....''

The *Midrash* continues: "Boaz played his part, Ruth played hers, Naomi played hers, whereupon the Holy One, Blessed is He, said: I, too, must play Mine.''

The word וְהִנֵּה, *just then*, suggests something unusual [see *Comm.* of *Malbim* on 2:4]. The redeemer did not usually pass by the gate. Divine Providence guided him that day אֲשֶׁר דִּבֶּר בֹּעַז, *of whom Boaz had spoken*, to enable the righteous Boaz to fulfill his promise to Ruth (*Malbim*).

סוּרָה שְׁבָה־פֹּה — *Turn aside, sit down here. Turn aside* from your planned destination and sit here (*Malbim*).

פְּלֹנִי אַלְמֹנִי — *Ploni Almoni.* [A pseudonym. Sometimes translated *So-and-so.* Compare *I Samuel* 21:3, and *II Kings* 6:8.]

His real name was withheld because he did not discharge his duty as redeemer. The meaning of *Ploni* is *hidden; Almoni, nameless.* Another interpretation: *Almoni,* mute and devoid of Torah. He should have known the law of *Moabite not Moabitess* but instead he asserted,

lest I imperil my own inheritance [verse 6] (*Rashi; Midrash*).

Rav Shmariah Halkriti explains the word אַלְמֹנִי as "fit for an אַלְמָנָה, *widow.''*

Boaz probably addressed him by his real name, Tov; it is Scripture that disguised his name to avoid his embarrassment (*Rav Alkabetz*).

According to *Ima Shel Malchus,* it was only proper that he was not called by his real name, Tov; he did not deserve to be called *Tov,* good, because he ignored his familial obligation.

וַיֵּשֵׁב — *And he sat.* Even though Ploni Almoni was Boaz's uncle [see *Comm.* 3:13 s.v. אִם יִגְאָלֵךְ], he did not take a seat until told to do so by Boaz, who was the head of the Sanhedrin.

He sat and waited, because Boaz did not tell him why he wanted him until the quorum of ten assembled (*Alshich*).

2. וַיִּקַּח עֲשָׂרָה אֲנָשִׁים מִזִּקְנֵי הָעִיר — *He then took ten men of the elders of the city.* Rav Elazar ben Rav Yose said: From here we learn that the blessing of the bridegroom [a wedding ceremony] requires a מִנְיָן,

פרק ד
ד-ג

וַיֵּשֵׁבוּ: וַיֹּאמֶר לַגֹּאֵל חֶלְקַת הַשָּׂדֶה
⟨ of the ⟨ The ⟪ to the ⟨ Then he 3 ⟪ and they
field portion redeemer, said sat down.

אֲשֶׁר לְאָחִינוּ לֶאֱלִימֶלֶךְ מָכְרָה נָעֳמִי
⟨ by ⟨ is being ⟨ Elimelech, ⟨ belonged to ⟨ which
Naomi, sold our brother,

---

quorum of ten. Rav Yuden ben
Pazzi said: Not only the marriage of
a bachelor to a maiden, but even the
marriage of a widower to a widow
[as Boaz and Ruth] requires a quorum of ten (*Midrash*).

According to others in the
Talmud, the presence of ten elders
was required to publicly confirm
the halachah permitting a *female*
Moabite into the community of
Israel. [This auspicious public gathering made the law clear to all, and
thus Boaz could marry Ruth the
Moabite] (*Kesubos* 7b).

According to the *Malbim*, Boaz
wanted to make sure he would not be
subject to accusations of partiality toward Ruth in promulgating the law
allowing her to enter the Assembly
of God. He therefore expounded the
law while the responsibility of redemption still lay upon *Ploni Almoni*.

שְׁבוּ־פֹה וַיֵּשֵׁבוּ — *''Sit here,'' and they
sat down*. Boaz was head of the
Sanhedrin, and though they were
older than he, they did not sit until
he asked them to because ''an inferior has no right to take a seat until
his superior grants him permission''
(*Midrash; Zos Nechemasi*).

He bid them to remain there and
be present for a wedding ceremony
which, regardless of who the re-

deemer turned out to be, was sure to
take place (*Malbim*).

3. חֶלְקַת הַשָּׂדֶה — *The portion of
the field*. Possibly, there was a large
field, a part of which belonged to
Elimelech (*Ibn Ezra*).

Perhaps the reason why it is referred to as חֶלְקַת הַשָּׂדֶה, *the portion
of the field*, is that the three brothers, Elimelech, Tov, and Salmon,
inherited a large field from their
father and divided it among themselves. Boaz inherited a portion of
land from his father, Salmon [see
2:3], Tov had his, and Naomi was
administering her late husband's
portion. Boaz had therefore advised
the kinsman that he should purchase
the piece adjacent to both their prop-
erties so that a non-relative should
not intrude on the family property
(*Iggeres Shmuel*).

לְאָחִינוּ לֶאֱלִימֶלֶךְ — *Belonged to our
brother, Elimelech*. [The *Talmud*
and *Midrash* note that Elimelech
was not Boaz's brother, but his uncle
— the brother of Boaz's father, Salmon — but he called him *brother* in a
general sense, as the *Midrash* puts it,
''because one does not refrain from
calling his uncle 'brother.' '']

מָכְרָה נָעֳמִי — *Is being sold by Naomi*.
[The literal translation of the Hebrew

IV
3-4

הַשָּׁבָה מִשְּׂדֵה מוֹאָב: ‏ד‏וַאֲנִ֤י אָמַ֔רְתִּי

⟨ have ⟨ Now I **4** ⟪ of Moab. ⟨ from ⟨ who has
resolved the fields returned

אֶגְלֶ֤ה אָזְנְךָ֙ לֵאמֹ֔ר קְנֵ֞ה נֶ֣גֶד הַיֹּֽשְׁבִים֒

⟨ of those ⟨ in the ⟨ 'Buy [the ⟪ saying: ⟨ to your ⟨ that I
sitting here presence portion] ears, should reveal
[the matter]

---

is *Naomi has sold*, but the context of the verse, according to most of the commentators, demands our translation, because Naomi had not in fact sold the field, as it appears from verse 5. Rather, מָכְרָה נָעֳמִי here means *Naomi was determined to sell*. The commentators discuss the halachic status of such a sale and suggest that in a classic sense "redemption" would imply that the field had *already* either been sold or was in the process of being sold to someone else, and it is the duty of the next of kin to "redeem" its sale. In the strict halachic sense, however, had the property already been sold to another, there would have to be a two-year waiting period between sale and redemption (which certainly was not the case here). Therefore, in the final analysis, most commentators (*Rashi, Ramban, Ibn Ezra, Alkabetz, Alshich*) agree that in this case, a prior sale had not taken place.]

הַשָּׁבָה מִשְּׂדֵה מוֹאָב — *Who has returned from the fields of Moab*. Destitute, hungry, and barefoot (*Iggeres Shmuel*).

4. וַאֲנִי אָמַרְתִּי — *Now I have resolved* [lit., *I said*]. Since I wanted to avoid having the field fall into the hands of strangers — and you precede me — I decided to give you the first option to act as redeemer (*Malbim*).

אֶגְלֶה אָזְנְךָ לֵאמֹר — *That I should reveal [the matter] to your ears, saying:* I personally, not *via an intermediary* (*Midrash Lekach Tov*).

קְנֵה נֶגֶד הַיֹּשְׁבִים ... — *Buy [the portion] in the presence of those sitting here* .... Note that here Boaz uses the word קְנֵה, *buy*, and later in the verse גְּאָל, *redeem*. There is a difference: *One who buys* looks for a bargain, and tries to purchase at the lowest possible price. A גְּאָל, *redeemer*, however, is more magnanimous; to keep his family estate intact he will graciously pay more. Boaz, therefore, said: "*In the presence of the elders,* etc., *I officially advise you to 'buy';* but, between ourselves, my advice is *'redeem it';* act more magnanimously, because if you won't, I will" (*Iggeres Shmuel*).

Boaz was apprehensive that before their departure to Moab, Machlon and Chilion might have sold their estates. He therefore insisted that this transaction take place *in the presence of those sitting here and in the presence of the elders of my people*, in public, to prevent the pos-

פרק ד
ה-ו

וְנֶגֶד זִקְנֵי עַמִּי אִם־תִּגְאַל גְּאָל וְאִם־
⟨ But if ⟨⟨ redeem. ⟨ you will ⟨ If ⟨⟨ of my ⟨ of the ⟨ and in the
redeem, people.' elders presence

לֹא יִגְאַל הַגִּידָה לִּי וְאֵדְעָה [ואדע כ']
⟨⟨ that I may ⟨ me, ⟨ tell ⟨⟨ will ⟨ no
know. redeem it, one

כִּי אֵין זוּלָתְךָ לִגְאוֹל וְאָנֹכִי אַחֲרֶיךָ
⟨⟨ after you. ⟨ and I am ⟨⟨ to redeem it, ⟨ other ⟨ there is ⟨ For
than you no one

וַיֹּאמֶר אָנֹכִי אֶגְאָל: ה וַיֹּאמֶר בֹּעַז בְּיוֹם־
⟨ On the ⟨⟨ Then 5 ⟨⟨ will ⟨ I ⟨⟨ And
day Boaz said, redeem. he said,

קְנוֹתְךָ הַשָּׂדֶה מִיַּד נָעֳמִי וּמֵאֵת רוּת
⟨ Ruth ⟨ and ⟨⟨ of ⟨ from the ⟨ the field ⟨ you buy
from Naomi, hand

sibility of an unknown purchaser arising later and laying claim to the field (Meishiv Nefesh).

אִם־תִּגְאַל גְּאָל — If you will redeem, redeem. Immediately, and without delay (Alshich) [as it is your primary right and obligation to do according to Leviticus 25:25].

וְאִם־לֹא יִגְאַל — But if no one will redeem it. [According to the Midrash, Boaz said this phrase directly to the elders.]

כִּי אֵין זוּלָתְךָ לִגְאוֹל — For there is no one other than you to redeem it. There is no one else from among our relatives (Rashi) — just the two of us (Alshich).

And according to the Torah, you, as the closest relative, are given the first option (Akeidas Yitzchak).

וַיֹּאמֶר אָנֹכִי אֶגְאָל — And he said, ''I

will redeem.'' He consented because he was aware only of his obligation to redeem Naomi's field. At that time, he knew nothing of Ruth (Malbim).

According to the Midrash, he assumed that he had no obligation vis-a-vis Ruth's portion of the estate (Yefe Anaf).

5. בְּיוֹם־קְנוֹתְךָ הַשָּׂדֶה מִיַּד נָעֳמִי — On the day you buy the field from the hand of Naomi. When Boaz heard the kinsman was accepting his obligation, he told him of the condition attached to the redemption: he must also, at the same time, marry Ruth (Midrash Lekach Tov).

''When you buy Naomi's field, don't think you thereby have fulfilled your obligation. Naomi owns only half the estate; [according to the Zohar Chadash (that Ruth converted when she married Machlon) — see

IV
5-6

הַמּוֹאֲבִיָּה אֵשֶׁת־הַמֵּת֙ קָנִ֔יתָ [קניתי כ׳]

‹‹ *you must also* ‹ *of the* ‹ *the wife* ‹ *the Moabite,*
buy [her field], *deceased,*

לְהָקִ֥ים שֵׁם־הַמֵּ֖ת עַל־נַחֲלָת֑וֹ וַיֹּ֨אמֶר

‹ *Said* **6** ‹‹ *his* ‹ *upon* ‹ *of the* ‹ *the* ‹ *to*
inheritance. *deceased* *name* *perpetuate*

הַגֹּאֵ֗ל לֹ֤א אוּכַל֙ לִגְאָל־לִ֔י [לגאול־לי כ׳]

‹‹ *for* ‹ *to* ‹ *Then I am* ‹‹ *the*
myself, *redeem [it]* *not able* *redeemer,*

Overview] the other half belongs to Ruth — and it is absolutely essential that when you redeem Naomi's portion you must also redeem Ruth's'' (*Pri Chaim*).

וּמֵאֵת רוּת הַמּוֹאֲבִיָּה אֵשֶׁת־הַמֵּת קָנִיתָ — *And from Ruth the Moabite, the wife of the deceased, you must also buy [her field].* [The translation of this obscure Hebrew phrase follows *Rashi*, who continues: ''and she is not willing [to sell] unless you marry her.'']

''And just as we cannot leave the redemption of the field to an outsider, so can we not allow a righteous woman like Ruth to be married to an outsider'' (*Zos Nechemasi*).

The *Iggeres Shmuel* notes that Boaz stressed מוֹאֲבִיָּה, *the Moabite* [even though female Moabites had already been officially permitted], and he also mentioned אֵשֶׁת־הַמֵּת, *wife of the deceased*, invoking the memory of the dead, in a further attempt to discourage the kinsman. Boaz hoped to keep the *mitzvah* of the redemption for himself.

[My father, Harav Aron Zlotowitz שליט״א [זצ״ל], pointed out that the *Shaarei Teshuvah* on *Orach Chaim*

484:1 quotes this *Iggeres Shmuel* to support a halachah: Although misleading someone is prohibited — in financial matters — however, in matters pertaining to the performance of a *mitzvah*, in a case where no one has *specifically* been appointed to perform that particular *mitzvah*, that *mitzvah* is considered open to all who wish to fulfill it. One should strive as much as possible, by whatever means, to perfect his soul and acquire that *mitzvah* for himself.]

The כְּתִיב, *k'siv*, traditional spelling, is קָנִיתִי, ''I'' *bought*, because Boaz prophetically foresaw that it was *he* who would ultimately consummate the transaction (*Torah Temimah*).

לְהָקִים שֵׁם־הַמֵּת עַל־נַחֲלָתוֹ — *To perpetuate the name of the deceased upon his inheritance.* Boaz made clear that the main purpose of this entire transaction was *to perpetuate the name of the deceased upon his inheritance*; acquisition of the field itself was secondary (*Vilna Gaon*).

6. לֹא אוּכַל לִגְאָל־לִי — ''*Then I am not able to redeem [it] for myself.*'' Machlon and Chilion died

פֶּן־אַשְׁחִית אֶת־נַחֲלָתִי גְּאַל־לְךָ אַתָּה

פרק ד

ז

‹‹— you —‹‹   for ‹ Redeem ‹‹   my [own]   ‹   I imperil   ‹ lest
yourself   inheritance.

only because they took them [Ruth and Orpah — Moabite women] as wives; shall *I* then go and take her?" (*Midrash*).

I cannot allow myself to take on a second wife and destroy the harmony of my home (*Targum*).

The *Iggeres Shmuel* stresses לֹא אוּכַל as meaning *I am not able* — "my merits are insufficient to effect a redemption of Machlon's soul; his sin was great and he needs זְכֻיּוֹת, *merits*, like yours, Boaz, to effect true redemption." The *Malbim* stressing לִי, *for myself*, translates: "I cannot redeem because it will not remain לִי, *in my name*, but rather in the name of the deceased, and *I will thus imperil my own inheritance.*"

פֶּן־אַשְׁחִית אֶת־נַחֲלָתִי — *Lest I imperil my [own] inheritance.* [The *Midrash* takes נַחֲלָה to mean *children* (comp. *Psalms* 127:3, נַחֲלַת ה' בָּנִים, *the heritage of HASHEM is children*).]

"Heaven forfend that I should take her; I will not contaminate my seed — even if I myself will not die for the sin [of marrying a Moabite woman], my children may suffer. I will not cause my children to become disqualified." But, the *Midrash* continues, he was unaware of the newly publicized law, *Moabite but not Moabitess* [see *Overview*].

The *Chidah* discusses this *Midrash* and asks the obvious question: If he was unaware, why didn't they tell it to him? Furthermore, they had just finished confirming it [see *Comm.* to 4:2]. Didn't he hear? Rather, he was unlearned in Torah and could not comprehend how the law could have been unknown for so long until it was just now repromulgated. He thought they were mistaken in their ruling; therefore he used the uncertain term פֶּן, *lest*. He was uncertain himself, and he refused to put his progeny in jeopardy, hence he "made himself unaware."

The *Bach* questions how the kinsman could have been so brazen as to disagree with a ruling of the Sanhedrin, an act which is rebellious and, under some circumstances, punishable by death! Also, if according to the kinsman the ruling permitting a female Moabite was improper, how dare he suggest that Boaz take her? Rather, he acknowledged the ruling as valid, but he considered himself insignificant to execute it, for were the ruling ever disputed [as it was when Doeg later attempted to disqualify David; see *Overview*], his seed would be disqualified, and he would have been of insufficient stature to combat the slur. Therefore he stressed לִי, *for myself*, I, a commoner, cannot take this awesome responsibility upon myself. He felt that such a precedent-setting act must be done by a great man, a leader and judge such as Boaz himself. גְּאַל־לְךָ, "*Redeem for yourself,*" he said to Boaz, "because as a man

IV
7

אֶת־גְּאֻלָּתִי כִּי לֹא־אוּכַל לִגְאָל: וְזֹאת

⟨ Now, 7 ⟩⟨ to ⟨ I am not able ⟨ for ⟩⟨ that which I
this was redeem. was to redeem,

לְפָנִים בְּיִשְׂרָאֵל עַל־הַגְּאוּלָה וְעַל־

⟨ and for ⟨ [cases of] ⟨ for ⟩⟨ [the practice] ⟨ of old
redemption in Israel,

הַתְּמוּרָה לְקַיֵּם כָּל־דָּבָר שָׁלַף אִישׁ

⟨ A man would ⟩⟨ matters: ⟨ all ⟨ to ⟩⟨ exchange
take off validate [transactions],

of great stature *your* deeds are less prone to be disputed."

According to *Rav Velvele Brisker* [pointed out to me by my friend Harav David Cohen], *Ploni Almoni* mistakenly thought that this law was *interpreted* by the Sanhedrin and, as such, open to possible later reinterpretation. He was not aware that it was a never-before-invoked tradition from Moses at Sinai, and hence uncontestable.

גְּאַל־לְךָ אַתָּה אֶת־גְּאֻלָּתִי — *Redeem for yourself — you — that which I was to redeem].* "Boaz, you are a man of merits; you accept the responsibility" (*Iggeres Shmuel*).

"You don't have a wife and children; you do it!" (*Alshich*).

"I feel a female Moabite is prohibited and I don't want to contaminate my seed thereby. If you permit it, *take over my right of redemption yourself,* because under the circumstances *I am not able to redeem*" (*Pri Chaim*).

The greater the selfishness of the egoist, the more generous the measure of altruism he allows to others (*Rav Breuer*).

7. וְזֹאת לְפָנִים בְּיִשְׂרָאֵל — *Now this was of old [the practice] in Israel* — in ancient times (*Ibn Ezra*).

The next verse goes on to tell us that Boaz removed his shoe to consummate the transaction. This verse introduces the custom, explaining that, although it is not Biblical in origin, it is nevertheless an ancient and well-founded one (*Iggeres Shmuel*).

Rav Alkabetz notes that this ancient form of acquisition, once very much in mode, fell into disuse for some time, and Boaz reinstituted it on that occasion. Therefore the author found it appropriate to explain the custom as being old, and וְזֹאת הַתְּעוּדָה בְּיִשְׂרָאֵל, *this was the attestation in Israel* having the strength of Torah-law: עֵדוּת, *testimony, ratification.*

עַל־הַגְּאוּלָה וְעַל־הַתְּמוּרָה — *For [cases of] redemption and for exchange [transactions]. Redemption* — sales; *exchange transactions* — חֲלִיפִין (*Rashi*).

[This verse parenthetically discusses קִנְיָן, the mode of *acquisition of property* which was in vogue at that time. According to halachah, whenever a transaction occurs, the

פֶּרֶק ד נַעֲלוֹ וְנָתַן לְרֵעֵהוּ וְזֹאת הַתְּעוּדָה
ח-י
‹ the attestation ‹ This was ‹‹ to his fellow. ‹ and give it ‹ his shoe,

בְּיִשְׂרָאֵל: וַיֹּאמֶר הַגֹּאֵל לְבֹעַז קְנֵה־
‹ Buy [it] ‹‹ to Boaz, ‹ [So when] the 8 ‹‹ in Israel.
redeemer said

transaction may be consummated —
even before money changes hands
— by a symbolic barter, an example
of which is חֲלִיפִין, *exchange*. In our
times it is called קִנְיָן סוּדָר, lit., *acquisition of a scarf*, during which a
garment is symbolically grasped by
both parties to the transaction.]

[According to the *Rambam*: "Real
estate ... may be acquired by symbolic barter. This act is called *kinyan*. The fundamental principle of
this mode of acquisition is that the
transferee should give the transferor
an article of some utility no matter
how small its value and say to him,
'Acquire this article in exchange for
the yard ... you sold me for so much
and so much.' If this is done, then
the moment the vendor lifts the article and takes possession of it, the
purchaser acquires title to the land
... though he has not paid its price.
Then neither party may renege.'']

שָׁלַף אִישׁ נַעֲלוֹ וְנָתַן לְרֵעֵהוּ — *A man
would take off his shoe and give it to
his fellow*. A shoe was used because it
was always convenient and available;
a shirt or other necessary garment
could not very well be removed leaving the purchaser bare! (*Ibn Ezra*).

The *Targum*, without further elucidation, translates נַעַל, *shoe*, as *glove*.
[It must be made clear that the
transference of a shoe described in

this verse is not to be confused with
the act of *chalitzah* (*Deut.* 29:9)
where a similar symbolic action takes
place. *Chalitzah* is applicable only in
the case of a sister-in-law, where the
brother of the deceased does not want
to perform יִבּוּם, *levirate marriage*.
This procedure "frees her to marry
whomsoever" she desires. Note, also,
that in reference to *chalitzah* (ibid.)
the Torah uses the word חָלַץ for
"removal" instead of its synonym
שָׁלַף used in this verse, suggesting a
different procedure.] Therefore, the
verse describes this procedure as one
accompanying *every* exchange and
sales transaction, so as not to confuse
it with *chalitzah* (*Meishiv Nefesh*).

וְזֹאת הַתְּעוּדָה בְּיִשְׂרָאֵל — *This was the
attestation in Israel*. תְּעוּדָה stems
from עֵדוּת, *testimony* (*Ibn Ezra*);
and the transference of the shoe,
once completed, was *testimony* hallowed by Biblical tradition, that the
transaction was complete and irrevocable (*Ralbag; Alshich*).

[The halachos stemming from this
verse are fully treated in *Choshen
Mishpat* 195.]

8. קְנֵה־לָךְ — *Buy [it] for yourself*. The
Bach observes that (in verse 6) the
kinsman renounced his right of redemption, but Boaz did not immediately respond. He was apprehensive

IV
8-10

לֶךְ וַיִּשְׁלֹף נַעֲלוֹ: ‹ וַיֹּאמֶר בֹּעַז לַזְּקֵנִים

‹ to the ‹ And Boaz said **9** « his ‹ he took « for
elders   shoe.   off   yourself,

וְכָל־הָעָם עֵדִים אַתֶּם הַיּוֹם כִּי קָנִיתִי

‹ I have ‹ that ‹ this day, ‹ you are ‹ Witnesses « the ‹ and all
bought   people,

אֶת־כָּל־אֲשֶׁר לֶאֱלִימֶלֶךְ וְאֵת כָּל־אֲשֶׁר

‹ that ‹ and all ‹ belonged to ‹ that ‹ all
Elimelech

לְכִלְיוֹן וּמַחְלוֹן מִיַּד נָעֳמִי: וְגַם אֶת־רוּת

‹ Ruth ‹ And **10** « of ‹ from the ‹ and ‹ belonged
also   Naomi. hand   Mahlon   to Chilion

---

that the kinsman would later regret it and lay claim to the redemption. Only after the kinsman, noting Boaz's silence, *specifically* said, *"Buy it for yourself"* — *before the elders and the entire community* — did Boaz formalize his acceptance by drawing off his shoe.

וַיִּשְׁלֹף נַעֲלוֹ — *He took off his shoe.* Whose shoe, Boaz's or the kinsman? It is more likely Boaz's shoe, for according to the established halachah, it is the purchaser who gives the pledge (*Bava Metzia* 47a; *Midrash*). The *Talmud* [*Bava Metzia* 47a] records a minority opinion that it was the kinsman who drew off his shoe and gave it to Boaz as if to say, "As I hand you the shoe, I hand over the rights of redemption" (*Ibn Ezra*).

9. וְכָל־הָעָם — *And all the people.* [Obviously, a crowd had assembled by this time, to witness the events.]

עֵדִים אַתֶּם הַיּוֹם — *Witnesses you are this day.* This phrase is repeated twice (in this and the next verse).

The *Malbim* explains that he summoned two groups of witnesses: one for the purchase of the land, and the other for the marriage of Ruth.

Boaz thus took every possible precaution to ensure the legality of the proceeding (*Nachlas Yosef*).

לְכִלְיוֹן וּמַחְלוֹן — *Chilion and Machlon.* Their names are recorded here in seemingly reverse order from the other places where they are mentioned. They are listed in this verse in the order of their death and the succession of their inheritance (*Vilna Gaon; Bach; Iggeres Shmuel*).

According to *Alshich*, Boaz mentioned Chilion first to stress that his property had also been redeemed so that no descendant of his widow Orpah would ever be able to dispute Boaz's absolute right of ownership. One must be concerned with the inferior members of the family. Hence he mentioned him first (*Zos Nechemasi*).

מִיַּד נָעֳמִי — *From the hand of*

פרק ד   הַמּוֹאֲבִיָּה אֵשֶׁת מַחְלוֹן קָנִיתִי לִי לְאִשָּׁה
יא
‹ as a   ‹ for   ‹ have I   ‹ of   ‹ the wife   ‹ the Moabite,
wife,   myself   acquired   Mahlon,

לְהָקִים שֵׁם־הַמֵּת עַל־נַחֲלָתוֹ וְלֹא־
‹ that   «   his   ‹ upon   ‹ of the   ‹ the   ‹ to
not   inheritance,   deceased   name   perpetuate

יִכָּרֵת שֵׁם־הַמֵּת מֵעִם אֶחָיו וּמִשַּׁעַר
‹ and from   ‹ his   ‹ from   ‹ of the   ‹ be the   ‹ cut off
the gate   brethren,   among   deceased   name

Naomi, with Naomi's consent (*Zos Nechemasi*).

These commentators point out that according to halachah, the estates of Machlon and Chilion would not have reverted to Naomi. What then is the significance of מִיַּד נָעֳמִי, *from the hand of Naomi?* Several explanations are given. According to the *Bach* it was given back to Naomi as a *gift*; the *Chida* suggests that it remained part of the marriage settlement in her care.

10. וְגַם אֶת־רוּת הַמֹּאֲבִיָּה ... קָנִיתִי לִי לְאִשָּׁה — *And also Ruth the Moabite ... have I acquired for myself as a wife.* The act of taking Ruth as his wife was separate from the redemption of the field. For this event he enlisted them as separate witnesses (*Malbim*).

[Boaz mentions the "acquisition" of Ruth with great delicacy. The acquisition of a wife and property are referred to with the same legalisms, but there the similarity ends. A Jewish wife is a respected and beloved partner in the sacred task of building a home. Therefore, Boaz mentions his marriage separately to

make it clear that he does not lump Ruth with his newly acquired land.]

He referred to her as הַמֹּאֲבִיָּה, *the Moabite,* to stress to the populace — who might not as yet have heard the ruling permitting female Moabites — that although she was a Moabite, she was nevertheless permitted to him (*Shaar Bas Rabim*).

אֵשֶׁת מַחְלוֹן — *The wife of Machlon.* She is still considered Machlon's "wife" because, as the *Zohar* states, her husband's "spirit" still stirred within her [see *Comm.* on 3:1] (*Malbim*).

לְהָקִים שֵׁם־הַמֵּת — *To perpetuate the name of the deceased.*

[Here again Boaz emphasizes the sincerity with which he embarked on this transaction. His purpose was not selfish, but to perpetuate Machlon's memory — not with *actual* levirate marriage, for that did not apply here, but symbolically.]

By his wife going about the inheritance doing her business, all who see her will say, "She was the wife of Machlon." His name is thereby perpetuated because of her (*Rashi*).

IV
11

מְקוֹמְוֹ עֵדִים אַתֶּם הַיּוֹם: יא וַיֹּאמְרוּ

‹ Then declared   **11** ≪ this day. ‹ you are ‹ Witnesses ≪ of his place.

כָּל־הָעָם אֲשֶׁר־בַּשַּׁעַר וְהַזְּקֵנִים עֵדִים

≪ [We are] witnesses! ≪ and the elders, ‹ at the gate, ‹ who were ‹ the people ‹ all

יִתֵּן יהוה אֶת־הָאִשָּׁה הַבָּאָה אֶל־בֵּיתֶךָ

‹ your house ‹ into ‹ who is coming ‹ the woman ‹ May HASHEM make

כְּרָחֵל ׀ וּכְלֵאָה אֲשֶׁר בָּנוּ שְׁתֵּיהֶם

≪ — both of them — ≪ built up ‹ who ≪ and like Leah, ‹ like Rachel

---

11. כָּל־הָעָם — *All the people.* [The blessing was a spontaneous response offered in unison by all present.]

They witnessed the proceedings and also blessed him in three ways: a. הָאִשָּׁה, *the woman* — despite the fact that she is of foreign stock and upbringing, by virtue of her *coming into your house*, the house of a righteous man like yourself, she will become *like Rachel and like Leah* — also foreigners, daughters of Laban the Aramean, who married Jacob and *built up the House of Israel.* So will Ruth, too, merit righteous and royal descendants. b. *Boaz* himself should *prosper* as *an Ephrathite* — his distinguished family name, bringing further glory to his family [see *Comm.* 1:2 s.v. אֶפְרָתִים] *and be famous in Bethlehem,* — may your own accomplishments bring such praise to Bethlehem that all will say, "The great man Boaz was born here!"; and c. [next verse] *your house* — the children you will have from this marriage, may they be considered as if they were the children of Machlon be-

cause you are taking Ruth in the spirit of levirate marriage (see *Overview*); nevertheless, just *as the house of Perez whom Tamar bore* [*Genesis* Ch. 38] was ascribed to *Judah,* so may your "house" be honored and distinguished *through the offspring which* HASHEM *will give you from this young woman* (*Malbim*).

כְּרָחֵל וּכְלֵאָה — *Like Rachel and like Leah.* Although those present were of the tribe of Judah, descendant of Leah, they agreed that Rachel was the mainstay of the house, and they mentioned Rachel first (*Rashi*).

The *Gishmei Berachah* suggests that the people compared Ruth to Rachel and Leah because they too came from non-righteous parents. Sarah and Rivkah were not mentioned because each of them had one evil son — Yishmael and Esav — whereas Rachel and Leah had only righteous children; also Ruth, like Rachel and Leah, deserted her parents' home to cling to God and a righteous husband.

פרק ד
יב-טו

אֶת־בֵּית יִשְׂרָאֵל וַעֲשֵׂה־חַיִל בְּאֶפְרָתָה
⟨ in Ephrath ⟨ May you prosper ⟨⟨ of Israel. ⟨ the House

וּקְרָא־שֵׁם בְּבֵית לָחֶם: יב וִיהִי בֵיתְךָ
⟨ And may 12 ⟨⟨ in Bethlehem. ⟨ and may your
your house be name be famous

כְבֵית פֶּרֶץ אֲשֶׁר־יָלְדָה תָמָר לִיהוּדָה
⟨⟨ to Judah, ⟨ Tamar bore ⟨ whom ⟨ of Perez ⟨ like the
house

מִן־הַזֶּרַע אֲשֶׁר יִתֵּן יהוה לְךָ מִן־
⟨ from ⟨ you ⟨ HASHEM will give ⟨ which ⟨ the ⟨ through
offspring

הַנַּעֲרָה הַזֹּאת: יג וַיִּקַּח בֹּעַז אֶת־רוּת
⟨ Ruth ⟨ And so Boaz took 13 ⟨⟨ this young woman.

וַתְּהִי־לוֹ לְאִשָּׁה וַיָּבֹא אֵלֶיהָ וַיִּתֵּן יהוה
⟨ HASHEM ⟨⟨ unto her. ⟨ and he ⟨ a wife; ⟨ to ⟨ and she
granted came him became

וּקְרָא שֵׁם בְּבֵית לָחֶם — *And may your
name be famous in Bethlehem.* The
Alshich offers: May she no longer
be called "Ruth the Moabite" but
"Ruth of Bethlehem."

12. וִיהִי בֵיתְךָ כְּבֵית פֶּרֶץ — *May your
house be like the house of Perez
whom Tamar bore to Judah.* By
evoking Tamar's memory, they
meant to allay any guilt Boaz might
have felt about the propriety of the
circumstances leading to his marriage to Ruth (*Gishmei Berachah*).

13. וַיִּקַּח בֹּעַז אֶת־רוּת וַתְּהִי־לוֹ לְאִשָּׁה
— *And so Boaz took Ruth and she
became to him a wife.* This was
not a true levirate marriage. Boaz
first *took* her as his wife, formally,
with קִידוּשִׁין, *sanctification,* and
only *then* וַיָּבֹא אֵלֶיהָ, *did he consummate the marriage* (*Malbim*). [See

Rambam: According to *Scriptural
Law,* there need be no marriage ceremony for levirate marriage, since she
is his wife already, married to him
by Heaven.] The verse makes it clear
that Boaz did not act in accordance
with the custom [see *Rambam*] of
יבּום, *levirate marriage.*

On that very night, Boaz died
(*Yalkut Shimoni*).

[With Ruth's marriage and the
birth of her child, her place in Jewish
history is secure. Ruth's name is no
longer mentioned in the *Megillah.*
The Sages maintain she enjoyed unusual longevity. She lived to see her
royal descendant Solomon on the
throne (*Bava Basra* 91b).]

וַיִּתֵּן ה' לָהּ הֵרָיוֹן — *HASHEM granted her
conception.* God, in His Providence,
allowed her to conceive immediately,

IV
12-15

לָהּ הֵרָיוֹן וַתֵּלֶד בֵּן: יד וַתֹּאמַרְנָה הַנָּשִׁים

> And the women said 14 《 a 〈 and 〈 conception, 〈 her son. she bore

אֶל־נָעֳמִי בָּרוּךְ יהוה אֲשֶׁר לֹא הִשְׁבִּית

> 〈 withheld 〈 has not 〈 Who 〈 HASHEM 〈 Blessed be 《 Naomi, 〈 to

לָךְ גֹּאֵל הַיּוֹם וְיִקָּרֵא שְׁמוֹ בְּיִשְׂרָאֵל:

> 《 in Israel. 〈 May his name be famous 《 today! 〈 a redeemer 〈 from you

טו וְהָיָה לָךְ לְמֵשִׁיב נֶפֶשׁ וּלְכַלְכֵּל

> 〈 and one who sustains 《 [your] soul, 〈 one who refreshes 〈 for you 〈 He will be 15

although with her first husband — who had been a young man — she never conceived (*Malbim*).

The numerical value of הֵרָיוֹן, *conception*, equals 271: the number of days which, according to the Sages [*Niddah* 38b], a pregnant woman carries (*Nachal Eshkol*).

וַתֵּלֶד בֵּן — *And she bore a son.* Rav Alkabetz comments that "unto him" is not mentioned because Boaz was already dead when the child was born.

14. אֲשֶׁר לֹא הִשְׁבִּית לָךְ גֹּאֵל — *Who has not withheld from you a redeemer.* The child will *redeem* you from dying childless as he carries the soul of your son Machlon. Also, since Boaz died on the night of his marriage, had the child not been conceived that very night, Naomi would truly have been cut off completely (*Alshich*).

הַיּוֹם — *Today.* This phrase is seemingly superfluous, and the *Midrash* interprets it as an additional blessing: Just as the day [the sun] holds dominion in the skies, so may your

seed produce one [the Messiah from the House of David] who will hold sway over Israel forever ....

Rav Chunya said: It was the result of the blessings of these women that the line of David was not cut off entirely in the days of Ataliah [see *II Kings* 11:1-4] (*Midrash*).

וְיִקָּרֵא שְׁמוֹ בְּיִשְׂרָאֵל — *May his name be famous in Israel* [lit., *may his name be called in Israel*]. He will be righteous, and people will name their children after him (*Iggeres Shmuel*).

Pri Chaim observes that had this child been born during Machlon's lifetime — before Ruth's conversion [according to those who maintain that Ruth' conversion took place after her husband's death (see *Overview*)] — the child would have been considered a non-Jew following the nationality of his mother; now, after Machlon's death and Ruth's conversion, *his name is called in Israel* — he is a full-fledged Jew.

15. וְהָיָה לָךְ לְמֵשִׁיב נֶפֶשׁ — *He will be for you one who refreshes [your]*

פרק ד
טז-יח

אֶת־שֵׁיבָתֵךְ כִּי כַלָּתֵךְ אֲשֶׁר־אֲהֵבָתֶךְ

‹ loves you, ‹ who ‹ your daughter- ‹ for ‹‹ your old age;
in-law,

יְלָדַ֫תּוּ אֲשֶׁר־הִיא֙ טוֹבָה לָ֔ךְ מִשִּׁבְעָ֖ה

‹ than seven ‹ to you ‹ is better ‹ she ‹ wherein ‹‹ has borne
him,

בָּנִ֑ים: טז וַתִּקַּ֨ח נָעֳמִ֤י אֶת־הַיֶּ֙לֶד֙ וַתְּשִׁתֵ֣הוּ

‹ and held it ‹ the child, ‹ Naomi took 16 ‹‹ sons.

בְחֵיקָ֔הּ וַתְּהִי־ל֖וֹ לְאֹמֶֽנֶת: יז וַתִּקְרֶ֩אנָה֩

‹ They called 17 ‹‹ a nurse. ‹ for ‹ and she ‹‹ in her
him was bosom,

ל֨וֹ הַשְּׁכֵנ֥וֹת שֵׁם֙ לֵאמֹ֔ר יֻלַּד־בֵּ֖ן לְנָעֳמִ֑י

‹‹ to ‹ A son has ‹‹ saying, ‹ a ‹‹ —the ‹‹ him
Naomi, been born name, neighborhood
women [did] —

soul, a comforter, after so many years of trials and suffering.

The *Malbim* explains that his birth, in a sense, "revived" the soul of her son Machlon.

וּלְכַלְכֵּל אֶת־שֵׁיבָתֵךְ — *And one who sustains your old age.* As a son of Ruth, who so selflessly sustained you in her youth, he will certainly sustain you in your old age (*Alshich*).

He will sustain you in your old age with delicacies (*Targum*).

אֲשֶׁר־הִיא טוֹבָה לָךְ מִשִּׁבְעָה בָּנִים — *Wherein she is better to you than seven sons.* The *Midrash* differs on whether this refers to the seven sons of Jesse (enumerated in *I Chronicles* 2:13) or to the seven generations listed in verses 18-21.

16. וַתְּהִי־לוֹ לְאֹמֶנֶת — *And she was for him a nurse.* The *Alshich* explains that Naomi was miraculously

enabled to nurse the child. It became manifestly clear to all that Machlon's memory had been perpetuated through the child and, in a spiritual sense, a *son has* truly *been born to Naomi.*

17. וַתִּקְרֶאנָה לוֹ הַשְּׁכֵנוֹת שֵׁם — *They called him — the neighborhood women [did] — a name.* Seeing the miracle God wrought for Naomi, allowing her to nurse the child, they realized that a continuity of Machlon's soul had been implanted in the child; it was truly Naomi's child (*Zos Nechemasi*).

יֻלַּד־בֵּן לְנָעֳמִי — *A son has been born to Naomi.* The *Talmud* remarks: Was it then Naomi who bore him? Surely it was Ruth who bore him! But Ruth bore and Naomi brought him up; hence he was called after Naomi's name (*Sanhedrin* 19b).

It was through her counsel that

IV
16-18

⟨ of ⟨ was the ⟨ he ⟪ Obed; ⟨ his ⟨ and they called
Jesse, father name

⟨ Perez ⟪ of ⟨ are the ⟨ Now **18** ⟪ of ⟨ the
Perez: generations these David. father

the marriage came about, and so it was proper that the child should be called after her (*Nachlas Yosef*).

The neighbors described the child as "a son born to Naomi," with reference to the legitimacy of the child, which some questioned, for he had been born from a Moabitess. That is to say, it is not the name of the Moabite mother which is called on this child, but the name of Naomi — a granddaughter of Nahshon son of Amminadab, a prince among his people. And Ruth had also become to Naomi like her own child from birth — how dare anyone slur this noble child! (*Sefer HaTodaah*).

וַתִּקְרֶאנָה שְׁמוֹ עוֹבֵד — *And they called his name Obed*, as a blessing that this child will *serve* [עוֹבֵד] God with a full heart (*Iggeres Shmuel*).

אֲבִי דָוִד — *The father of David*. According to *Iggeres Shmuel* this phrase refers back to Obed: it was not merely by the merit of Jesse that David was born; but, by the merit of Obed were both Jesse and David born. He was the *father of Jesse* and the *father of David*.

"This story was the cause of severe harassment to the house of David. 'How long,' said David to God, 'will they speak angrily and say: Is he

not of unworthy lineage? Is he not descended from Ruth the Moabite?' (*Ruth Rabbah* 8:1) ... A man-made story would have attributed the privilege of David's birth to an aristocratic Israelite mother, in accordance with the dignity of Boaz, the descendant of the illustrious Nahshon ben Amminadab. The gentile monarchs had their lineage traced to gods or celestial bodies (the sun or the stars), and this was taught to the people as a religious principle. But this is another monument to the truthfulness of the prophetic books, *wherein the voice of prophecy spoke without fear of man*. It was only because of the prestige of prophecy in Israel that this narrative was able to be told and was preserved" (*Behold A People*).

18. Having detailed David's descent from Ruth the Moabite, the author now traces his lineage to Judah (*Rashi*).

וְאֵלֶּה תּוֹלְדוֹת פָּרֶץ — *Now these are the generations of Perez* [the son of Judah]. Judah is avoided here; the listing of generations begins with Perez to avoid evoking the memory of the Judah-Tamar incident which is embarrassing to many (*Iggeres Shmuel; Meishiv Nefesh*).[See *Comm.* of *Gishmei Berachah* on verse 12.]

פֶּרֶק ד
יט-כב

הוֹלִיד אֶת־חֶצְרוֹן: יט וְחֶצְרוֹן הוֹלִיד
《 begot 〈 and Hezron 19 《 Hezron; 〈 begot

אֶת־רָם וְרָם הוֹלִיד אֶת־עַמִּינָדָב:
《 Amminadab; 〈 begot 〈 and Ram 《 Ram,

כ וְעַמִּינָדָב הוֹלִיד אֶת־נַחְשׁוֹן וְנַחְשׁוֹן
〈 and Nahshon 《 Nahshon, 〈 begot 〈 and Amminadab 20

הוֹלִיד אֶת־שַׂלְמָה: כא וְשַׂלְמוֹן הוֹלִיד
〈 begot 〈 and Salmon 21 《 Salmah; 〈 begot

אֶת־בֹּעַז וּבֹעַז הוֹלִיד אֶת־עוֹבֵד:
《 Obed; 〈 begot 〈 and Boaz 《 Boaz,

כב וְעוֹבֵד הוֹלִיד אֶת־יִשַׁי וְיִשַׁי הוֹלִיד
〈 begot 〈 and Jesse 《 Jesse, 〈 begot 〈 and Obed 22

אֶת־דָּוִד:
《 David.

חֶצְרוֹן — *Hezron.* [Mentioned in *Genesis* 46:12.]

19. וְחֶצְרוֹן הוֹלִיד אֶת־רָם — *And Hezron begot Ram.* The *Midrash* points out that Yerachmiel, not Ram, was the elder son. Having married a Canaanite woman (*I Chronicles* 11:26), Yerachmiel was unworthy to be an ancestor of the House of David.

[Ram is not mentioned in the Torah. In *I Chronicles* 2:9 he is identified as the second son of Hezron.]

עַמִּינָדָב — *Amminadab.* [One of the greatest personalities of the tribe of Judah during the slavery in Egypt. His daughter, Elisheva, was the wife of Aaron the *Kohen* (*Exodus* 6:23).]

20. נַחְשׁוֹן — *Nahshon.* [The leader of the tribe of Judah. The Sages credit him with being the first one to

plunge into the Red Sea. According to *Seder Olam Rabbah* he died in the second year in the Desert.]

שַׂלְמָה — *Salmah.* [Sometimes called *Salmon.* He was the brother of Elimelech and Tov.]

21. וּבֹעַז הוֹלִיד אֶת־עוֹבֵד — *And Boaz begot Obed,* who served [עָבַד, *avad*] the Master of the Universe with a perfect heart (*Targum*).

22. וְיִשַׁי הוֹלִיד אֶת־דָּוִד — *And Jesse begot David.* So said the Holy One, Blessed is He, to David: "What need have I to record the genealogy of Perez, Hezron, Ram, Amminadab, Nahshon, Salmon, Boaz, Obed, Jesse? Only on account of you; מָצָאתִי דָּוִד עַבְדִּי, *I have found David, My servant* [*Psalms* 89:21] (*Midrash*).

תם ונשלח שבח לאל בורא עולם

Bibliography / Biographical Sketches

Bibliography
of Authorities Cited in the Commentary

Italics are used to denote the name of a work. **Bold italics** within the biography indicate the specific book of that particular author cited in the commentary.

An asterisk (*) precedes the names of contemporary figures

Alkabetz, Rav Shlomo HaLevi

(b. 1505 Salonica; d. 1576 Safed)

One of the greatest Kabbalists and mystical poets of his day. Author of the *piyyut "L'chah Dodi"* recited every Friday evening. He was a contemporary and friend of Rav Yosef Karo, author of *Shulchan Aruch*.

His commentary on *Ruth*, **Shoresh Yishai**, published in 1561, is quoted by nearly every commentator on *Ruth* after him.

He is cited constantly in *Iggeres Shmuel*, who refers to him in various ways: "Rashba HaLevi"; "Rav Shlomo HaLevi"; "HaRav ibn Alkabetz HaLevi."

He wrote commentaries on most of the Bible, the Passover Hagaddah, on *Kabbalah*, and was a noted *paytan*.

In his *piyyut*, *"L'chah Dodi,"* he speaks of the sufferings of the Jewish people and their aspirations for Redemption. Probably no other *piyyut* has reached the popularity of *"L'chah Dodi"*; it is recited every Friday evening by all Jewish congregations throughout the world.

Alshich, Rav Moshe

[Also spelled Alshekh]

Rav, *Posek*, and Bible Commentator. Born in Adrionople in 1508; studied Torah there in yeshivah of Rav Yosef Karo. Settled in Safed where he spent most of his life and was ordained there by Rav Karo with the full *semichah* reintroduced by Rav Yaakov Berav. Among his pupils was Rav Chaim Vital, whom he ordained in 1590.

He died in Damascus, where he was traveling, before 1600.

He wrote commentaries on most of the Bible, and published a collection of 140 of his halachic Responsa.

His **Eynei Moshe** on *Ruth* was published in 1615.

Alter, Rav Yitzchak Meir

(1789-1866)

Gerrer Rebbe; founder of the Gerrer Chassidic dynasty. Rav Yitzchak Meir was a disciple of the Maggid of Koznitz, and later of Rav Simcha Bunem of Peshish'cha, and of Rav Menachem Mendel of Kotzk.

After the Kotzker's death in 1859, Rav Yitzchak Meir was acknowledged Rebbe by the majority of Kotzk chassidim. His influence was far reaching. Although his leadership lasted only seven years, he had a formative influence on the development of Chassidus in Poland. Gerrer Chassidus became a powerful element in Orthodox Polish Jewry.

He is most famous for *Chiddushei HaRim*, novellae on the Talmud and *Shulchan Aruch*, and was frequently referred to as "the Chiddushei HaRim," after the name of his work.

Alter, Rav Yehudah Aryeh Leib

(1847-1903)

Gerrer Rebbe; known by his work, *Sfas Emes*.

His father, Rav Avraham Mordechai, a great but chronically ill man, died when Yehudah Leib was only 12 years old. His upbringing fell to his grandfather, the illustrious Chiddushei HaRim. Yehudah Aryeh would study eighteen hours a day as a youth. It became widely known that a fitting successor was being groomed for the Chiddushei HaRim.

He was 19 years old when his grandfather died and, despite the pleas of the chassidim, insisted he was unworthy to become Gerrer Rebbe. Several years later, after the death of Rav Henach of

Alexandrow, he acceded to their wishes and molded Ger into the largest Chassidus in Poland.

A prodigious and diligent scholar, he nevertheless found time to counsel tens of thousands of disciples every year and to become an effective leader in Torah causes. His discourses were distinguished for profundity and originality.

Although he never wrote for publication, his writings were posthumously published as *Sfas Emes*, separate volumes of novellae on Talmud, and chassidic discourses on Torah and festivals.

Anaf Yosef

see *Rav Chanoch Zundel ben Yosef*

Arama, Rav Yitzchak ben Moshe

(1420-1494)

Spanish Rav, philosopher, and preacher. He was Rav of Calatayud where he wrote most of his works. After the expulsion of the Jews from Spain in 1492, he settled in Naples where he died.

He is best known for his book *Akeidas Yitzchak*, a collection of allegorical commentaries on the Torah. First published in 1522, it has been reprinted many times and has exercised great influence on Jewish thought.

Because of this work he is often referred to as the *Baal Akeidah* ["author of the *Akeidah*"].

He also wrote a *Commentary on the Five Megillos* which was printed together with his *Commentary to the Torah* in Salonica, 1573.

He wrote *Yad Avshalom*, a commentary on *Proverbs*, in memory of his son-in-law Avshalom, who died shortly after his marriage.

Ashkenazi, Rav Shmuel Jaffe

16th-century Rav in Constantinople.

Not being satisfied with any commentary to the *Midrash*, Rav Shmuel devoted himself to writing a comprehensive commentary to *Midrash Rabbah* and to the *Aggados* in the *Talmud*.

His first published work was *Yefe Mar'eh* on the *Aggados* in the Jerusa-

lem *Talmud* (1597); *Yefe To'ar* to *Midrash Rabbah: Genesis, Exodus, and Leviticus* (1606); *Yefe Anaf* to *Ruth, Esther,* and *Lamentations* (1691); and *Yefe Kol* to *Song of Songs* (1739).

His commentary to *Ecclesiastes* and his halachic writing are still in manuscript form.

Avodah Zarah

Talmudic tractate on *Seder Nezikin*.

Azulai, Rav Chaim Yosef David

Known by his Hebrew acronym CHIDA.

Born in Jerusalem in 1724; died in Leghorn in 1806.

Halachist, Kabbalist, and bibliographer-historian, he possessed great intellectual powers and many-faceted talents.

He went abroad as an emissary and he would send large sums of money back to Israel. He ended his mission in 1778 in Leghorn where he spent the rest of his life.

His fame as a halachist rests on his glosses to *Shulchan Aruch*, contained in his *Birkei Yosef,* a work constantly cited by later authorities.

He was the author of the famous bibliographic work *Shem HaGedolim*. Among his many works is the homiletical *Nachal Eshkol* on the *Five Megillos,* and *Simchas HaRegel* on *Ruth*.

Baal HaTurim

see *Rav Yaakov ben Asher*

Bach

see *Sirkes, Rav Yoel*

*Bachrach, Rav Yehoshua

Contemporary Bible scholar on Israeli scene.

Educated in Lithuanian Yeshivos, the first of which was the Yeshivah of Rav Shimon Shkop in Grodno.

He is senior lecturer in *Neviim Rishonim* at the Jerusalem College for Women (Michlalah). He published a monumental study of David and Saul; a book on Jonah and Elijah; and a commentary on *Esther.* His commentary on Ruth, *Ima*

Shel Malchus (*Mother of Royalty*), is a poetically profound synthesis of *p'shat* (plain meaning) and *d'rash* (homiletical interpretation).

Bamidbar Rabbah

The *Midrash Rabbah* to *Numbers*. See *Midrash Rabbah*.

Bava Basra

Talmudic tractate in *Seder Nezikin*.

Bava Kamma

Talmudic tractate in *Seder Nezikin*.

Behold a People

see **Miller, Rav Avigdor*

Besuras Eliyahu

see *Rav Eliyahu Shlomo Avraham Ha-Kohen*

Binyan Ariel

see *Rav Shaul ben Aryeh Leib of Amsterdam*

Breuer, Rav Raphael

(1881-1932)

Grandson of Rav S.R. Hirsch; son of Rav Shlomo Breuer; and late brother of Rav Joseph Breuer, shlita, of Washington Heights.

Rav Breuer was born in Papa, Hungary. He was district Rabbi at Aschaffenburg, Bavaria.

He published a commentary (in German) on many books of the Bible. His **Commentary on Ruth** was published as part of his commentary to the *Five Megillos* between the years 1908-1912.

Rav Chanoch Zundel Ben Yosef

(d. 1867)

Rav Chanoch lived in Bialystock, Poland, where he devoted his life to writing commentaries on the *Midrash* and the *Ein Yaakov.*

He published two commentaries which appear side by side in the large editions of the *Midrash Rabbah* and *Ein Yaakov*: *Eitz Yosef,* in which he strives to give the plain meaning of the text; and **Anaf Yosef** which is largely homiletical.

Rav Chanoch also published a commentary to *Pirkei Avos,* but his commentaries to *Yalkut Shimoni* and the *Mechilta* are still in manuscript.

Chasman, Rav Yehudah Leib

(1869-1935)

Born in Lithuania, he studied in Slobodka, Volozhin, and Kelm. He was strongly influenced by three of the *Mussar* giants of the era: Rav Simcha Zisel Ziev of Kelm; Rav Yitzchak Lazar of St. Petersburg — both of whom were among the foremost disciples of Rav Yisrael Salanter; and Rabbi Nosson Tzvi Finkel of Slobodka.

Rav Chasman held several positions as Rav and lecturer of Talmud. He found his place in Shtutzin, Lithuania, where, after assuming the rabbinate in 1909, he established a yeshivah that grew to 300 students. However, the destruction and dislocation brought about by World War I destroyed the Torah life of the city.

After the war, Rav Chasman was a vital activist in rebuilding Torah life in Europe.

The call to become "*Mashgiach*" (spiritual guide) of the Hebron Yeshivah in Eretz Yisrael gave him the opportunity to become a seminal figure in the development of the Torah Yishuv.

Ohr Yohel, published posthumously by his students, is a collection of his lectures and writings.

Chayes, Rav Zvi Hirsch

(1807-1856)

Born in the Galician region of Poland. Even at the age of 5 he was known as a prodigy, having mastered the entire *Tanach* by heart.

He was ordained at 21 by Rav Ephraim Zalman Margolios of Brody. Rav Chayes's most famous rabbinical position was in Kalisch. He wrote extensively and originally in addition to glosses on the Talmud and halachic responsa. Noteworthy was his *Mevo HaTalmud* (Introduction to the Talmud), printed in most editions of the Talmud; Responsa; *Imre Binah; Darkei Horaah.*

Among his most basic writings were a series of monographs called *Toras HaNevi'im*, in which he dealt with and clarified many obscure topics in the Torah and post-Biblical tradition.

Chida

see *Azulai, Rav Chaim Yosef David*

Chiddushei HaRim

see *Alter, Rav Yitzchak Meir*

Derech Hashem

see *Luzatto, Rav Moshe Chaim*

Dessler, Rav Eliyahu Eliezer

(1891-1954)

One of the outstanding personalities of the *Mussar* movement. He was born in Homel, Russia.

In 1929 he settled in London. He exercised a profound influence on the teaching of *Mussar*, not only because of the profundity of his ideas, but also on account of his personal, ethical conduct.

In 1941 he became director of the Kollel of Gateshead Yeshivah in London.

In 1947, at the invitation of Rav Yosef Kahaneman, he became *Mashgiach* of Ponovezh Yeshiva in Bnei Brak, Israel, and there remained until his death.

His teachings reflect a harmonious mixture of *Mussar*, *Kabbalah*, and Chassidus. Some of his ideas were published by his pupils in *Michtav Me'Eliyahu* (3 vols. 1955-64).

Dubno Maggid

see *Kranz, Rav Yaakov*

Eidels, Rav Shmuel Eliezer ben Yehudah HaLevi

(1555-1631)

Known as Maharsha — Moreinu HaRav Shmuel Eliezer — He is one of the foremost Talmud commentators, whose commentary is included in almost every edition of the Talmud.

Born in Cracow, he moved to Posen in his youth. In 1614 he became Rav of Lublin, and in 1625 of Ostrog, where he founded a large yeshivah.

Einhorn, Rav Zev Wolf

Rav in Vilna, end of 19th century.

Author of *Peirush Maharzu*, a comprehensive and well-detailed commentary to *Midrash Rabbah* appearing in the Romm edition.

Rav Elazar ben Yehudah of Worms

[Heb.: Elazar of Germizah.] Also known as *Baal HaRokeach*.

(1160-1237)

Scholar in the field of Halachah and *Kabbalah*, and *paytan* in medieval Germany. Student of Rav Yehudah HaChassid, the author of *Sefer Chassidim*.

Rav Elazar is known primarily for his authoritative halachic work *Sefer Rokeach*, which is quoted extensively in the *Shulchan Aruch*.

His students were many, among them Rav Yitzchak of Vienna, author of *Or Zarua*. Among his exegetical works are *Shaarei Binah*.

Rav Eliyahu Shlomo Avraham HaKohen

(d. 1729)

Born in Smyrna, he spent most of his life there as *Dayyan* and *Rav*.

His most famous works are *Shevet Mussar* on ethics and homiletics, and *Midrash Haltttamari*, a homiletical work on ethical subjects. Because of this work, he became known as "Rav Eliyahu Halttamari." He also wrote *Midrash Talpiyos*, novellae on various subjects arranged alphabetically; and *D'na Pashra* [abbreviation of *Peirush Shir HaShirim, Ruth, Esther*], a commentary on three Megillos: *Song of Songs, Ruth,* and *Esther*.

The commentary on *Ruth* is entitled *Besuras Eliyahu.*

Rav Eliyahu ben Shlomo Zalman of Vilna [Vilna Gaon]

Also known by his acronym HaGRA = HaGaon Rav Eliyahu.

(Born first day Passover 1720; died third day of Chol HaMoed Sukkos 1797.)

One of the greatest spiritual leaders of Jewry in modern times. A child prodigy and man of phenomenal genius, his knowledge of every facet of Torah learning was without equal. His glosses and commentaries encompassed nearly every one of the important classical writings.

The Gra also familiarized himself with astronomy, algebra, and geography in order to better understand certain Talmudic laws and discussions.

According to his sons, he did not sleep more than two hours a night, and never for more than half an hour at a time. He would often study with his feet in cold water to prevent himself from falling asleep.

More than 70 of his works and commentaries have been published. His *Commentary to Ruth* has been reprinted several times.

His influence was immense. According to the testimony of one of his contemporaries, "Without his knowledge, no important activity can be carried out."

Epstein, Rav Baruch HaLevi

(1860-1940)

Born in Bobruisk, Russia. He received his early education from his father, Rav Yechiel Michel Epstein, author of *Aruch HaShulchan*.

Rav Baruch later studied under his uncle, Rav Naftali Zvi Yehudah Berlin [the "Netziv"].

He was the author of several works, but he is best known for a brilliant commentary to Chumash, *Torah Temimah*, in which he quotes and explains the halachic and Aggadic passages on the various verses. He also wrote *Gishmei Berachah* on the *Five Megillos*.

Eshkol HaKofer

see *Saba, Rav Avraham ben Yaakov*

*Feinstein, Rav Moshe

Contemporary *Posek* and Rosh Yeshivah, Harav Feinstein is considered by many to be the *Gadol Hador* — Torah leader of the generation.

Born in Russia in 1895, Harav Feinstein was known as a child prodigy. He came to America in 1937 and became Dean of Mesivtha Tifereth Jerusalem on New York's Lower East Side. Harav Feinstein responds to halachic inquiries from around the world daily. Author of *Igros Moshe* — 5 volumes of his halachic responsa; and an ongoing series of *Dibros Moshe* — his novellae on Talmud.

Gans, Rav David

(1541-1615)

Chronicler and mathematician.

Rav David was a student of the Rama (Rav Moshe Isserles) and the Maharal of Prague (Rav Yehudah Loewe), where he mastered his Talmudic studies.

He spent most of his life in Prague where he wrote many works, most of which have been lost.

Encouraged by the Rama, Rav David published the historical work for which he is most famous: *Tzemach David*. The book is in two parts: one part deals with Jewish history; the other with general history.

This work has become a standard reference work for later chroniclers.

Gishmei Berachah

see *Epstein, Rav Baruch HaLevi*

Halkriti

see *Rav Shemariah ben Eliyahu Halkriti*

Heilprin, Rav Yechiel ben Shlomo

(1660-1746)

Lithuanian Rav, Kabbalist, and historian.

He was a descendant of Rashal (Rav Shlomo Luria), and traced his ancestry back through Rashi to the Tanna, Rav Yochanan HaSandlar.

He was Rav and Rosh Yeshivah at Minsk, where he studied *Kabbalah* and published several works.

He is most known for his *Seder HaDoros*, a history from Creation down to his own time.

He based his work on *Sefer HaYuch-sin* of Rav Avraham Zaccuto; *Shalshe-les HaKabbalah* of Rav Gedaliah ibn Yachya; and *Tzemach David* of Rav David Gans, as well as on an abundance of Talmudic and Midrashic references.

Hirsch, Rav Shamshon Raphael

(1808-1888)

The father of modern German Orthodoxy. He was a fiery leader, brilliant writer, and profound educator. His greatness as a Talmudic scholar was obscured by his other monumental accomplishments. After becoming chief Rabbi and member of Parliament in Bohemia and Moravia, he left to revitalize Torah Judaism in Frankfurt-am-Main which he transformed into a Torah bastion.

His best-known works are the classic six-volume *Commentary on Chumash* noted for its profound and brilliant philosophical approach to Biblical commentary; and *Horeb*, a philosophical analysis of the *mitzvos*.

Ibn Ezra, Rav Avraham

(Born 1089 in Toledo; died 1164)

Famous poet, philosopher, grammarian, astronomer, and — above all — Biblical commentator. He also wrote a *Commentary on the Megillos* — including *Ruth*.

In all his Bible commentaries he strived for the plain, literal meaning of the verse. His aim was to explain the etymology of difficult words within their grammatical context. Next to Rashi, his commentary on the Torah is most widely studied, and appears in almost all large editions of the Bible.

In France, he met Rav Yaakov Tam ["Rabbeinu Tam," grandson of Rashi], and a deep friendship between the two followed.

According to some, he married the daughter of Rav Yehudah HaLevi, and had five sons.

Legend has it that he once met the Rambam and dedicated a poem to him on the day of his death.

Ibn Shushan, Rav Yehudah

Rav in Magnesia, about 1500.

Member of illustrious Ibn Shushan Spanish family of Toledo, which can be traced back to the 12th century.

Little is known about Rav Yehudah. He is the author of a *Commentary on Ruth,* and is quoted extensively in many halachic works, and by *Iggeres Shmuel.*

Ibn Yachya, Rav Yosef

Bible commentator; member of the famous Ibn Yachya family of which many scholars were descendants.

He was born in Florence, Italy in 1494, his parents having fled to that country from Portugal.

He relates in his preface to his *Torah Or* that in her first month of pregnancy with him, his mother, under threat of being ravished, had thrown herself off a roof in Pisa, in order to preserve her modesty, and she was miraculously saved.

She then fled to Florence where he was born.

He published his *Commentary to the Five Megillos.* Two of his other works, *Derech Chaim* and *Ner Mitzvah,* were consigned to flames at the burning of the Talmud in Padua in 1554.

Rav Yosef had three sons, one of whom was Gedaliah, the author of *Shalsheles HaKabbalah.*

Rav Yosef died in 1534. Ten years after his death his remains were brought to Eretz Yisrael. Rav Yosef Caro arranged for his burial in Safed.

Iggeres Shmuel

see *Uzeda, Rav Shmuel de*

Ima Shel Malchus

see *Bachrach, Rav Yehoshua*

Josephus, Flavius

[Hebrew: Yosef ben Gorion HaKohen]

Jewish, Roman general and historian (born in 37 or 38; died after 100).

He boasted of belonging to the Hasmo-

nean dynasty on his mother's side. As a boy he was distinguished by his profound memory.

During the great Jewish war in 66, he was entrusted by the Sanhedrin with the defense of the Galilee.

Captured in the war and led before Vespasian, he prophesied that Vespasian would become Emperor (just as Rav Yochanan ben Zakkai had also done) — and Vespasian released him, rewarding him with a command in the Roman army.

He spent the rest of his life writing a history and "apology" of the Jews which is a classic, eyewitness account of the period. The accuracy, however, of the religious sections is questionable. He was generally despised as a traitor and turncoat by the Jews.

It is said that a statue of him was erected in Rome after his death.

Kimchi, Rav David

French grammarian; known by his acronym RADAK.

Born in Narbonne, 1160; died there in 1235. His father, Rav Yosef, also a grammarian, died when Rav David was a child, and he studied under his brother, Rav Moshe, who had also published several volumes on grammar.

Radak's commentary on Bible is profound, and is included in most large editions of the Bible.

Many have applied to him the saying from *Pirkei Avos:* "Without *kemach* ['flour,' i.e., 'Kimchi'], no Torah"; such was his great influence.

His main work was the **Michlol,** the second edition of which came to be known independently as the *Sefer HaShorashim.*

In his commentary, he stressed the *derech ha'peshat,* the plain sense, wherever possible, striving for clarity and readability, rather than for the compression and obscurity of some of his contemporary commentators.

His **Commentary to Ruth** was published in Paris, 1563.

Kitov, Rav Eliyahu

Israeli scholar and author; died 1976.

Famous for his *Ish uBeiso (The Jew and His Home)* and **Sefer HaTodaah** *(The Book of Our Heritage),* both of which have been translated into English by Rav Nathan Bulman; and his series of *Sefer HaParshiyos* on the Five Books of the Bible.

Kol Yaakov

see *Kranz, Rav Yaakov*

Kol Yehudah

Kabbalistic and philosophical commentary to **Ruth,** *Lamentations,* and *Esther,* by Rav Yehudah Leib ben Eliezer, published in 1727.

Rav Yaakov Kranz

(1741-1804)

Known as the "Dubno Maggid." Born near Vilna; Rav Yaakov demonstrated his skill as a preacher at an early age, and was barely 20 years old when he became *darshan* in his city. He later became *darshan* in several cities, but he achieved his fame as preacher in Dubno where he served for 18 years. He came into frequent contact with the Vilna Gaon, who, it is said, enjoyed his homiletical interpretations, stories, and parables.

The Dubno Maggid's works were printed posthumously by his son Yitzchak, and his pupil Baer Flahm. Among these works were: *Ohel Yaakov* on *Chumash;* **Kol Yaakov** on the *Five Megillos;* Commentary on the Passover Haggadah; and *Mishlei Yaakov,* a collection of his parables.

Rav Levi ben Gershom

(Acronym: RALBAG).

Born in Bangols, France in 1288; died 1344.

One of the most important Bible commentators of his time, he was also a mathematician, astronomer, philosopher, and physician.

He wrote commentaries to *Job, Song of Songs, Ecclesiastes; Ruth; Esther;* the

Five Books of the Torah; Early Prophets; *Proverbs; Daniel; Nechemiah;* and *Proverbs.*

His commentary to *Job* was one of the first books printed in Hebrew (Ferrara, 1477).

Lipowitz, Rav Yosef

Noted Israeli Bible scholar and lecturer of the last generation.

Rav Lipowitz was one of the outstanding pupils of Rav Nosson Finkel *(der Alter)* of Slobodka.

He published several works on the Bible, among them the very philosophical *Nachalas Yosef,* his commentary on *Ruth.* Written in poetic Hebrew, the author appears to be lecturing, as it were, weaving the various *Midrashim* and philosophical *hashkafos* [perspective] into a flowing, lucid commentary.

Luria, Rav David

(1798-1855; known as RADAL)

Lithuanian Rav and *Posek.* Student of Rav Shaul Katzenellenbogen of Vilna.

After the death of his mentor, the Vilna Gaon, Radal was considered one of the Torah leaders of his generation. His scholarly writings embrace almost all of Torah literature. Among his works is his commentary to the *Midrash,* **Chiddushei Radal,** printed in the Romm edition of the *Midrash Rabbah.*

Luzatto, Rav Moshe Chaim

(1707-1746)

Kabbalist, author of *Mussar* ethical works, and poet.

Born in Padua, Italy, Rav Moshe Chaim was regarded as a genius from childhood, having mastered *Tanach, Midrash,* and Talmud at an early age. He later went on to delve into Kabbalistic and ethical studies.

He is most famous for his profound ethical treatise, *Mesilas Yesharim (The Path of the Upright),* which has, alongside the *Chovos HaLevavos* of Rav Bachya ibn Paquda, become the standard ethical-*Mussar* work.

Among his Kabbalistic works were: *Razin Genizin,* **Megillas Sesarim;** *Maamar HaGeulah;* **Derech Hashem.**

In 1743, he immigrated to Eretz Yisrael. He lived a short time in Acre, and died there, with his family, in a plague.

Maharal

see *Rav Yehudah Loewe ben Bezalel*

Maharsha

see *Eidels, Rav Shmuel Eliezer ben Yehudah HaLevi*

Malbim, Rav Meir Leibush

(1809-1879)

Rav, preacher, and Biblical commentator.

The name Malbim is an acronym of "Meir Leibush ben Yechiel Michel."

The Malbim was also known as the *"ilui* (prodigy) from Volhynia": He was Rav in several cities, but he suffered much persecution on account of his uncompromising stand against Reform, leading to his short-term imprisonment on a false accusation. He wandered much of his life, serving as Rav in various cities for several years at a time.

His fame and immense popularity rest upon his commentary to the Bible which was widely esteemed. His first published commentary was on *Megillas Esther* (1845). His commentary to the remaining books of the Bible were published between then and 1876. His commentary to *Ruth* is entitled **Geza Yishai.**

Margolios, Rav Chaim Mordechai

Polish Rav and *Posek;* died in 1818.

Rav Chaim was Rav in Great Dubno, where he operated a printing office.

Together with his brother Rav Ephraim [author of *Bais Ephraim* and *Mattei Ephraim*], he published **Shaarei Teshuvah,** a digest of the Responsa literature dealing with the laws of the *Shulchan Aruch Orach Chaim,* from the time of Rav Yosef Karo until his day.

This work was continued on the three remaining sections of *Shulchan Aruch*

by Rav Tzvi Hirsch Eisenstadt and published under the name *Pis'chei Teshuvah.*

Mashal Umelitzah

Collection of homiletic interpretations on the Torah by Rav Avraham Naftali Galanti. Published in New York City during the last generation.

Matanos Kehunah

see *Rav Yissachar Berman HaKohen*

Megillas Sesarim

see *Luzatto, Rav Moshe Chaim*

Meishiv Nefesh

see *Sirkes, Rav Yoel*

Michlol

see *Kimchi, Rav David*

Michtav Me'Eliyahu

see *Dessler, Rav Eliyahu Eliezer*

Midrash

see *Midrash Rabbah*

Midrash HaNe'elam

see *Zohar Chadash*

Midrash Lekach Tov

Early *Midrash* on various Books of the Bible. This *Midrash* has been published at separate times on the various books of the Bible as the manuscripts have been discovered. *Ruth* was published in 1867.

Midrash Rabbah

[Lit., "The Great Midrash."]

The oldest Amoraic classical *Midrash* on the Five Books of the Bible and the *Megillos.*

[Note: Throughout the commentary of this Book, whenever *"Midrash"* alone is shown as the source, the reference is to *Midrash Ruth Rabbah.*]

Midrash Tanchuma

The ancient *Midrash* on the Torah which has come down to us in two versions.

One of the versions is the oldest collections of *Midrashim* known.

Midrash Zuta

Also called *Ruth Zuta* ("Minor Ruth"). This *Midrash* was probably compiled before the 10th century. It is quoted by the author of *Midrash Lekach Tov* which was written in the 11th century.

It was published by Buber from a Parma manuscript in 1894.

*Miller, Rav Avigdor

Contemporary Rav, noted lecturer and author. A major force on the American Orthodox scene. Rav in Brooklyn, New York. Author of *Rejoice O Youth!; Sing You Righteous; **Torah Nation; Behold a People.***

Minchas Shai

see *Rav Yedidiah Shlomo of Norzi*

M'lo HaOmer

see *Zuenz, Rav Aryeh Leib*

Rav Moshe ben Maimon

(1135-1204)

Known by his acronym, RAMBAM; Maimonides.

One of the most illustrious figures in Judaism in the post-Talmudic era, and among the greatest of all time. He was a rabbinic authority, codifier, philosopher, and royal physician. According to some, he was a descendant of Rav Yehudah HaNasi.

Born in Cordoba; moved to Eretz Yisrael and then to Fostat, the old city of Cairo, Egypt.

At the age of 23 he began his commentary on the *Mishnah,* which he authored all through his wanderings. His main work was ***Mishneh-Torah Yad HaChazakah,*** his codification of the spectrum of Halachah until his day. This was the only book he wrote in Hebrew, all his other works having been written in Arabic, a fact he regretted later in life.

He is also known for his *Moreh Nevuchim (Guide for the Perplexed),* and for his many works in the field of medicine, hygiene, astronomy, etc.

Truly it may be said, "from Moshe to Moshe there arose none like Moshe."

Rav Moshe ben Nachman

(1194-1270)

Known by his acronym, RAMBAN; Nachmanides.

One of the leading Torah scholars and authors of Talmudic literature during the generation following Rambam; also a renowned philosopher, Biblical commentator, poet, and physician.

Born in Gerona, to a famous rabbinic family. He is sometimes referred to, after his native town, as Rabbenu Moshe Gerondi, where he spent most of his life, supporting himself as a physician. He exercised extensive influence over Jewish life. Even King James I consulted him on occasion.

Already at the age of 16 he had published works on Talmud and Halachah.

Among his works were: *Milchemes Hashem*, in defense of the Rif against the *"hasagos"* of Rav Zerachiah HaLevi in his *Sefer HaMaor; Sefer HaZechus,* in response to the *"hasagos"* of the Ravad on the Rif; *Sefer HaMitzvos; Iggeres HaRamban; Iggeres HaKodesh;* and his profound and encyclopedic **Commentary on the Torah**, which is printed in all large editions of the Bible.

In 1263 he was coerced by King James I into holding a public disputation with the apostate Pablo Christiani which led to a victory for the Ramban, but which aroused the anger of the Church and resulted in his barely succeeding to escape from Spain. He then immigrated to Eretz Yisrael. In 1268 he became Rav in Acco, successor to Rav Yechiel of Paris.

He died in 1270; his burial site has not been definitely ascertained.

Nachalas Yosef

see *Lipowitz, Rav Yosef*

Nachal Eshkol

see *Azulai, Rav Chaim Yosef David*

Niddah

Talmudic tractate in *Seder Nashim*

Ohr Yohel

See *Chasman, Rav Yehudah Leib*

Pirkei Avos

"Chapters" or *"Ethics"* of the Fathers. A Talmudic tractate in *Seder Nezikin*. Read in the synagogue on Shabbos afternoons from Passover to Rosh Hashanah.

Pirkei d'Rabbi Eliezer

Ancient aggadic work attributed to the first-century *Tanna,* Rabbi Eliezer ben Hyrcanos.

Pri Chaim

Commentary to the Five *Megillos* by Rav Chaim Knoller, published in Peremyshlan, Poland c. 1903.

The **Commentary on Ruth** is based on the approach of the *Malbim* whom the author quotes extensively and upon whom he elaborates in a most original manner.

Also by the same author is *Kavod Chachamim* in which he explains what may seem to be discrepancies between the *aggados* of the Talmud and quoted verses in the Bible, as well as Masoretic differences.

Pri Tzaddik

See next entry.

Rabinowitz, Rav Tzadok HaKohen

(1823-1900)

Born in Kreisburg, Latvia, young Tzadok attracted attention as a phenomenal genius. Orphaned at the age of 6, he was raised by his uncle near Bialystock. Such was the child's reputation, that Rav Yitzchak Elchanan Spektor of Kovno made a point of testing him when he happened to be nearby. He prophesied that "the boy will light a great torch of knowledge in Israel."

In later years, Rav Tzadok lived in Lublin where he became acquainted with Rav Leibele Eiger, a disciple of Rav Mordechai Yosef of Izbica. Rav Tzadok became their disciple, and, with their

passing, became Rebbe of the Chassidim of Izbica. He became known far and wide as the "Kohen of Lublin." The breadth and depth of his thought were astonishing. Many considered him the greatest Torah scholar in all of Poland.

Pri Tzaddik is a collection of his discourses on the weekly portion and festivals. He was a very prolific writer. Although much of his works have been published, he left many unpublished manuscripts that were destroyed during World War II.

Among his other works are Responsa *Tiferes Zvi, Meishiv Tzaddik,* and *Resisei Layla.*

Radak

see *Kimchi, Rav David*

Ralbag

see *Rav Levi ben Gershom*

Rambam

see *Rav Moshe ben Maimon*

Ramban

see *Rav Moshe ben Nachman*

Rashba HaLevi

see *Alkabetz, Rav Shlomo HaLevi*

Rashi

see *Rav Shlomo ben Yitzchak*

Saba, Rav Avraham ben Yaakov

15-16th-century Kabbalist, Bible commentator, and *Darshan.* Rav Avraham was among those expelled from Spain in 1492. He moved to Portugal where he wrote his commentary *Eshkol HaKofer* to the *Chumash,* the *Five Megillos,* and *Pirkei Avos.*

In his youth, many of his works were lost, and he was forced to rewrite them later in life from memory.

His commentary to the *Chumash* was entitled *Tzror HaMor.*

According to the *Shem HaGedolim,* he died on board a ship on Erev Yom Kippur 1508.

Sanhedrin

Talmudic tractate in *Seder Nezikin.*

Seder HaDoros:

see *Heilprin, Rav Yechiel ben Shlomo*

Seder Olam

Early Midrashic-chronological work. *Seder Olam* is mentioned in the Talmud (*Shabbos* 88a; *Yevamos* 82b et al.) and is ascribed to the *Tanna* Rav Yose ben Chalafta.

Sefer HaTodaah

see *Kitov, Rav Eliyahu*

Sfas Emes

see *Alter, Rav Yehudah Aryeh Leib*

Shaar Bas Rabim

Scholarly and erudite anthology of commentaries on the Torah and *Megillos* by Rav Chaim Aryeh Leib Yedvavnah; late-19th century.

Shaarei Binah

see *Rav Elazar ben Yehudah of Worms*

Shaarei Teshuvah

see *Margolios, Rav Chaim Mordechai*

Shabbos

Talmudic tractate in *Seder Moed.*

Rav Shaul ben Aryeh Leib of Amsterdam

Born 1717 in Risha; died in Amsterdam, 1790.

Member of famous rabbinical family. Served as Rav in many important cities, and upon the death of his father he replaced him as Rav of the prestigious Ashkenazi community of Amsterdam, where he served until his death.

He published many works on Bible, Talmud, and Halachah, most famous of which was *Binyan Ariel.*

When the Chida visited Amsterdam, he stayed at the home of Rav Shaul and was so awed by his erudition and righteousness, that he praised him most flourishingly in his *Shem HaGedolim.*

Shem HaGedolim

see *Azulai, Rav Chaim Yosef David*

Rav Shemariah ben Eliyahu Halkriti

(1275-1355)

Italian Bible commentator and philosopher. When he was a child, his family moved to Crete where his father was appointed Rabbi; hence his surname "Halkriti" ["the Cretan"] or, as he is also known, "HaYevani" ["the Greek"].

Until the age of 30 he studied Bible almost exclusively; then he immersed himself in *Talmud* and philosophy. His reputation as a Bible scholar was so great that he was invited to the court of King Robert of Naples, a patron of Jewish learning, where he devoted himself to his studies, and published *Philosophical Commentaries* on the Bible, of which his commentary to *Song of Songs* is still extant.

He is quoted extensively by the early commentators, among them: *Rav Alkabetz, Alshich,* and *Iggeres Shmuel.*

Among his other works were *Elef Ha-Magen,* a commentary on the *Aggadah* in tractate *Megillah;* and *Piyyutim.*

He tried to reconcile the Rabbanites and Karaites, and because of this certain zealots leveled accusations against him, and he died in prison.

Rav Shlomo ben Yitzchok

(RASHI)

Leading commentator on the Bible and Talmud.

He was born in Troyes, France in 1040 — the year in which Rabbeinu Gershom Meor HaGolah died. According to tradition, Rashi's ancestry goes back to Rav Yochanan HaSandlar and to King David.

The summit of Rashi's commentaries was his commentary on the Talmud — an encyclopedic and brilliant undertaking. Nothing can be compared to the impact this commentary has had upon all who study the Talmud. Rashi's commentary has opened to all what otherwise would have been a sealed book. Without his commentary, no one would

dare navigate the "Sea of Talmud." Every word is precise and laden with inner meaning. Rashi's corrections of the Talmud text were, for the most part, introduced into the standard editions and became the accepted text.

Rashi's *Commentary to the Bible,* too, made a similar impact — and virtually every printed Bible contains his commentary which is distinguished by its conciseness and clarity.

Many halachic works from the "School of Rashi" have come down to us: *Sefer HaOrah; Sefer HaPardes; Machzor Vitry; Siddur Rashi;* and Responsa.

Rashi died on Tammuz 29, 1105. His burial place is not known.

Shoresh Yishai

see *Alkabetz, Rav Shlomo HaLevi*

Sirkes, Rav Yoel

Known as BACH from his work *Bayis Chadash.*

Polish Rav, *Posek,* and Commentator.

Born in Lublin in 1561.

Student of Rav Shlomo, Rav of the City, he then studied in the Yeshivah of Brisk under Rav Meshullam Feivish (later Rav of Cracow), and Rav Zvi Hirsh Shur, a student of the Rama.

Rav Sirkes was Rabbi in many cities, among them Lublin, Brisk, and Cracow.

His most famous works are *Bayis Chadash* (BACH) on the *Tur, Hagahos Ha-Bach* on the *Talmud,* and his Responsa.

He published an analytical commentary of *Ruth* entitled **Meishiv Nefesh** along with his supercommentary on *Rashi, Be'er Mayim.*

In his old age he wanted to immigrate to Eretz Yisrael, but he never did. He died in Cracow at the age of 79 in 1640.

Soloveichik, Rav Yitzchak Zev HaLevi

(1889-1960)

Known as Rav Velvele Brisker.

Son of Rav Chaim Brisker, Rav Velvele was regarded by many to be the supreme *Talmudic* authority of his day.

Born in Volozhin, he was the student of his father Rav Chaim, who was his only teacher.

His erudition and acumen were evident in his early youth, and upon the death of his father, he succeeded him as Rav in Brisk where he became a central figure in the Torah world. During World War II his wife and four of his children were murdered in Brisk; he fled to Vilna with his surviving five sons and two daughters, and managed to flee from there to Eretz Yisrael.

He settled in Jerusalem, where he founded a kollel for a group of select young men. Later a yeshivah was founded which was administered by his son, Rav Yosef Dov.

He confined himself to his studies, and was considered the spiritual heir of the Chazon Ish (Rav Yeshaya Karelitz).

He exercised a great influence over extensive circles in the Torah world.

Sotah

Talmudic tractate in *Seder Nashim*.

Tanchuma

see *Midrash Tanchuma*

Targum

The ancient, authoritative translation of the Bible into Aramaic.

Torah Nation

see *Miller, Rav Avigdor*

Torah Temimah

see *Epstein, Rav Baruch HaLevi*

Tzemach David

see *Gans, Rav David*

Uzeda, Rav Shmuel de

Born in Safed c. 1540.

He studied Kabbalah with Rav Yitzchak Luria [ARI zal] and Rav Chaim Vital.

In 1557 he traveled to Constantinople where he published his commentary, an encyclopedic supercommentary on

Ruth, *Iggeres Shmuel,* which has been reprinted many times and appears in large editions of the Bible.

His most famous work is *Midrash Shmuel,* a detailed commentary on *Pirkei Avos* with reference to many connecting sources such as Rabbeinu Yonah of Gerondi, Meiri, Rav Yosef Ibn Shushan, and Rashbam, which were at that time in manuscript, but have since been printed.

Rav Velvele Brisker

see *Soloveichik, Rav Yitzchak Zev Ha-Levi*

Vilna Gaon

see *Rav Eliyahu ben Shlomo Zalman of Vilna*

Rav Yaakov ben Asher

(1270-1340)

Posek and codifier.

Son of Rav Asher ben Yechiel (the Rosh), under whom he studied. He was born in Germany, and in 1303 he accompanied his father to Toledo, where he lived in great poverty, and devoted his life to Torah.

Rav Yaakov's enduring fame rests on his encyclopedic halachic codification *Arbaah Turim,* which is the forerunner of our *Shulchan Aruch* today, and as a result of which he is referred to as the "Baal HaTurim."

The arrangement and wealth of content made it a basic work in halachah and it was disseminated greatly through the Jewish world. It became so widely accepted, that when Rav Yosef Karo wrote his major work, *Bais Yosef,* he decided to "base it upon the *Turim* because it contains most of its views of the *Poskim.*"

Rav Yaakov also wrote a comprehensive commentary on the *Chumash* anthologizing the literal explanations (*p'shat*) by earlier Bible commentators. To the beginning of each section he added "as a little appetizer, *gematrios* and explanations of the *Masorah,* in order to attract the mind." Ironically the

whole work was printed only twice. It was just these "appetizers" that were popularly published alongside most editions of the Bible under the title **Baal HaTurim.**

Among Rav Yaakov's students was Rav David Abudraham.

According to *Shem HaGedolim* Rav Yaakov died en route to Eretz Yisrael.

Yalkut Shimoni

The best-known and most comprehensive Midrashic anthology covering the entire Bible.

It is attributed to Rav Shimon HaDarshan of Frankfurt who lived in the 13th century.

The author collected *Midrashim* from more than 50 works, arranging them into more than 10,000 statements of *Aggadah Halachah* according to the verses of the Bible.

Yavetz, Rav Yitzchak ben Shlomo

Turkish Bible commentator in the second half of the sixteenth century. He published commentaries on *Pirkei Avos* and most of the Bible.

His commentary on *Ruth* is called *Tzemach Tzaddik*. He is quoted extensively by *Iggeres Shmuel.*

Rav Yedidiah Shlomo of Norzi

Rav and Commentator.

Born in Mantua 1560; died in 1626. Became Rav in Mantua in 1585.

Rav Yedidiah consecrated the greater part of his life to studying the *Masorah* of the Bible — and by studying every previously printed *Masorah* text, comparing the various readings scattered through Talmudic and Midrashic literature, as well as in published and unpublished manuscripts.

The resulting work was entitled *Poretz Geder* but was published under the name *Minchas Shai.*

This work, which was as perfect as thorough learning and conscientious industry could make it, has become the most accepted work in establishing the Masorah. The *Minchas Shai* is printed in the back of all large Bibles.

Yefe Anaf

see *Ashkenazi, Rav Shmuel Jaffe*

Rav Yehudah Loewe ben Bezalel

Known as the Maharal of Prague.

One of the seminal figures in the last 500 years of Jewish thought, Rav Yehudah was born c. 1512 and died in Prague in 1609. His genealogy can be traced to King David.

Although he was universally acknowledged as one of the rabbinic greats of the era, his life was not an easy one. He delayed his marriage for 20 years due to financial difficulties. He was Chief Rabbi of Moravia, residing in Nikolsburg, for 20 years. Then, in 1573, he transferred his yeshivah to Prague, the Torah metropolis of Europe. Upon two different occasions, he accepted the rabbinate of Posen in order to settle communal strife.

He was elected Chief Rabbi of Prague in 1597 as a very old man. It appears that the position had been denied him up to then because of his outspokenness in attacking social evils and religious laxity.

Though commonly known as a folk hero and miracle worker, his greatest contribution was his formulation of a self-contained system of Jewish thought. His many books and lengthy sermons formed the basis for much of the significant writing of succeeding centuries.

Among his many erudite works were: *Novellae* on *Shulchan Aruch Yoreh Deah,* **Gur Aryeh** on the Torah, *Be'er HaGolah* on the Passover Hagaddah, *Derech Chaim, Netzach Yisrael, Nesivos Olam,* etc. Many of his works are extant and were recently republished in an 18-volume set: *Sifrei Maharal.*

Yerushalmi, Peah

Tractate *Peah* in the Jerusalem Talmud.

Yevamos

Talmudic tractate in *Seder Nashim.*

Rav Yissachar Berman HaKohen

Known as Berman Ashkenazi.

16-17th-century commentator on the *Midrash.*

Very little is known about him except that he was born in Sczebrzesyn, Poland, and that he was a student of the Rama (Rav Moshe Isserles).

He is the author of the famous commentary to the *Midrash Rabbah, Matanos Kehunah,* first published in 1584, and appearing subsequently in nearly every edition of the *Midrash.*

Rav Yissachar makes it very clear in his introduction that he was very concerned with establishing the correct text for the *Midrashim,* basing his text upon all the various printed editions up to his time and on various manuscripts.

Zohar Chadash

A part of the *Zohar* which was printed slightly later than the main body of the text. Incorporated within the *Zohar Chadash* is the **Midrash HaNe'elam** on the *Torah* and **Midrash Ruth HaNe'elam.**

Midrash Ruth HaNe'elam also appeared as a separate work called *Tapuchei Zahav.*

Zos Nechemasi

Commentary on *Ruth* by Rav Shlomo ben Chaim Chaykl Yanovsky of Warsaw; early 19th century.

Zuenz, Rav Aryeh Leib

(1773-1833)

Polish Rav and Kabbalist. At a young age his genius was recognized and he became known as Leib Charif ("sharp-witted").

For a time he was Rav of Prague, then Warsaw, then he became Rosh Yeshivah in Praga, a suburb of Warsaw.

He was the author of many works, and on his deathbed he promised to intercede in Heaven on behalf of anyone who published his works, with the result that many Jews came forward to publish them.

He is known for his *Get Mekushar* and *Geresh Yerachim.* His commentary on *Ruth* is called **M'lo HaOmer**